THE ECONOMIES OF LATIN AMERICA:
NEW CLIOMETRIC DATA

Perspectives in Economic and Social History

Series Editors: Robert E. Wright
Andrew August

Titles in this Series

Forthcoming Titles

THE ECONOMIES OF LATIN AMERICA: NEW CLIOMETRIC DATA

EDITED BY

César Yáñez and Albert Carreras

LONDON AND NEW YORK

First published 2012 by Pickering & Chatto (Publishers) Limited

Published 2016 by Routledge
2 Park Square, Milton Park, Abingdon, Oxfordshire OX14 4RN
711 Third Avenue, New York, NY 10017, USA

First issued in paperback 2015

Routledge is an imprint of the Taylor & Francis Group, an informa business

BRITISH LIBRARY CATALOGUING IN PUBLICATION DATA

The economies of Latin America: new cliometric data. – (Perspectives in
economic and social history)
1. Latin America – Economic conditions – 20th century. 2. Latin America –
Economic conditions – 20th century – Statistics.
I. Series II. Yanez, Cesar. III. Carreras, Albert.
330.9'80033–dc23

ISBN-13: 978-1-138-66199-8 (pbk)
ISBN-13: 978-1-8489-3323-1 (hbk)
Typeset by Pickering & Chatto (Publishers) Limited

CONTENTS

LIST OF FIGURES AND TABLES

LIST OF CONTRIBUTORS

Marc Badia-Miró (PhD: University of Barcelona, 2008) is lecturer in the Department of Economic History and Institutions in the University of Barcelona (Spain) and member of the board of the Centre d'Estudis Antoni de Capmany. His latest publications are: C. Yáñez and M. Badia-Miró, 'El consumo de automóviles en América Latina y el Caribe, 1902–1930', *El Trimestre Económico*, 310 (2011); M. Badia-Miró, Y. Blasco, S. Lozano and R. Soler, 'Centrality and Investment Strategies at the Beginnings of the Industrialization, Catalonia at Mid 19th Century', *Business History*, 52 (2010), pp. 493–515; M. Badia-Miró, E. Tello, F. Valls and R. Garrabou, 'The Grape Phylloxera Plague as a Natural Experiment: The Upkeep of Vineyards in Catalonia (Spain), 1858–1935'. *Australian Economic History Review*, 10 (2010), pp. 133–42; A. Carreras-Marín and M. Badia-Miró, 'La fiabilidad de la asignación geográfica en las estadísticas de comercio exterior: América Latina y el Caribe (1908–1930)', *Revista de Historia Económica–Journal of Iberian and Latin American Economic History*, 26 (2008), pp. 355–73; C. Aravena, M. Badia-Miró, A. Hofman, C. Hurtado and J. Jofré, 'Growth, Productivity and Information and Communications Technologies in Latin America, 1950–2005', in M. Cimolo, A. Hofman and N. Mulder (eds), *Innovation and Economic Development: The Impact of Information and Communication Technologies in Latin Americat* (Cheltenham, Edward Elgar, 2010), pp. 118–38; M. Badia-Miró, 'The Ports of Northern Chile: A Mining History in a Long-Run Perspective', in T. Dins de Bergholm, L. R. Fischer and M. E. Tonizzi (eds.), *Making Global and Local Connections: Historical Perspectives on Ports* (St John's, 2007), pp. 153–70.

Albert Carreras (PhD: Universitat Autonoma de Barcelona, 1983) is full professor, Department of Economics and Business, Universitat Pompeu Fabra, Barcelona. Dean of the School of Economics and Business. Prince of Asturias Visiting Professor, BMW Center for German and European Studies, Edmund A. Walsh School of Foreign Service, Georgetown University (2007–8). Professor, Department of History and Civilization, European University Institute, Florence (1989–94). Visiting scholar at University of California, Barkeley (1988–9). President, European Business History Association (2010–11). Vice-president, Asociación Española de Historia Económica (2009–11). Chairman (since 2009), Research Council, European University Institute, Florence. His latest publications are: with C. Josephson 'Aggregate Growth, 1870–1914: Growing at the Production Frontier', in S. Broadberry and K. O'Rourke (eds), *Cambridge Economic History of Modern Europe*, 2 vols (Cambridge: Cambridge University Press, 2010), vol. 2, pp. 30–58; M. Rubio, C. Yáñez, M. Folchi and A. Careras 'Economic Modernization in Latin America and the Caribbean between 1890 and 1925: A View from Modern Energy Consumption', *Economic History Review*, 63:3 (2010), pp. 769–804; with E. Felice, 'L'industria italiana dal 1911 al 1938: ricostruzione della serie del valore aggiunto e interpretazioni', *Rivista di Storia Economica*, 26:3 (2010), pp. 285–333; with X. Tafunell, *Historia económica de la España contemporánea (1789–2009)* (Barcelona: Crítica, 2010).

Anna Carreras-Marín (PhD: University of Barcelona, 2008) is lecturer in the Department of Economic History and Institutions at the University of Barcelona (Spain) and member of the board of the Centre d'Estudis Antoni de Capmany. Her latest publications are: A. Carreras-Marín and M. Badia-Miró, 'La fiabilidad de la asignación geográfica en las estadísticas de comercio exterior: América Latina y el Caribe (1908–1930)', *Revista de Historia Económica–Journal of Iberian and Latin American Economic History*, 26 (2008), pp. 355–73; A. Carreras-Marín and M. Badia-Miró: 'The First World War and Coal Trade Geography', in *Jahrbuch fur Geschichte Lateinamerikas. Anuario de Historia de América Latina* (2008).

Santiago Colmenares (MA: Universidad Autónoma de Barcelona, 2008) is a PhD candidate and Scholar of the Project on Teaching Innovation (2009MQD 00186), in the Department of Economic History and Institutions in the Universitat de Barcelona, Spain. His latest papers are: *El Banco Mundial y las políticas económicas en Colombia: de Bretton Woods al neoliberalismo* (unpublished thesis, Universidad Nacional de Colombia, 2005); 'Apuntes sobre los procesos de asistencia para el desarrollo en el capitalismo y socialismo subdesarrollados: una comparación de Colombia y Cuba', in *Proceedings of XIII Colombian Congress of History*, (Bucaramanga: Universidad Industrial de Santander, 2006); *El debate empírico sobre los términos de intercambio y los términos de intercambio factoriales de Colombia, 1975–2006* (Bellaterra: Departamento de Economía e Historia Económica, Universidad Autónoma de Barcelona, 2008); and translator of J. G. Williamson, *Desarrollo Global e Historia* (Saragossa: Prensas Universitarias de Zaragoza, in press).

Cristián Ducoing is a PhD Candidate in Economic History at the University of Barcelona and lecturer at the Universitat Pompeu Fabra, Barcelona. He is writing his thesis about capital formation in machinery and capital productivity in

Chile for the period 1830–1938. His latest work is his Master's thesis 'Machinery Investment and Economic Growth: Chile 1890–2005' (2009).

Mauricio Folchi (PhD, Universidad Autónoma de Barcelona, 2006) currently teaches in the Department of History at the Universidad de Chile, where he is also a visiting lecturer in the School of Economic and Business Administration and the Master's Degree Programme in Environmental Management and Planning. He has taught at the Department of Economics and Business at the Universitat Pompeu Fabra, in Barcelona. His main areas of interest are the history of energy, mining, technology and the environment. Among his recent publications are M. Rubio, C. Yáñez, M. Folchi and A. Careras 'Economic Modernization in Latin America and the Caribbean between 1890 and 1925: A View from Modern Energy Consumption', *Economic History Review*, 63:3 (2010), pp. 769–804; 'La gestación de la política ambiental minera antes de la "revolución ambiental de los noventa"' ('The Formation of an Environmental Policy for the Mining Sector Prior to the "Environmental Revolution of the 1990s"') (2010); 'Industria, salud y salubridad: la visión original sobre las condiciones de vida de la clase obrera' ('Industry, Health and Wellness: Early Views of the Living Conditions of the Working Class') (2009); 'El consumo aparente de energía fósil en los países latinoamericanos en 1925' ('The Apparent Consumption of Fossil Fuels in Latin America, 1925') (2008).

André Hofman (PhD: Universidad de Groningen) has worked in the ECLAC since 1986, first in the joint technology Division of ECLAC/UNIDO and later in the Division of Economic Development and the Division of Statistics and Economic Projections as Head of the Centre of Economic Projections. Currently he is Director of the ECLAC magazine. His recent publications are: 'Productividad Total de los Factores en Chile: Una Perspectiva Comparativa' (Programa Innovación Tecnológica, Ministerio de Economía, 1997); with N. Mulder, 'The Comparative Productivity Performance of Brazil and Mexico, 1950–1994' in J. H. Coatsworth and A. M. Taylor (eds), *Latin America and the World Economy Since 1980* (Cambridge, MA: The David Rockefeller Center on Latin American Studies, Harvard University, 1998); 'Capital Stocks Estimates in Latin America: A 1950–1994 Update', *Cambridge Journal of Economics*, 24:1 (January 2000); *The Economic Development of Latin America in the Twentieth Century* (Cheltenham and Northampton, MA: Edward Elgar Publishing, 2000); with H. Tapia, *Potential Output in Latin America: A Standard Approach for the 1950–2002 Period* (Santiago: Cepal, 2003); with A. Solimano and C. Aravena, 'Economic Growth in the Andean Region: The Role of Economic and Governance Factors', in A. Solimano (ed.), *Vanishing Growth in Latin America* (Cheltenham: Edward Elgar Publishing, 2006).

José Jofré is economic analyst in the Department of Price Studies at the National Statistics Institute of Chile. He is simultaneously preparing his doctoral thesis for the interuniversity doctoral program at the Department of History and Economic Institutions at the Universidad de Barcelona-Universidad Autónoma de Barcelona. His thesis is on 'Patterns of Apparent Modern Energy Consumption in Latin America, 1890–2003' under the directorship of Doctor César Yáñez Gallardo. His latest publication is 'Regularidades empíricas entre el consumo de energía y el Producto en América Latina durante el siglo XX', in M. Rubio and R. Bertoni (eds), *Energía y Desarrollo en el largo siglo XX. Uruguay en el marco latinoamericano* (Universitat Pompeu Fabra, Barcelona, and the Social Sciences Faculty of the Universidad de la República, Montevideo, 2008), ch. 4, pp. 121–52.

Vicente Neira is a PhD candidate in Economic History at Universitat de Barcelona. Associate lecturer, Department of Economics and Business, Universidad Pompeu Fabra in 2007–2008. At present, he is writing his thesis about factorial distribution of income in Latin America between 1950 and 2000. His latest work, 'Distribución factorial del ingreso en América Latina, 1950–2000. Nuevas series a partir de las cuentas nacionales', won the Barcelona Chamber of Commerce Prize 'VI Premi Fons Bibliogràfic de la Cambra de Comerç de Barcelona'.

Frank Notten (PhD: Universidad de Barcelona, 2010; MA: University of Groningen, 2002) is a macroeconomics editor in the department of National Accounts of the Centraal Bureau voor de Statistiek (CBS) in The Hague, Holland, since June 2010. Title of thesis: 'La influencia de la Primera Guerra Mundial sobre las economías centroamericanas, 1900–1929. Un enfoque desde el comercio exterior'.

José Peres is a scholarship student in the Department of History and Economic Institutions, Universidad de Barcelona. His latest publications are: 'Repensando el desarrollo boliviano desde la historia económica. ¿La lucha de los débiles?', in *Repensando el desarrollo* (La Paz: CIDES/UMSA, 2011); 'Estado y Carnaval de La Paz en el siglo XX', in *Carnaval Paceño y J'iska Anata (Fiesta Popular Paceña)* (La Paz: IEB/ASDI-SAREC, 2009).

Carolina Román is a researcher in the areas of Development and Economic History in the Economics Institute of the Faculty of Economic Sciences and Administration of the Universidad de la República (Uruguay). Lecturer in the Faculty of Economic Sciences and Social Sciences, Universidad de la República. Doctoral candidate in History and Economic Institutions of the Universidad de Barcelona, where she obtained her Diploma in Advanced Studies. Her latest publications are: R. Bertoni, C. Román and M. Rubio, 'El desarrollo energético de España y Uruguay en perspectiva comparada: 1860–2000'. *Revista de Historia Industrial*, 41 (2009), pp. 161–96; R. Bertoni and C. Román, 'La transición energética en Uruguay' and R. Bertoni, M. Camou, S. Maubrigades and C. Román, 'Energía eléctrica y calidad de vida en Uruguay', both in M. Rubio and R. Bertoni (eds), *Energía y Desarrollo en el largo siglo XX: Uruguay en el marco Latinoamericano* (Montevideo, 2008).

Maria del Mar Rubio (PhD: London School of Economics, 1997 and 2002), is lecturer at Unviersidad Publica de Navarra. Fulbright Visiting Scholar, Department of Economics, UC Berkeley, 2001–2. Assistant professor at Universitat Pompeu Fabra, Barcelona, 2002–8. Her area of interest moved from energy-producing countries to energy-consuming countries, particularly to the relationship between energy consumption, pollution and economic growth over the very long run, firstly in Spain within the European context, and lately, in Latin America and the Caribbean over the twentieth century. The results of her research have been published in Spanish, Latin American and international journals such as *Economic History Review*; *European Review of Economic History* and *Journal of Environmental Economics and Management*.

Xavier Tafunell (PhD: Universidad Autónoma de Barcelona, 1988) is full professor of Economic History in the Department of Economics and Business at the Universitat Pompeu Fabra, Barcelona (Spain). He has published several books, including: *Historia Económica de la España, 1789–2009*, together with Albert Carreras, with whom he edited the *Estadísticas Históricas de España, siglos XIX–XX*. He has written numerous articles and chapters of books on financial and business history, the construction sector and the history of Latin American economies during the first globalization. Among these, it is worth mentioning: 'On the origins of ISI: The Latin American cement industry, 1900–30', *Journal of Latin American Studies*, 2 (2007); 'América Latina y El Caribe en 1913 y 1925: Un enfoque desde las importaciones de bienes de capital', *El Trimestre Económico*, 299 (2008); 'La inversión en equipo de transporte de América Latina, 1890–1930: una estimación basada en la demanda de importaciones', *Investigaciones de Historia Económica*, 14 (2009); and 'Capital Formation in Machinery in Latin America, 1890–1930', *Journal of Economic History*, 4 (2009).

César Yáñez (PhD: Universitat Autonoma de Barcelona, 1994) is full professor, Department of Economic History and Institutions, University de Barcelona (Spain) and member of the board of the Centre d'Estudis Antoni de Capmany. His latest publications are: with M. Badia-Miró, 'El consumo de automóviles en América Latina y el Caribe, 1902–1930', *El Trimestre Económico*, 310 (2010); M. Rubio, C. Yáñez, M. Folchi and A. Careras, 'Economic Modernization in Latin America and the Caribbean between 1890 and 1925: A View from Modern Energy Consumption', *Economic History Review*, 63:3 (2010); 'Importaciones de bienes de consumo duradero en América Latina en 1925: los relojes y los automóviles', *Revista de Historia Económica*, 2 (2008); C. Yáñez, M. Rubio and A. Carreras, 'Modernización económica en América Latina y el Caribe entre 1890 y 1925: una mirada desde el consumo de energía', in M. Rubio and R. Bertoni (eds), *Energía y desarrollo en el siglo XX. Uruguay en el marco latinoamericano* (Universitat Pompeu Fabra, Barcelona, and Universidad de la República, Montevideo, 2008); C. Yáñez and M. Badia-Miró, 'Las importaciones de relojes y automóviles en América Latina durante 1925. Una aproximación desde el punto de vista de la renta y su distribución', in *Revista de Historia Industrial*, 35:3 (2008).

PREFACE

César Yáñez and Albert Carreras

One decade into the twenty-first century, and thirty years since the worst economic crisis in Latin America (the debt crisis of the 1980s – 'the lost decade'), it is time to have another look at the economic history of Latin America and the Caribbean from a long-term perspective. We firmly believe that many of the ideas used to study Latin American backwardness, are twentieth-century rather than twenty-first-century ideas. In this sense, Latin American economic historiography has been marked by a period of pessimism about Latin America's chances of overcoming economic backwardness. The tendency to take a short-term perspective or to focus only on a few national cases has meant that research has been heavily influenced by debates centring on the failure of industrialization, the political cost of the military dictatorships, the social and economic impact of the 'lost decade' and the limitations of the subsequent recovery. The poor performance of Latin American economies in recent times has also influenced those who study the earlier stages, which helps to understand the success of a book entitled 'How Latin America Fell Behind' published in 1997.

This backwardness is apparent in the widening gap between GDP per inhabitant in Latin America and the Caribbean and that of wealthy countries. The ideas most frequently used in an attempt to explain Latin American backwardness point to institutional reasons, on the one hand, and the theory of 'the curse of natural resources', on the other, or to both simultaneously. These ideas share a certain sense of doom with regards Latin America's economic prospects: institutions inherited from centuries of colonization whose modernization is slow and barely noticeable gave way to 'macroeconomics of populism' (to quote another influential title in Latin America) from which these countries have not been able to break free; or the abundance of natural resources distributed arbitrarily around the New Continent meant those countries attempting to move towards development by exporting their most prolific factor were at the mercy of this 'lottery'. And in the event that the Latin American country is a coffee exporter, exporter of mining resources, or of wheat, maize or sugar, and has had recurrent de facto military governments, all this conspires to make it a given that its past, like its present is the result of an inevitable destiny.

These types of interpretations of Latin American economic history are certainly not arbitrary. They were conceived of and disseminated by historians who relied on a not insignificant accumulation of empirical evidence. However, it is evident that there is still a substantial lack of quantitative data and that, in some way, this accumulated evidence falls far short of what is needed to provide a conclusive explanation for the causes of Latin American and Caribbean economic backwardness. In this regard, we are convinced that there is a delay in obtaining relevant information about this historical path. This delay is shaping the debate, and the dominant ideas are also spin-offs of the absence of this indispensable information. Evidence of this is the knowledge we have about the economic growth of Latin America and the Caribbean. In this sense, we know that research has moved forwards with regards to the big countries in the region, such as Brazil, Mexico and Argentina, and also about some medium-sized countries like Colombia, Chile, Peru and Venezuela, and one small country – Uruguay.

For all of these cases, we have GDP estimations from Maddison's compilation since at least 1900, although they are not always solid enough or sufficiently comparable. For the remaining countries, there is still a lack of knowledge of the effect on them – positive, negative or neutral – of their growing integration into the international economy until 1913. The information available for the period known as the 'transwar' period (1914–45) is better, but suffers from several limitations:

- the GDP estimations are not easily comparable since they were made according to specific procedures for each country;
- we do not have information for the entire period;
- nor is there information for all countries; and
- existing information is often incomplete.

All of these limitations were progressively overcome in the post-war period after the Second World War when the System of National Accounts of the United Nations came to predominate. But without doubt, what we already know is far less relevant than what remains to be discovered.

In short, in order to improve our understanding of the causes of economic backwardness of Latin American and the Caribbean, we must revise both the ideas with which we have dealt with the problem, as well as the empirical evidence on which they are based. The collection of contributions we have selected for the edition of this book are a step in this direction – they offer new quantitative evidence compiled with extreme rigour and take on with audacity (but without rashness) the interpretation of the past. Another novelty about the texts presented for this edition is the wide territorial coverage and their tendency to study those cases for which information gathering is difficult (generally small or medium-sized countries), without losing the reference of the 'big' economies in the region. We must underline the coherence there is among all the contributions in this volume, in terms of territorial coverage, historical periods and sectors of the economy. We provide a perspective from the cutting edge of knowledge about economic backwardness of Latin America and the Caribbean. We have before us a new vision of the economic history of the whole of Latin America and the Caribbean throughout the nineteenth and twentieth century.

Below, we briefly review each of the contributions to the book. They are grouped according to whether they are regional or national studies. The following papers give a perspective of the whole of the subcontinent. Albert Carreras (Universitat Pompeu Fabra) looks for new interpretations for the Latin American economic evolution in the twentieth century, in the tensions caused by changes on the world economic stage. The comparison between the degree of openness of Europe and Lain America permits Carreras to reinterpret the reasons for accumulated economic backwardness during the years of highly protectionist policies. Mar Rubio (Universidad Pública de Navarra) and Mauricio Folchi (Universidad de Chile) resort to sophisticated statistical techniques (the Wilcoxon Matched-Pairs test) and resume an optimistic perspective on foreign trade statistics as a source for the study of Latin American economic history. With this work, Rubio and Folchi lay the foundations for a new wave of research work with one of the best available sources of quantitative knowledge about the economy of Latin America and the Caribbean in the near future. Marc Badia-Miró (Universidad de Barcelona) and Anna Carreras-Marín (Universidad de Barcelona), making full use of foreign trade statistics, review the idea – predominant until now – that the United Kingdom had totally dominated Latin American trade relations before the First World War. With their new data, they bring to the fore the United States' participation in this trade relation from early on. Xavier Tafunell (Universitat Pompeu Fabra) deals with investment in equipment goods in Latin America during the first globalization (1890–1930), offering a rigorous estimation of the investment in machinery for all (twenty) of the Latin American countries. This represents an important leap forward in the elaboration of a basic input for economic growth. The series on industrial and agricultural machinery, as well as electric and transport equipment, which Tafunell presents, estimated using trade statistics, promises to be a reference for economic historians dealing with the subject in the future. Vicente Neira (Universidad de Valparaíso, Chile), calculates the functional income distribution for fourteen countries in Latin America in the second half of the twentieth century. Neira's groundbreaking series proposes a new vision of Latin America during its industrialization and deindustrialization, which changes our way of seeing the economic and social policies of the period. Frank Notten (Centraal Bureau voor de Statistiek, The

Hague) deals with the group of small Central American economies and explains the changes brought about by the First World War in their international economic relations. Notten is the first to take advantage of the full potential of the foreign trade statistics of the United States, the United Kingdom and Germany in order to understand the dynamics of the economies of Costa Rica, El Salvador, Honduras and Guatemala at a critical time in their history. The chapters that follow take a perspective that focuses more on national cases. César Yáñez (Universidad de Barcelona), for example, studies the paths of Chile and Cuba throughout the nineteenth century, from the final stages of the colonial regime in Chile to Cuban Independence in 1898. Yáñez reviews the idea of the Hispanic colonial order and relates the oligarchic order of the nineteenth century with opportunities for economic growth in the two countries – both successful exporters of their natural resources. As an indicator, Yáñez uses growth in apparent consumption of modern energies, following in this sense the proposal of Rubio, Yáñez, Folchi and Carreras of 2009. André Hofman (ECLAC) and Cristián Ducoing (Universitat Pompeu Fabra), in the wake of Tafunell's work, carry out an in-depth study of machinery investment in Chile up to the early years of the twenty-first century, thereby offering a new assessment of what machinery investment meant for economic growth in the long run. The work of Hofman and Ducoing can be repeated for the other Latin American countries which have good foreign trade statistics, which is why this study is so important. José Jofré (Instituto Nacional de Estadísticas, Chile), does an in-depth study concerning energy consumption in Cuba in the eighteenth and nineteenth centuries, and its impact on the environment, particularly on tropical forests. Jofré, who studied the transition from the consumption of organic energies to fossil energies, is the first to provide us with complete energy accounting for Cuba at an early stage in its history. Santiago Colmenares (Universidad de Barcelona) retrieves a classical subject in Latin American economic history with his estimation using the 'double factorial' technique of the terms of reference of Colombia between 1975 and 2006. Colmenares' work achieves a decisive improvement in the reconstruction of historical series of terms of trade, which could also be imitated for other national cases. José Péres (Universidad de Barcelona) achieves extraordinary results in the elaboration of Bolivian fiscal series – a country we know little about from a perspective of quantitative economic history. The fiscal structure of Bolivia in the first three decades of the twentieth century allows us to see the progress of the country while at the same time outlining the obstacles of its past, Carolina Román (Universidad de la República, Uruguay), examines the complex question of the demand function for durable consumer goods in six Latin American countries during the first globalization. Román's work stands out for its originality, in estimating consumption by means of the importation of goods in

Argentina, Brazil, Chile, Cuba, Mexico and Uruguay, and the difficulty in deter-mining the income and price elasticity of the demand for these types of goods.

To end this preface, we would like to express our gratitude to the institu-tions and the people who have believed in the scientific capacity of this research team. In the first place, the Spanish Ministry of Science and Technology, which between 2003 and 2006 backed the projects led by Albert Carreras, 'Importaciones y modernización económica en América Latina, 1890–1960' (BEC2003–00412) and between 2007 and 2010, 'Energía y economía en Amé-rica Latina y el Caribe, entre mediados del siglo XIX y mediados del siglo XX' (SEJ2007-60445/ECON). Likewise, the Spanish Ministry of Science and Inno-vation supported the project led by Xavier Tafunell (2011–13), 'Formación y stock de capital y consumo de energía en América Latina y el Caribe entre 1850 y 2010' (ECO2010–15882). In the final stage, these studies have received the backing of Conicyt of Chile, through the MEL project led by César Yáñez, 'Estado ciudadanía y atraso económico en Chile durante el siglo XX.La con-tribución de la historia económica a la comprensión del desarrollo chileno', at the Universidad de Valparaiso, Chile. We would also like to acknowledge Anya Doherty for the translation of texts by José Jofré, César Yáñez and Xavier Tafu-nell, and the Preface and Introduction by César Yáñez and Albert Carreras, as well for the overall style revision. Likewise, we acknowledge the collaboration of Alejandra Rojas in compiling the notes.

INTRODUCTION: LATIN AMERICAN ECONOMIC BACKWARDNESS REVISITED

César Yáñez and Albert Carreras

Introduction

Prior research into Latin American economic growth was undertaken mainly by Luis Bértola and José Antonio Ocampo,[1] using Angus Maddison's GDP per capita data in the OECD data base.[2] These authors focused primarily on the estimation of periods of convergence and divergence in relation to the leader countries. Our book revisits the subject, making use of the same data, but focusing on the magnitude of economic backwardness in order to highlight the degree of difficulty Latin American countries face when attempting to move beyond their current level of development. This research does not aim to question the value of the convergence criterion. On the contrary, it values the accumulation of historiographical knowledge and looks carefully at Maddison's research data. It is surprising to note that in 2008 Haiti's GDP per capita was US$686 at purchasing power parity (PPP), which is less than that estimated for all the countries in that region for 1820 (US$691 at PPP). This is not too different from Leandro Prados de la Escosura's[3] proposal of US$649 for the same year. This would indicate that the poorest part of Latin America (represented by Haiti) has the same level of wealth as Latin American countries had at the time of independence, roughly 200 years ago. Among the leader economies, the United Kingdom had a similar figure of US$761 at PPP in 1500, five centuries ago. Haiti however, is most certainly not representative of the whole of Latin America. Maddison's Latin American average for 2008 is US$6,973 at PPP – ten times greater than that of the region in 1820. This figure is nonetheless worrying, since the United States had reached this level in 1929 and the United Kingdom in 1950. Economic backwardness has, however, only increased over time with the Latin American GDP of 1820 at half that of the US, in 1913 at one-third, and in 2000 at one-fifth.

Latin America, however, is highly diverse, as Bértola and Ocampo[4] among others, observed. Latin America today has an enormous dispersion in GDP per capita values. The Chilean economy is twenty times bigger than that of Haiti, whereas the Norwegian economy is only 1.4 times bigger than that of Italy. This indicates that some Latin American countries have had a strong growth path, with GDP multiplying by a factor of twenty-one as did Chile between 1820 and 2008. At the other extreme, however, Haiti has stagnated for centuries. In contrast, the twelve Western European economies have tended to converge around average values.

It is worth mentioning that there is diversity of wealth levels within Latin America, but this does not make the average regional GDP per capita values less representative. The majority of the Latin American population, and most of the absolute GDP, sits at between US$6,000 and US$8,000 at PPP. Brazil, Colombia, Mexico, Venezuela, Costa Rica and Panama, which make up two-thirds of the Latin American population and wealth in general terms, also fall within the above-mentioned segment. Only three countries stand out above the regional average, namely Argentina, Chile and Uruguay with over US$10,000 at PPP according to Maddison's data. The remaining countries are at below US$6,000 at PPP with enormous differences among them.

What does this say in terms of the magnitude of economic backwardness accumulated over two centuries of independence, and the difficulty of overcoming it? Our position is that each of the three blocks introduced above should be dealt with differently. Each group shows strong path dependence related to when the process of economic modernization took place, which in turn corresponds to the different times at which the process of economic modernization took place.

The economic performance of the dominant group of Latin American countries was precarious until the 1920s, which meant their economic modernization was postponed until the implementation of state-directed policies for industrialization. It should be noted that the GDP per capita at PPP of Brazil, Colombia, Mexico, Costa Rica and Venezuela from 1920 or 1929 was below that of the United Kingdom and the United States in 1820 (for Panama there is no data until 1945). However, the economic boost initially generated by the first and second Industrial Revolution and the first globalization, lost impetus.

Unlike the previous group, the trio made up of Argentina, Chile and Uruguay did manage in 1929 to reduce the relative gap in GDP per capita. These three countries took the lead in the region thanks to early economic modernization which intensified in the decades preceding the First World War. This lead was to be relatively long-lasting. Prior to 1960 Venezuela left its original GDP grouping to join the leaders of the region, only to return to it with a downswing at the end of the twentieth century.

There was a large group of laggard countries made up predominantly of the smaller economies whose process of capitalist modernization had been very slow in getting off the ground. Of this group, Peru was the only economy that cannot be defined as small. Until the second half of the twentieth century this set of countries' GDP per capita remained below that of 1820 Britain. Here we include economies such as Haiti and Nicaragua which, even until most recently, have experienced sharp and prolonged processes of regression in their GDP per capita at PPP. Without doubt, this is the group with the most serious problems in terms of the economic development gap, and for which prospects are the most pessimistic.

Path Dependence: The Problem of Economic Modernization

The main problem the Latin American economy has, when analysing its long-term path, is the difficulty of initiating a process of modern economic growth. Most countries in the region have been excessively slow in definitively putting behind them the features of a pre-capitalist economy. This has made it difficult for Latin American countries to experience high rates of lasting economic growth. Three factors condition the history of Latin American economic backwardness. First, the late adoption of technology from the Industrial Revolution, with most of Latin America remaining unaffected by productivity increases associated with the use of fossil energy until the twentieth century. Second, and linked with the previous point, one notes the absence of synergies generated by the establishment of institutions guaranteeing modern property rights with regard to both the means of production as well as labour. The third factor was external. Smaller and weaker Latin American countries were not always able to internalize the external shocks coming from the international economy, which at specific moments in history cut off the upward trajectories of these economies.

This lack of economic growth reached the first critical point in the nineteenth century. The majority of the Latin American population continued working within a technological paradigm with very low levels of productivity. Coal consumption figures for 1890 showed that working with modern machinery was quite alien to a great majority of Latin Americans.[5] Not only was the GDP per capita more typical of pre-industrial times, as we saw above, but also the material and technical bases which would push up the GDP through more efficient labour had not yet been established. If we look carefully at the results of Table I.1, we can conclude that in 1890 a significant number of Latin American countries were still in a technological paradigm which could be defined as having almost total dependence on biomass energies. This is important because without coal it was impossible to run machines that increased productivity in a sustainable manner. The consequence, therefore, is that only those countries which incorporated modern machinery into their productive systems were able to initiate processes of economic growth that were not interrupted by repeatedly diminishing long-term yields.

In other words steam engines, the big coal consumers which were responsible for the improvement in labour productivity during the Industrial Revolution, were introduced too late into the Latin American economies. Consequently, economic modernization in these countries was delayed, with important consequences for the future. The tardiness of the introduction of modern machinery had implications other than just GDP slowdown in the short run. In the long run, it was also a limitation for the technical training of the population, reducing incentives for the formation of advanced human capital, and it was an obstacle for the formation of modern enterprises with new ways of organizing capital and labour.

Table I.1: Levels of modern energy consumption per capita in Latin America and the Caribbean: ranking for years 1890, 1900, 1913 and 1925

1890		1900		1913		1925	
Country	TOE/cap.*	Country	TOE/cap.*	Country	TOE/cap.*	Country	TOE/cap.*
Latin American Republics							
Uruguay	278.6	Uruguay	360.3	Panama	1.276.4	Panama	2.197.9
Chile	171.5	Chile	189.5	Chile	503.8	Chile	490.3
Argentina	116.9	Cuba	158.3	Uruguay	449.8	Cuba	484.0
Cuba**	114.3	Argentina	122.9	Cuba	391.7	Argentina	331.0
L.A. and C.	44.3	Mexico	70.6	Argentina	335.0	Uruguay	287.2
Brazil	33.3	L.A. and C.	63,4	L.A.and C	142.9	Mexico	251.6
Peru	17.3	Brazil	34.5	Mexico	111.1	L.A. and C.	176.9
Puerto Rico**	16.2	Peru	27.5	Peru	91.4	Honduras	127.5
Costa Rica	13.3	Costa Rica	26.4	Costa Rica	89.3	Costa Rica	113.6
Venezuela	11.6	Puerto Rico	16,9	Brazil	76.7	Peru	89.6
Nicaragua	10.4	Dominican R.	8,3	Puerto Rico	26.1	Brazil	75.1
Mexico	10.1	Nicaragua	6.4	Guatemala	24.1	Puerto Rico	55.6
Colombia	8.7	Colombia	5.5	Dominican R.	16.9	Dominican R.	41.4
Dominican R.	5.8	Venezuela	5.5	Honduras	11.2	Guatemala	39.5
Haiti	3.1	Haiti	3.0	Ecuador	10.2	Colombia	26.5
Honduras	0.8	Honduras	2.8	Nicaragua	9.7	Venezuela	26.4
Ecuador	0.5	Guatemala	1.5	Venezuela	9.2	Ecuador	21.1
El Salvador	0.4	Ecuador	0,9	Haiti	5.4	Nicaragua	19.6
Guatemala	0.4	El Salvador	0.5	Colombia	3.4	El Salvador	12.6
				El Salvador	1.9	Haiti	2.1
Pro memoria: United States and Spain							
United States	3.571.6	United States	4.913.2	United States	7.869.8	United States	8.889.9
Spain	123.0	Spain	194.2	Spain	274.3	Spain	255.1

Notes: TOE: Tonnes of oil equivalent. *TOE/cap is actually TOE per 1000 habitants. **Cuba and Puerto Rico were Spanish colonies up to 1898. The former obtained independence in 1902 and the latter remained under US influence till today. Modern energy includes fossil plus hydroelectric consumption. M. Rubio, C. Yáñez, M. Folchi and A. Carreras, 'Energy as an Indicator'.

Even today, some Latin American countries are still suffering the consequences of this radical backwardness. These can be found at the end of Figure I.1: Haiti, Honduras, Nicaragua, El Salvador, Ecuador and Guatemala, and probably if data existed, Bolivia and Paraguay would be there too. In these countries the use of modern energies is still very unevenly spread. Not all homes have electricity, motorized transport has not yet fully replaced draught animals, many agricultural activities are still carried out without the help of machinery and manufacturing still shows features of craft production that does not use the most efficient machinery available. In these countries firewood, charcoal and draught animals still occupy a central position in economic activities. The evidence of development is so tenuous in these economies that it is as if modernization in the past never occurred at a pace that could ensure sustained, long-term development.

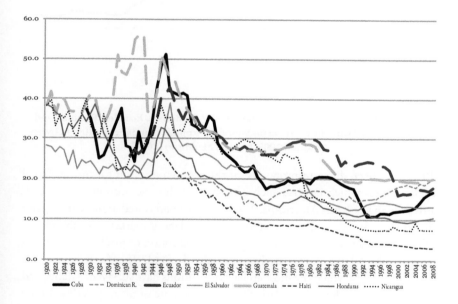

Figure I.1: Evolution of GDP per capita at PPP for the Central American and Caribbean countries, compared with the twelve main Western European economies (= 100) between 1920 and 2008. Source: Maddison (2010)

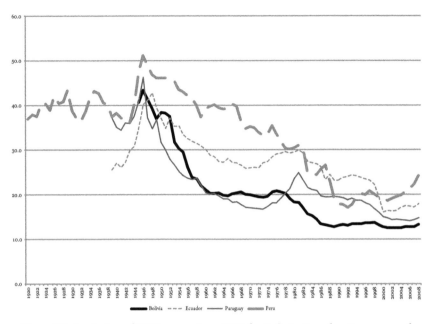

Figure I.2: Evolution of GDP per capita at PPP for Bolivia, Ecuador, Paraguay and Peru, compared with the twelve main Western European economies (= 100) between 1920 and 2008. Source: Maddison (2010)

There have been different proposals for the economic reason for this technical backwardness which has had such consequences for the economy and standards of living of Latin Americans. The most tried and tested arguments suggest that the reason lies in the characteristics of the labour market. The abundance of labour has acted as an incentive against the adoption of machinery. In Latin America the labour supply easily outweighs demand. The consequence is a labour market in which the most archaic institutions have survived. Salaries and pay scales are very low particularly for the lower strata of the population. In the poorest countries, as well as in the lowest income groups in the most advanced countries of the region, the labour market was poorly institutionalized, dominated by personal relations where the employers imposed their will without space for workers to use the law to defend their interests.

Latin America's historical trajectory is full of events highlighting its institutional problems. It has been perceived that the traditionally high level of corruption is the problem which has characterized Latin American countries' trajectories from the start. Today, the main argument identifies technological factors, together with the political environment as being responsible for the instability which has inhibited investment and entrepreneurial attitudes and has perpetuated social conflicts. Alan Dye's essay 'The Institutional Framework'[6] is an eloquent illustration of the degree of consensus this idea has achieved among specialists. The essence of the idea is that institutions are the 'rules of the game' of formal or informal origin, generated through time, which decisively influence the behaviour of economic agents. In this sense, institutions form part of the economic, political and social structures and have a long-term validity, changing at a much slower pace than the short-term context. In this sense, institutions have become an object of analysis – of growing importance within economic history and Latin American economic history in particular.

Stanley Engerman and Kenneth Sokoloff's 1997 article[7] proposed that the Spanish colonial institutions established a tradition of economic inequality in Latin America due to the abundance of productive factors. This inequality, which still exists today, has become a hallmark of the New World economies. Theoretically, this describes an economic path dependence which united the Spanish colonial past with Latin America's contemporary backwardness. The same authors, in their article of 2000, insist that endogenous factors of Hispanic colonial origin have held back Latin America on its path to progress. Over the past ten years debate has continued to produce new versions on the differential impact of the different colonial traditions on economic growth. Douglass C. North, William Summerhill and Barri Weingas, in their controversial article of 2000 'Order, Disorder and Economic Change: Latin American versus North America',[8] propose that a comparison of the British colonial past of the United States and the Hispanic colonial past of Latin America reveals that in the latter it was impossible to build early political consensus among the elites which emerged with independence. This was because unlike the British in North America the Hispanic institutions had failed to provide the local people with the experience of self-government. Subsequently, Daron Acemouglu, Samuel Johnson and James A. Robinson[9] returned to the theme of colonial determinism, broadening the comparison to include Asia and Africa. They concluded that there was little difference between the different types of colonialism. There were however, important differences in the economic development of colonies situated in the tropical zones in contrast to those in the temperate zones. Emigrants with knowledge and incentives to increase productivity had settled in the temperate areas, but not in the tropical zones. Robert Bates, John Coatsworth and Jeffrey Williamson[10] offer the latest contribution to the debate, in which they emphasize the comparison of colonial legacies as an explanation for economic backwardness. They contrast the meagre economic results of Latin America after its independence and the equally low results of post-independence Africa. For these authors, the difficulty in constructing 'political orders' with stable, credible and accepted institutions in the cycles after colonial emancipation had common features in Latin America and Africa, with negative effects on the economy.

A milestone in the analysis of institutions in Latin American economic history was the publication in 1997 of the book compiled by Steven Haber.[11] What these studies had in common was the emphasis on the rent-seeking behaviour of Latin American businesspeople of the nineteenth century. The legacy of the past, in this case, was apparent in the absence of incentives for creating economic structures based on the continuous increase of productivity, which directed the business sector toward rent-seeking behaviour. That is to say, they opted not to make an effort at investments to improve productivity in a context of open competition. Instead, they were inclined to take advantage of their relationship with the state, co-opting political leaders from the oligarchy to safeguard their group interests. In a way, one could say that these works ushered in studies of pressure groups in Latin American economic history.

Most recently, these studies point to the weakness of state creation in Latin America from a long-term historical perspective. Theories point to the importance of mechanisms of exclusion in the competition for political power as a key element in understanding the reasons for economic backwardness. The de facto interest groups formed through long historical processes, would have monopolized the exercise of power and given shape to a type of state 'usurped' by an oligarchy unwilling to expose itself to open political competition.

Without doubt, technological and institutional backwardness together obstructed better performance by the Latin American economies. These factors were more serious in the case of weaker and poorer economies. However, in Latin American economic history there were also good periods, good practices and countries which escaped, at least for some periods, this 'pessimistic' path which ties these countries to the past and obstructs modernization. Although the majority of the region took an extremely long time to reap the benefits of modern technologies, and corruption has been ever-present in their history, there are other examples of countries where institutional order did exist and which invested in technological modernization from relatively early in the nineteenth century.[12] Of the three Latin American Southern Cone countries (Argentina, Uruguay and Chile), with GDP per capita levels of US$10,000, Chile and Uruguay's corruption levels differ from the rest of the region and in 1890 they were already located at the top end of the table of modern energy consumption (see Table I.1). This illustrates that it is not just a circumstantial situation, despite the fact that the gap with advanced countries widened in the long run.

Figure I.3 illustrates the examples of Argentina, Uruguay and Chile whose economic performance in the eighty years before the Second World War kept them at a level of nearly 80 per cent of Western European economies, with Chile briefly exceeding 90 per cent and Uruguay at 100 per cent. Therefore, the question arises as to why these economies declined so severely in the twentieth century. The inadequacy of economic policies in the new international arena appears to be greatly responsible according to Albert Carreras.[13]

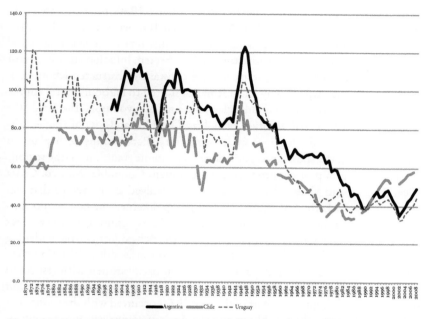

Figure I.3: Evolution of GDP per capita at PPP of Argentina, Uruguay and Chile, compared with the twelve main Western European economies (= 100) between 1870 and 2008. Source: Maddison (2010)

In 1940, the manufacturing sector in Argentina and Chile, and to a lesser extent Uruguay, made up about 20 per cent of GDP. These countries continued the industrialization process in subsequent decades, boosted by government policies that were decisively pro-industrialization, until manufacturing reached 30 per cent of GDP.[14] The advantage accumulated by these leader countries before 1940 enabled them to move forward with industrialization, which spread and became established in the 1950s. Unfortunately however, despite industrialization and the advanced economic growth of these countries (the highest in their history), the gap of economic backwardness continued to widen with respect to the leading world economies. In other words, the main capitalist economies grew much faster and there was long-term divergence between them and Latin America. Certainly, it was a period in which the terms of trade evolved against Latin American products. But is it possible to attribute all responsibility for insufficient growth to the type of international insertion? For Bértola and Ocampo[15] the economic volatility of this period was extremely important, and they highlight economies with a very fragile external commercial structure which were totally dependent on international prices. Endogenous tensions which were also responsible for high levels of inflation. Of importance was that the consumer price index in the decades of the 1940s, 1950s and 1960s increased above 30 per cent for Chile and Argentina, and surpassed 100 per cent annually in the 1970s.[16] No economy can withstand such high inflation over such a long period of time without its productive structures being affected. Inflation absorbed most of the growth, discouraged investment and constantly obstructed labour relations. These issues explain why Latin America started to harbour desires (in the lower classes and part of the middle class) for a social revolution. The Cold War context produced a radicalization of political options and loss of fragile pro-democracy pacts, ushering in a cycle of military dictatorships with plans to radically reform the short-lived political and economic traditions of the region.

The third group of countries (including Brazil, Colombia, Mexico, Costa Rica, Panama and Venezuela, as a special case) evolved at an average that was very close to the Latin American one. This group obtained the best results during the period of state-driven industrialization policies, resulting in growth rates that were high enough to prevent the gap with the rich countries from widening in the 1950s and 1960s. However, these efforts towards industrialization were insufficient and did not significantly reduce their backwardness with respect to the rich countries. They suffered the consequences of a demographic explosion which absorbed a significant part of the growth (as occurred with the economies of Central America, the Caribbean and the Andean countries), and Argentina, Chile and Uruguay also had problems of volatility and inflation. However, the influence of their trajectory, characterized by a historically low GDP per capita, was such that their progress with industrialization pushed total GDP upwards more than in those countries which had industrialized earlier.

The crisis of the 1980s, known as the foreign debt crisis, marked the worst period in history for Latin America's economic gap with the rich world.[17] This crisis forced the application of tax adjustments which had a homogenizing effect on Latin America, which until then had been characterized by its heterogeneity. At the end of the twentieth century, Latin America implemented policies that were unprecedented, both in their standardization, and because they were decided outside of the region. The Washington Consensus united the countries under a uniformizing packet of policies, and simultaneously situated them all below 40 per cent of the GDP per capita of the twelve richest countries in Europe. More recent history, since 2003, documents Latin America's economic recovery. Rising prices of raw materials help the region, to the point that the severe crisis affecting the most developed countries, appears not to have affected the Latin American region – historically sensitive to external shocks. This recovery has left its mark in statistics, but not yet in history.

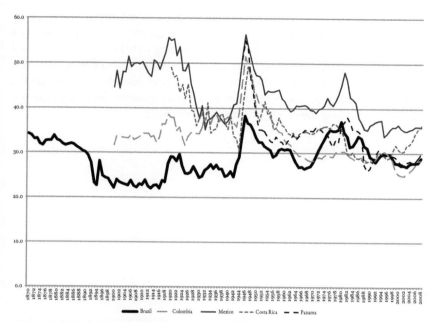

Figure I.4: Evolution of GDP per capita at PPP of Brazil, Colombia, Mexico, Costa Rica and Panama, compared with the twelve main western European economies (= 100) between 1870 and 2008. Source: Maddison (2010)

Conclusion

At the beginning of the nineteenth century, the GDP per capita of Latin America and the Caribbean was 30 per cent that of the twelve most developed countries in Europe. In the long run, this was the worst point in its history, together with the decade of the 1980s. The recovery over recent years does not yet indicate a trend. In addition, nowadays, the level differences which had been so important in the past have been reduced. Comparatively, Chile is at the one extreme, with a GDP per capita of 60 per cent while Haiti is at the other extreme with an index of 3 per cent of the GDP per capita of the European countries.

In a perspective of centuries, the national trajectories tend to differentiate themselves from each other. Those countries which adopted modern technical procedures which industrialization had made available to the markets – and especially those that facilitated the shift from biomass to fossil energy – managed from the start to prevent their economic backwardness from growing excessively.[18] In contrast, those countries which adopted modern procedures late fell behind from very early on compared to European countries. This established path dependence with long-term effects, leading to a wide variety of national experiences.

No Latin American country kept pace with the international progress after the Second World War. Twenty-five years of the 'golden age of capitalism' saw the gap of Latin American backwardness widening. Although it was a period of economic growth for the region, with a high prominence of state initiatives supporting industrialization, these were not vigorous enough to counteract the dynamism of the capitalist economies which were growing, reducing inequalities and establishing democratic forms of government.

1 EXPECTATIONS, INSTITUTIONS AND ECONOMIC PERFORMANCE: LATIN AMERICA AND THE WESTERN EUROPEAN PERIPHERY DURING THE TWENTIETH CENTURY[1]

Albert Carreras

Introduction

My hypothesis is that the increasing difficulties found by Latin American and Caribbean (LA&C) governments to promote growth enhancing policies via foreign trade during the first half of the twentieth century completely changed their system of incentives. Until quite late – for the smallest countries until the late 1940s – they hoped for the return of the old free trade order. The agreements reached at Bretton Woods – with a strong Latin American presence – were highly promising for all of them. The disappointment over the failure to launch the Organization of International Trade was enormous. While in the aftermath of the Second World War western European countries were able to expand their markets, to build a full employment consensus and to keep under control the challenge of the communist parties and the popular attraction of the Soviet Union, Latin American and Caribbean countries had to contend with the shrinking of their markets without any clear explanation as to why they were shrinking. The only reason was the opportunistic behaviour of the developed countries, taking advantage of the Cold War series of exceptions to the Bretton Woods agreements. I use the European southern peripheral countries as a counter-example.

If everybody in the literature accepts the importance of the 'carrot' for post-Second World War western Europe, what could be the importance of the 'stick' for Latin America? In my view, the diminished expectations that were increasingly built from the 1920s to the 1940s fuelled the decline of Latin American institutions. How can we expect the governments to behave if what they discover is that there is no room for good policies? I interpret LA&C failure from 1945 onwards as the other side of western European success.

Looking for the Origins of Latin American and Caribbean Backwardness

Latin American and Caribbean economies have fallen short of any expectation. There is a widespread consensus on this basic fact. The shortcomings appear when comparing LA&C economies with North America, with western Europe, or with east Asia. Only Africa provides a case of worse performance than LA&C. Has this always been the case? According to many scholars, from the Steins[2] to Landes[3] and to Acemoglu et al.,[4] yes, indeed, at least since the colonial era and because of it. There is a widespread shared belief in the colonial origins of LA&C underdevelopment. The encounter of the old world and the new world produced a distorted economy, polity and society. There were ethnic exclusions and segmented labour markets. This experience could have also happened to the United States had slavery remained in force and had the Confederate States survived as an independent entity.[5] It happened to Brazil and a number of Caribbean colonies and countries. It also happened to all those countries with a large proportion of native Indian population. Only the southern temperate and mostly native Indian-free countries – Argentina, Chile and Uruguay – started almost free of this distortion and were able to develop without major political and social exclusions.

Authors like Engerman and Sokoloff have argued about the long-term consequences of the ethnic exclusions and of the concentration of political power in very few hands.[6] The lack of promotion of universal education, so harmful for long-term economic development, is rooted in the unwillingness of elites to diffuse the franchise and to allow all citizens to share the fruits of prosperity. Engerman and Sokoloff's reasons are all the more telling as they are based in a permanent comparison between Latin America and the United States. The roots of the divergence between the most northern part of America and the rest of the continent would be located in the period of US industrialization, from the mid-eighteenth century to the late nineteenth century. Even recognizing all the virtues of this argument, Prados de la Escosura[7] has found evidence that the divergence, if we can rely on the data available, occurs much later, mainly in the second half of the twentieth century, although starting perhaps in the mid-1930s.

There is ongoing research aiming at testing the 'colonial origins' hypothesis for LA&C underdevelopment. Both a classical essay by the Steins and a still recent volume edited by Bordo and Cortés-Conde are framed within the same hypothesis.[8] The authors arguing against it underscore the dynamism and progressiveness of Spanish colonies. It seems odd to suggest 'progressiveness', but this is exactly what comes out of a lot of cultural, economic and political research on eighteenth century Spanish America. The political and social stability based on a number of checks and balances within the colonies, the native Indian entitlements and the expanding economy of the eighteenth century, mainly of its last third, are presented as evidence to support a positive view on the achievements of the colonial era.[9] Those that point at the positive side of this epoch, insist on how destructive the independence and post-independence wars were. They elaborate on the negative economic impact of breaking the Spanish empire state into many pieces, most of them well below the optimal size. They also underline the loss of welfare that came out of introducing many different currencies, a number of different fiscal systems, and the multiplication of state military expenditure.[10] We still lack any proper quantitative estimate of the cost of independence and it could well be that all the current figures underestimate its real impact.[11] Historiography insists in the slowness of reaching a political equilibrium – half a century at the very least, if not sixty or seventy years – and in the economic costs of such a delay. But nobody has measured it for good. We only have a rough idea about it.[12] Those pointing at the most negative legacies of the Spanish imperial rule focus on its absolutist character and the lack of any previous experience of representative government.[13] This is a crucial issue highlighted at least since Adam Smith's *The Wealth of Nations*.

A second line of criticism to the colonial origins interpretation of LA&C underdevelopment is by pointing at its institutional failures during the first globalization era as the major explanation of current LA&C weaknesses. Coatsworth, in a number of essays has made a case for the importance of the long nineteenth-century as the origin of Latin American malfunctioning institutions.[14] Dye has elaborated on the same direction.[15] Countering this kind of approach it is worth reminding of De Long's[16] criticism of Baumol's[17] convergence hypothesis. De Long insisted on Argentina and the Southern Cone Latin American countries being very rich by 1870 and by 1913, and their subsequent failure being very much a surprise if assessed from that moment in time. If countries like those in the Southern Cone became so rich and prosperous, this implies that the issue on LA&C could be more on the tropical side – temperate regions are more likely to be successful than tropical[18] – or on the economic policy side – you can destroy your growth potential by continued economic policy mismanagement.[19]

We thus turn to a third line of criticism. If the culprit of LA&C backwardness is economic policy mismanagement, Argentina, Chile and Uruguay become important case studies as they provide a natural experiment to test this hypothesis. Assessing their performance against Canada, Australia and New Zealand has been the task of various generations of economic historians looking for the recipe of good economic policy management. But even in these cases, where much more and better information is available, we still miss a clear-cut answer.[20] The reasons for Latin American economic failure are pretty complex to disentangle, and this is a powerful factor behind the multiplication of recent research oriented towards testing various hypotheses on this matter.[21] All these authors tend to suggest that the major failures are a matter of the twentieth century. Some go as early as the turn of century.[22] Others focus on 1914 and the outbreak of the First World War.[23] There are also those who see the Great Depression as the most decisive watershed.[24] The suggestion made by Prados de la Escosura on the relative lateness of Latin America backwardness is consistent with the previously mentioned.[25] In this paper I will continue along this line, exploring some further foundations and some possible causes and consequences.

Evidence from Historical National Accounts

An important reason behind the dissatisfaction with these stories lies in the lack of proper data to test the hypothesis. Proper national accounting started, as elsewhere in the world, in the 1940s. LA&C countries were among the first to share the Bretton Woods and United Nations efforts to build a system of national accounts that could be applied to every single country in the world.[26] But the efforts devoted to building a system of historical national accounts have been far from comparable with those experienced by the OECD countries.[27] Even the Southern Cone countries are still confronted with big uncertainties. We know that they were rich by the early twentieth century – even very rich. This was clear since the very early Mulhall income estimates of the late nineteenth century.[28] Of course, this is not the case for the rest – but we really don't know for sure. Our uncertainties on, say, Cuban or Peruvian or Venezuelan GDP per capita are enormous for any period before 1945 or even a bit later.

Since the very first founding essay of Domínguez[29] LA&C countries have been assigned disappointingly low incomes per capita. Domínguez[30] puts it candidly when presenting the first results on per capital national income, in comparable purchasing power units: 'The relative smallness of the national income of Latin American countries is the most striking feature of [the] table'. Indeed, the highest LA&C country in per capita purchasing power adjusted income for 1940 is Argentina, at 56.7 per cent of the United States. Is it worth reminding that Prados de la Escosura,[31] in an exercise that estimates current per capita purchasing power adjusted income for a number of years, assesses Argentina's in 1938 as being 58.8 per cent of the United States. A very close fit! Prados de la Escosura[32] assesses the exchange-rate-based Argentinian income per capita for the same year as being the 29.6 per cent of the United States, while Maddison's estimate is 85.2 per cent.[33] Domínguez's purchasing power parity calculations were based on a basket of twelve food items, not including any manufactured good nor any service. How much distortion can this introduce we don't know, but it is worth investigating. Food items may not be representative of the whole basket of goods and services of an average individual. The year 1940 could also be a very dubious foundation for such a calculation if it was to be carried over many years. The international economy was particularly close and domestic food prices could reflect a set of quasi-autarchic economic situations. Nevertheless, the United Nations and ECLAC calculations had to start from this point when figuring out the income per capita levels of Latin American countries after the Second World War.

Stating early twentieth-century LA&C comparative high per capita levels is not straightforward. Astorga, Berges and Fitzgerald[34] begin their paper asserting that 'the leading Latin American economies started the twentieth century with living standards comparable to those of Southern Europe'. But some direct measures and international comparisons of the time, and the direction and intensity of the migration flows suggest strongly that their income per capita had to be in fact closer to the richest European countries than to the emigration countries of southern Europe. It is unlikely that the widespread Italian, Spanish and Portuguese emigration to the Southern Cone and to Brazil, contemporary with Italian migration flows to the United States, did not reflect notably higher per capita income levels in the receiving countries or regions. The international comparisons of real wages are compelling evidence in support of Southern Cone economic superiority relative to Southern Europe.[35] But this simple statement implies a significant change in our assessment of Southern America relative performance.

With the creation in 1948 of a specialized UN agency for the region – the Economic Commission for Latin America and the Caribbean (ECLAC)[36] – a lot was improved. We can safely rely on estimates after Second World War.[37] But the size of our ignorance is huge before that period. ECLAC made an initial effort to assess per capita GDP growth since circa 1925 for the largest economies of the region: Argentina, Brazil, Chile and a few more during the 1950s.[38] The effort, started in 1948 and extended until 1956, produced high quality monographs on a number of Latin American countries, but not all the reported countries – as happened with Mexico – accepted the resulting estimates or were willing to publish them under the ECLAC official seal. Even ECLAC was uncertain about publishing GDP estimates labelled as 'official' as they were highly politically sensitive.

Some individual scholars have tried their best to cope with the non-existence of proper historical national accounts.[39] They have relied on many other individual scholars who, in the wake of ECLAC attempts, published detailed estimates, mainly for the large regional economies. Unfortunately, we are still far from having full coverage and far from full consensus. The poorest countries do not have any data at all. Some have scanty data, and they have transformed them into a GDP estimate, but with a very fragile foundation. Even the population data is under suspicion. Now, in the early twenty-first century, when most of the developed and developing world is well documented with GDP per capita historical estimates, LA&C countries are still uncertain about their own.

The picture that we obtain from the available data provides room for various interpretations. As Prados de la Escoura in 2004 suggests, focusing on the three largest economies (Argentina, Brazil and Mexico) leads to a more pessimistic assessment of their long-nineteenth century (1850–1913) economic performance, while a broader view gathering data on as many economies as possible leads to a much more positive assessment with relative real GDP per capita growing at the same rate as what he names 'the Anglo New World' until as late as his 1938 benchmark. This makes sense: the size of all the LA&C countries was not big enough to trigger significant scale economies. Prados de la Escosura does not depict LA&C countries as growing at the same rate as the rest of the world during the twentieth century – Astorga, Berges and Fitzgerald's view.[40] He stresses the importance of the fall from 1938 to 1950 and from 1980 to 1990.

I present some figures comparing Latin American economic performance, as measured by Angus Maddison (2009), with the rest of the world and to some world regions. The data that he was able to gather allows for a comprehensive twentieth-century coverage in the case of eight countries: Argentina, Brazil, Chile, Colombia, Mexico, Peru, Uruguay and Venezuela (LA-8). Unfortunately there is no data on Cuba – a medium-size well-off economy, for Latin American standards, during most of the twentieth century. If we want to cover the whole region, we have to restrict ourselves to the post-1950 period. Indeed, this is my first approach. The first figure allows for both comparisons: the whole of LA and LA-8 on the world total.

Figure 1.1: Latin America on world total, GDP per capita 1950–2008

What we can see is a stable proportion from 1950 to 1980 and a declining trend afterwards. To be fair, the stable trend is made of two opposing trends: declining from 1950 to the late 1960s and growing from then to 1980. The golden age was underperforming for LA. The world downturn of the 1970s was comparatively much better for LA. After the debt crisis LA has been unable to reach a growth performance at the world average. It has lost its traditional situation above the world average to move to below the average during the last decade. I want to stress that the two periods that used to be considered as the best in overall performance – the golden age and the 2000s – are precisely those of worse comparative performance.

If we limit our comparison to the world leader – the United States – we obtain some features common to the previous figure: stability from 1950 to 1980 and decline afterwards. We can add that the comparative performance was quite similar since, at least, 1900, with the ups and downs of the Great Depression and the Second World War, but LA-8 remained around 30 per cent of the US per capita GDP.

**Figure 1.2: Eight Latin American republics on the Unites States,
GDP per capita 1900–2008**

The outcome is completely different if we compare with western Europe. There is stability in comparative performance from 1900 to 1940, but not after the

Second World War. The post-1945 trend is one of decline. The decline is very intense from 1945 to the late sixties as well as after 1980.

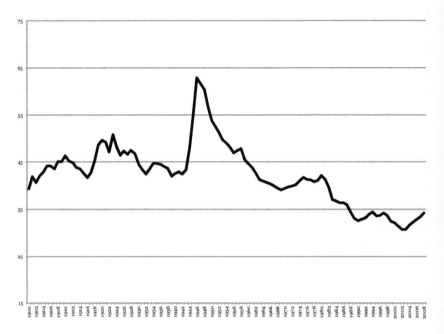

Figure 1.3: Eight Latin American republics on western Europe, GDP per capita 1900–2008

If we focus our attention to the Southern European periphery (Greece, Italy, Portugal and Spain) we can obtain some interesting nuances. These countries are closer to Latin America from various points of view. Italy, Portugal and Spain have provided most of their immigrants. Their levels of income are closer. In fact the relative income is quite similar for long periods of time. Italy behaves closer to western Europe, both in levels and in timing. The other three used to be poorer, and they were so, statistically speaking, for significant parts of the twentieth century. Greece catches up and forges ahead after 1945. But Portugal and Spain take a longer time to catch up with the largest Latin American republics. They only make decisive movements to improve their relative performance after 1958 (for Portugal) and 1960 (for Spain).

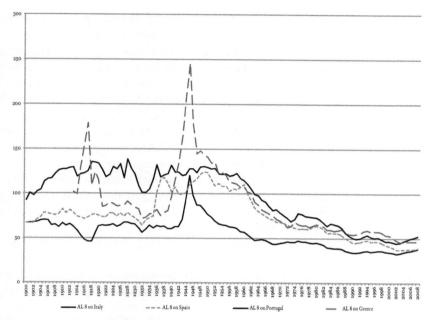

Figure 1.4: Relative GDP per capita of eight Latin American republics on Greece, Italy, Portugal and Spain 1900–2008

It occurs to me that these dates are very telling. They coincide with major policy changes in the two Iberian countries. Both Portugal and Spain made important steps to liberalize their economies in order to take more advantage of western European high growth rates. The Portuguese and Spanish dictatorships decided to change their economic policies as they felt very threatened by the European integration processes. They felt unable to keep completely to the side of what was an obvious economic success. This economic turn changed them from a Latin American destiny to a western European future.

The Breakdown of LA&C Expectations in the Aftermath of the Second World War

My hypothesis is that the increasing difficulties found by LA&C governments to promote growth, enhancing policies via foreign trade, completely changed their system of incentives. Even if their institutions were fragile, the experience of their distant and recent past pushed them to fully comply with international require-ments. Gaining the international 'seal of approval' was their priority. Until quite late – for the smallest countries until the late 1940s – they hoped for the return of the old free trade order. The agreements reached at Bretton Woods – with a strong Latin American presence as the major group of independent countries in

the world – were highly promising for all of them.[41] The disappointment over
the failure of the launching of the International Trade Organization was enormous – epochal. It is worth remembering that all of this happened in Havana,
the capital city of the country – Cuba – that we have estimated to have been
among those suffering the most from the closing of the markets of the economically advanced and politically democratic countries. While western European
countries were able to expand their markets, to build a full employment consensus and to keep under control the challenge of the Communist parties and
the popular attraction of the Soviet Union, the LA&C countries had to contend with the shrinking of their markets without any clear reason for it – or,
to be more precise, without any mistake of their own. Only the opportunistic
behaviour of the developed countries, taking advantage of the Cold War series of
exceptions to the Bretton Woods agreements, delivered economic success, and
only to those countries involved.

Let's briefly review one of these episodes. By June 1944, both US and UK
leaderships shared a view on the post-war order. It had to be built on such foundations that any temptation towards 'beggar-thy-neighbour' policies could be
avoided. Trade was recognized as the major single promoter of growth and welfare. The return to a world trade order based on free trade was fundamental.[42]
It is necessary to explain that free trade was not identified as an international
trade without tariffs. This high ideal of free trade was too far away at that stage.
It was initially designed to be a world of international trade without non-tariff
barriers. Tariff barriers are much less inimical to growth than non-tariff barriers.
The 1930s saw the multiplication of all kinds of non-tariff barriers: quotas, state-
managed trade, bilateral clearing mechanisms, trade permits, foreign exchange
intervention, and so on. Trade became a 'state' issue to be managed by state
officials. The outcome was the steep reduction of trade and the imposing of distorted, unnatural, anti-economical, trade patterns.

At Bretton Woods, and in a number of other grand occasions such as the signing of the Atlantic Charter and of the lend-lease agreements, the commitment
to a full return to free trade was settled, to be started with the dismantling of
non-tariff barriers.[43] Because of the war-reconstruction needs a transitory adaptation period of two years for international monetary adjustments was given to
be counted from the end of the war.[44] Plans to launch a new international trade
organization started immediately. Indeed, an international conference to discuss
the draft of the new organization (International Trade Organization (ITO)) was
called. It would meet in Havana starting 21 November. The 'Chart of World
Trade' was completed by 24 March 1948. Parliamentary ratifications started
subsequently.[45] Expert discussions took a lot of time and called for a range of
high level officers. The tensions between Western and Eastern powers (US vs.
USSR) were tough and resounded in the specialized journals. Highly politically
influential journals such as *Foreign Affairs* devoted important articles to push

forward the US proposal.[46] Feis, writing at the latest in January 1947, was mainly worried about the attitude of the Soviet Union.[47] Six months later, once it was clear that the USSR was not going to participate, Viner[48] (1947) was much more worried on the attitude of the Western countries. His final statement is a good summary of what was at stake:

> If it is rejected [the ITO Charter], whether by us or by other important countries, the consequences are clearly indicated: a return to the systematic economic warfare which prevailed in the 1930's, with its political tensions, its economic wasteful- ness, and its favourable setting for the launching by desperate leaders, on behalf of despairing peoples, of ventures fatal to the world at large as well as to themselves. The International Trade Organization Charter is the only available safeguard against such a development. There are no alternatives.[49]

This was published in July 1947, in the same issue where 'X' (George Kennan) published the famous article on 'the sources of Soviet conduct' that meant the start of the 'containment' doctrine that was to last throughout the Cold War.

Once the Chart was completed, the political discussion became more intense within the United States, as the political mood had changed and new concerns appeared. Criticisms were raised from various sides.[50] Some criticized the ITO Chart as close to socialism and economic planning. Other suggested that it would trigger massive imports from all over the world as it was too much free-trade oriented. Other complained about the loss of national sovereignty. All these criticisms could have been resisted if not for the outbreak of the Cold War. Western European pressure to assure electoral success for the pro-Western camp went in the same direction as US domestic fears about freer trade. The commitment to free trade vanished from the political environment and Cold War politics comfortably took the lead.

Indeed, what happened after the end of the war was much more complex than expected. The competition between the Soviet Union block and the United States allies became much tougher and demanding than expected. The reconstruction and the post-war business cycle were also more difficult to man- age than planned. The combination of fear of economic crisis in the United States with the fear of communist expansion in western Europe and the diffi- culties of the United Kingdom to adjust to the new peace economy and polity changed US priorities. US and western European governments, especially the UK and France, preferred to postpone the entrance into the Bretton Woods next stage – currency convertibility and trade liberalization – and decided to approve an exception. We know this exception as the European Recovery Pro- gram – ERP, the Marshall Plan – so successful for western European economic growth and for US economic transition to a new peace economy. But the ERP meant that LA&C countries had to wait many long years to come back to a freer international trade system (to be fair, they have never returned to such a system). In the meanwhile, western European farmers, as well as those of the US and Japan, succeeded in retaining the exceptional protection they obtained during the war years. Not only was the protection kept, but it was strongly increased because of the food scarcities that appeared during 1946 and 1947. No government was willing to cope with short-term food scarcities, and even less with a free trade solution to them. If food was missing, the politically correct argument was to provide stronger incentives to domestic peasants: higher domestic prices. They were obtained through tariff protection and through tough control of state trade policies. No wonder that they resisted the Havana agreement to create an Organization of International Trade with the goal of liberalizing trade in goods. Agricultural goods were immediately considered as exceptions. When the United States Congress refused to ratify the ITO chart, western European governments were relieved. They could keep on protecting their farmers, still crucial in any general election, and strongly motivated in their voting behaviour by purely economic factors.

The agricultural inefficiencies in western Europe brought about an important political outcome: the persistence of Western oriented, democratic, pro-market and pro-capitalist economies and polities. The political weight of farmers could never be challenged again. Furthermore, in a very short period of time, from 1948 to 1952, an alternative growth engine was discovered. Indeed, the reconstruction of German manufacturing capacity – especially important for the engineering sector – and increasing trade development among the ERP (Marshall Plan) countries produced an economic miracle. Manufacturing trade increased at an astonishingly rapid pace, as did GDP. Western Europeans enjoyed a number of exceptions to their Bretton Woods commitments. By 1947 they had the Marshall Plan. By 1949, the devaluation, against commitments previously accepted not to do so. Further to this was the creation of the European Payments Union (EPU) with extra ERP funding. In the meanwhile, the failure of the OIT was partly corrected by the creation of the GATT – another exception device against Bretton Woods agreements.[51]

The GATT and the successor organization in charge of ERP funding coordination – OEEC – extensively discussed trade liberalization. The solution was to forget about agricultural goods trade liberalization – and these were to remain excluded from any multilateral agreement until the creation of the WTO in 1995 – and to focus on manufacturing goods liberalization. Agricultural trade proved to be too difficult to liberalize because of the political levy of peasant interests in western Europe and across other industrial advanced democracies. Even manufacturing goods were very difficult to liberalize. A number of western European countries fiercely resisted liberalization – starting with France – and liberalization had to be negotiated step by step. First came, for a decade – the

1950s – the first round of liberalizations: the elimination of non-trade barriers. Then once these were significantly reduced came the Kennedy round, in the early 1960s, which consisted, finally, in a reduction of tariffs.[52] The impact of the tariff reductions agreed in the 1950s and 1960s fuelled western European economic growth in the 1960s and early 1970s. Some of the poorest countries in the world – mainly in east Asia – took advantage of the exporting manufacturing possibilities opened by GATT agreements. But the relatively medium and high income LA&C countries could not enjoy them. They had too much expensive labour to become competitive in world manufacturing markets.[53] GATT was never useful for them. The more the West and North developed, the more they were confronted with the real fact that they would never regain access to western European agricultural markets. Western European citizens could ignore this and criticize the abnormal weight that the United States had in LA&C life. But the importance of US markets was severely exaggerated, in relation to the complete closure of western European – mainly EEC – markets. Even those freer markets of the EFTA countries were well opened to Commonwealth countries, but not to the independent, non-recent colonial, Latin Americans. The more the Europeans increased their agricultural protection, the more the United States felt free to do the same with their own agriculture.

The absolute Europeanness of the political experiment of European integration meant very bad news for overseas countries.[54] They knew that they could never enjoy an open access to western Europe. They would be always considered as foreigners. Conversely, western European peripheral countries like Greece, Portugal or Spain fully realized that they were going to have a sit at the European table. Their pure locational advantage was enough to dissolve any major criticism once the dictatorships were to disappear and once they were willing to pay a price for the economic integration. This 'carrot' – the possibility to enter into the EEC as a way to impose self-discipline on the European peripherals – worked extremely well for all the peripheral countries with income per capita below the EEC average, but not for those that were richer (Norway and Switzerland) – but the latter did not care about becoming European Union member states.[55]

Spain and Western Europe as Counter-Examples

Let's consider for a while the contrasting set of incentives of, say, Spain and Cuba.[56] Spain decided to be neutral during the First World War, and enjoyed very much being so.[57] The 1920s were a very good expansion period. The Great Depression did not hurt the Spanish economy in a significant way. Foreign trade depression worsened trade expectations, but Spain did not suffer from financial contagion. The only major economic problem in the early 1930s in Spain was political uncertainty. Domestic problems were much more influential in explaining Spain's poor economic performance during those years. The Civil War was a real disaster in economic terms. So much so that Spain could not enjoy the new neutrality opportunities of the Second World War. Franco's Spain was heavily indebted to Hitler's Germany and Mussolini's Italy. As long as the World War lasted, Spanish exports were completely oriented towards Germany to repay war debts. Once the war was over, a long period of economic stagnation began, which was interrupted by changes in world geopolitics. Did Spain suffer from European exclusion? Against what used to be written and said, not really.[58] The Cold War and the Korean War made Spain much more attractive to the United States and to Western military defence.[59] The increasing economic openness of Spain starting in 1959 allowed for fifteen years of full Spanish exploitation of western European growth opportunities. When the oil crisis came in 1973, Franco's regime was at its very end. Indeed, Franco died in 1975. For a few years – 1977 to 1982 – it was unclear if western European countries were to quickly accept Spain's new democratic regime. But even in the worst moments, the general feeling among Spaniards was that European doors were opened in principle, and it was only matter of doing their own homework to have them fully opened. In some sense, this was exactly the case. The 'carrot' motivated Spanish citizens and Spanish political leaders to behave properly as all of them realized how much they could benefit from becoming members of the EEC and how much they could lose by not joining it.[60] As a Foreign Minister of these days (Francisco Fernández Ordóñez) put it bluntly responding to left-wingers' criticisms of Spanish application to EEC membership: 'it is true there are many problems in becoming part of the EEC, but it is much colder outside'. Latin America had to remain outside, and it was much colder, indeed.

Think now for a moment of the different opportunities available for Latin American countries during the same period. Like Spain, most of them were not directly involved in the wars – even if some were formally aligned with the Allies. But they did not obtain any major long-term advantage for their support. They were put aside in the Marshall Plan and their commercial expectations were completely frustrated. As I was mentioning, Cuba's case could provide a good illustration. Cuba, following the War of Independence with Spain, became heavily under US influence. The economic appeal of the US was, undoubtedly, its huge market.[61] The major setbacks in Cuba's economic life were the closings of the US market. First and foremost the Smoot-Hawley Tariff, passed 'in extremis' thanks to the highly successful sugar lobby.[62] US bad news arrived on further occasions, especially after the Second World War when Cuba was dreaming of coming back to a freer trade era and found herself abandoned and betrayed by the US Congress. No wonder the Cuban educated youth of the 1950s were so bitter about the United States. The comparison with Spain is increasingly tough. The more Spain could rely on western European markets to alleviate the toughness of Franco's dictatorship, the less Cuba was able to obtain any 'carrot' to sweeten Castro's political hardship. The political equivalent was even tougher. While Spaniards were very confident of their entitlement to become members of the EEC once they established a democratic regime, the Cubans were perhaps highly sceptical of the United States' stance to Cuba in a post-Castro world.

A number of books and articles have measured and praised the quicker western European growth of the golden years. There is widespread agreement that total factor productivity was a huge part of economic growth in western Europe during those years.[63] All of them show that increasing foreign trade was an engine of growth by means of increasing the size of the market and allowing for increased productivity thanks to specialization. Major research projects conducted by Crafts, Toniolo and van Ark located the main forces of the extraordinary western European productivity growth in the combination of expanding trade opportunities and expanding investment opportunities.[64] The domestic social agreements that cemented social cohesion and wage moderation were crucial to boom profits and their reinvestment. International agreements among the network of European institutions and of worldwide manufacturing trade liberalization allowed for ever-increasing markets.[65] What could have happened without the benefits of trade integration among the major industrial powers of western Europe? The stagnating growth performance of the interwar years provides an obvious answer. Another answer is suggested by western European growth performance compared to the rest of the world. Following Maddison's estimates summarized in Table 1.1, the major western European economies enjoyed not only an extraordinary high growth rate but an extraordinarily high proportion of this growth rate coming from total factor productivity – between 60 and 70 per cent. Growth miracles were rooted in the improvement and expansion of better allocation mechanisms, mainly through expanded trade. The importance of total factor productivity (TFP) is even larger when considering that the calculation is made out of total GDP growth rates. Had we estimated TFP on per capita GDP, its importance would be increased.

Table 1.1: Growth accounting, 1950–73

Country or region	GDP growth rate (%)	Factor contribution (%)			TFP contribution (%)
		land	labour	capital	
Latin America	5.2	3	35	27	34
OECD	5.4	0	12	26	62
US	3.7	0	31	28	41
UK	3.0	0	2	33	66
German FR	5.9	0	2	27	70
France	3.1	0	7	21	72

Source: Carreras (2006), elaborating on Maddison (1995).
OECD: Organization for Economic Cooperation and Development. By then it gathered all the most developed market economies, including all the western Europeans, the United States and Canada, Australia, New Zealand and Japan.

The table also provides data on other major economic regions. The United States – the economic leader at that time with a huge advance on the follower economies – was not able to exploit any of the catching up devices so useful for the western European economies. Its performance is still good. Latin America is as good a performer as the US, but this is highly disappointing as its average income per capita is much lower. Here we have an underperformance to be explained. The Soviet Union is the region with the poorest total factor productivity growth rate – almost nil. This is unsurprising. All that we know concurs in explaining that the Soviet economic model was based on the growth of inputs and not on the improved efficiency in their use.[66] The Asian region (excluding Japan) had a similar performance to Latin America – also a very disappointing record for a part of the world that came out of the Second World War devastated and with many catching up opportunities. As a region these opportunities were missed until the 1970s. Only very few economies – South Korea, Taiwan, Singapore and Hong Kong – were able to benefit from them.

Even if a number of authors that look at LA&C performance over the twentieth century stress that the region's performance was quite normal, the fact is that the region was a clear underperformer since the Great Depression.[67] Total factor productivity was more heavily reduced in LA&C, while the contribution of labour and land, far more significant.

Both LA&C and western European experiences suggest that western European success could be measured as some 1.5 yearly extra growth percentage points. This is the result of comparing OECD and Latin America TFPs. But if the comparison is focused on the more EEC-related western European countries, such as France or Germany (Federal Republic), the range goes from 1.5 to 2.5 yearly percentage points.[68]

The importance of trade expansion can also be assessed measuring trade openness. Astorga, Berges and Filtzgerald[69] provide an aggregate picture for the largest six LA&C economies through the twentieth century. Openness recovered from the lowest twentieth-century levels attained by the mid 1940s, but contrary to what happened in western Europe, recovery was very limited.[70] It failed, by a large degree, to come back to pre-Second World War and to pre-First World War levels. And the recovery in openness lasted only ten years. After the mid-1950s LA trade openness start to drop very quickly. It reached a new minimum (a secular minimum!) during the 1960s. The whole decade was a stagnating period in openness. Just when western Europe was reaching its maximum levels, LA was confined to its lowest. The contrast in experiences is dramatic.

I have come back to the OXLAD database (the one created and used by Astorga, Berges and Fitzgerald) to check this picture. With the data provided by OXLAD it is possible to assess openness as they include current data on imports and exports in US dollars, data on GDP at local currency and data on exchange rates to the US dollars (GDP at US current dollars is derived from there). Therefore openness is assessed at US dollars at current exchange rates. No PPP correction is introduced. These estimates are possible for the three largest Latin American economies from 1900 to 2000. But it is not possible to repeat the estimate for such a long period for all the other countries. Indeed, the twenty republics can only be covered from 1960. As this year could be too late to grasp the major changes that occurred after Second World War, I have made an effort to take full advantage of the available information to expand the time coverage of the openness index. Before 1960, and as we go back in time, there are fewer and fewer countries with adequate data. I have estimated the overall Latin American openness ratio out of the available data and adjusting it as we go back in time.

This is what I have estimated in the next figure. I compare the openness degree for the three largest Latin American economies (Argentina, Brazil and Mexico) with the whole of the region. The other countries enter at various moments: Peru in 1900, Cuba in 1903 (I interpolated GDP data between 1958 and 1962), Venezuela in 1920, Guatemala and Honduras in 1925, Chile, Colombia and Ecuador in 1940, Costa Rica, the Dominican Republic, El Salvador, Panama and Paraguay in 1950, and Bolivia, Haiti, Nicaragua and Uruguay in 1960.

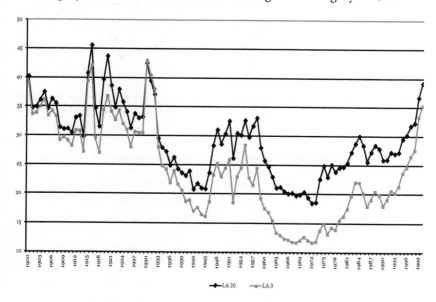

Figure 1.5: Openness of Latin America 20 vs Latin America 3 (Argentina, Brazil and Mexico), 1900–2000

The contrast of the three largest economies to the whole of the region is interesting. As could be expected, the large economies were less open than the medium and small economies. The import substitution turn was more intense in the large economies. The difference between these and the whole was at a maximum in the 1960s and 1970s. The liberalization of the 1990s brought openness differentials back to normal. These considerations make sense to hammer the point that there were many commonalities in the openness experience of Latin American economies, but that the large economies went through it in a more extreme way.

The Latin American openness ratio can be compared with western Europe.[71] Both have been estimated in a similar way, out of current export, import and GDP values. This is what is displayed in the next figure:

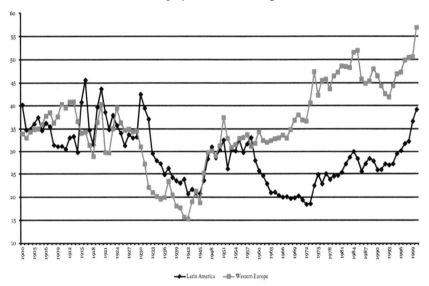

Figure 1.6: Openness of Latin America vs western Europe, 1900–2000 (%)

Up to the 1950s Latin America and western Europe had quite similar openness degrees. Much can be said about their differences, but the overall picture is of fluctuations around a similar level. The impact of the wars and of the Great Depression is felt in both regions. Post-war recovery is also common. The differences explode by the end of the fifties. To be precise, it is in 1959 that the two ratios start to diverge consistently. By 1960 the difference amounted to nine percentage points. By 1970 it jumped to eighteen and by 1973 to twenty-three. The next figure displays just the relative openness of the two regions:

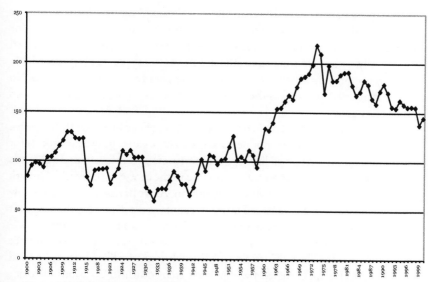

Figure 1.7: Relative openness of western Europe to Latin America, 1900–2000 (%)

From the relative low of 1958 to the high of 1973 we have fifteen years of systematic increase in the openness differential. After 1973 the differential had been partly reduced, but it remained very significant (50 per cent above the secular trend) by 2000.

The timing of openness differences is highly suggestive of the growth experiences of Portugal and Spain. It was exactly during these years that the two Iberian countries switched from a close economic regime to a more open ('cautiously open' in Donges words) one.

Institutional Consequences of Diminished Expectations

The huge European 'carrot' was a powerful engine in improving Spanish institutions and collective behaviour. It has been the same for Portugal, for Eastern European countries, and now it is the same for the new European enlargements. LA&C countries felt nothing else but a 'stick': reduced growth opportunities. The reason was as discretionary as 'bad luck' or 'bad location'. What could be the institutional effects of such a set of incentives? They could only be deleterious. No country can cope with pressing economic declining trends. There is no room for redistributive policies. The rise of the welfare state that in western Europe was deeply rooted in continuing productivity growth arising from market expansion and scale economies was impossible to establish in LA&C. There was no room for promoting savings. There was no room for promoting investment. There was no confidence in the future. Expectations were negative. Real wages declined, and real profits, too. Economic distribution became tighter. Each monetary unit to be gained became contentious. The gains for some were the losses for the others. Economic affairs became, at best, a zero-sum game; at worst, and more usually, a negative-sum game. The incentives to cooperate disappeared. No wonder if opportunistic behaviour became widespread and corruption usual. No wonder if political power was the major engine of economic redistribution and of monetary gains.

I am positing that this scenario is the consequence of negative growth prospects. Let me be more nuanced: it is not necessary to have negative growth prospects for such a disaster. It is enough to have growth prospects well below your neighbours – or the rest of the world if you are pretty close to the centre of the world. Growth prospects are comparative by their very definition. As we have seen how recent low growth prospects in the core large European countries are dissolving the scope for social cooperation to implement economic reforms, in a similar way the LA&C countries found themselves in a situation where nobody was willing to renounce their rights – or alter their expectations.[72] The rich countries like Uruguay, entered into a long decline punctuated by important steps down in occasions of major shocks (world economic commercial and/or financial crises).[73]

What can we expect from political leaders in such a scenario? Complete opportunism. Even the best intentioned of the political leaders, the most committed to his or her land and to its promotion would discover that the leaders of the Western world were completely uninterested with the destiny of LA&C. The LA&C countries did not trigger any positive cooperative game. US and western European policymakers were never interested in sacrificing the short-term interests of their agricultural producers in exchange for better economic prospects in LA&C and, eventually, in their own countries. Only in cases of dramatic challenges of their own economic and political interests, would Western leaders (mainly the US) react. This happened on a number of occasions, especially after Castro's revolution in Cuba. But whenever the LA&C leaders pressed their northern counterparts with the usual demands about the development of the Bretton Woods agreements, and about the liberalization of agricultural trade, the answers obtained were so sharply negative, that ignoring their consequences would be foolish for LA&C country leaders.

Political leaders as well as social and business leaders became, accordingly, increasingly opportunistic. In fact the whole population of LA&C countries became opportunistic. What we name 'populism' is about widespread opportunism – the other side of economic and political opportunism in the northern developed countries. Corruption is the other side of the same coin. When policy design is not sustained by the economic fundamentals, any agent – all agents, eventually – can decide to take care of their own private interests and to forget about cooperation. Cooperation stimuli disappear. Institutions decline and, eventually, collapse. The complex and disappointing political life of so many LA&C republics cannot be understood properly outside this framework. The increasing tightness of distributional conflicts was built in diminished economic expectations.

I should underscore that my argument goes from external expectations and constraints to domestic institution building. This is the reverse of what is usually told in the current literature. I also stress the fact that import-substituting policies were mainly reacting to external opportunities, and not framing them. In this I depart from a trend, rightly criticized by Haber,[74] of blaming 'Prebish' or 'CEPAL' because they defended what was no more than a 'pis aller' policy.[75]

It is easy to be proud, as many Europeans are, of your own institutions when you have enjoyed the progressive wind of history. LA&C countries had the wind of history blowing clearly against them. No wonder the quality of institutions declined. If my hypothesis is correct, the origins of LA&C backwardness need not be rooted in a distant past, but in the twentieth century, mainly in its second half. The institutional weaknesses of LA&C are a consequence of the diminishing expectations politically built by decisions taken by all the advanced Western countries – the OECD world – to build their own domestic consensus. In the same way that we can speak of segmented labour markets within a country, we have also had segmented world markets. Those that were not targeted by the protective rules of special international trade had to suffer a lot. The road down to impoverishment is not a good one to build a cooperative society, governed under the rule of law and with stable and democratic institutions. Such a hypothesis also suggests that the current LA&C bonanza based on the world's booming demand is as fragile as ever since the mid-twentieth century. Only substantial changes in expected access to the world's wealthiest markets could provide the lever to change the mind and, hence, the institutions of Latin America and the Caribbean. Indeed, we are seeing this mechanism at work in some countries.

The ambitious essay by North, Wallis and Weingast[76] (2006) reminds us how difficult it is to switch from a limited access social order – what they named 'natural state' – to an open access social order, and it could be easy to fall back from the natural state to chaos. They underscore the very few countries that have been able to make this transition after the Second World War; according to them, only a handful of European peripheral countries and a handful of Eastern Asian countries. Both groups were blessed by the second post-war arrangements or were indirectly benefited by them. Not a single one LA&C country was in the same lucky position, and they have paid a very high price for not being in the right place in the right moment.

Concluding Remarks

I put forward an explanation of the poor economic performance of LA&C region during a good portion of the twentieth century. There is wide consensus on the positive relevance of economic growth during the first economic globalization. Institution building would have been significant, allowing for a continuing diffusion of good practices, governance styles, well-rooted stability and commitment to property rights protection. The First World War shattered all these progresses, but it was considered as nothing more than a forced pause. The return to normality in the 1920s was sustained on very weak foundations. The great depression changed completely the state of world affairs, and the changes were to remain much longer than expected. The LA&C countries feared to lose forever their buoyant North Atlantic markets. The Second World War and, especially, its final steps brought new hopes that a new international economic order would bring a return to the good old pre-1914 era. Indeed, the Bretton Woods agreements went in this direction. Once the war was over, and after two years full of promise, the Bretton Woods commitments to liberalize world trade became more difficult to keep and, eventually, volatized. Latin American and Caribbean leaderships were shocked by this new turn that came to remain. Latin American institutions worsened as the hopes of good economic and political behaviour being compensated disappeared. As the leaders got a complete overview of the world, they realized that there was no room for cooperative behaviour. Only opportunistic behaviour would pay. Institutions suffered because of lack of positive incentives.

This negative picture has been mirrored with a counter-example: the economic success of post-war western Europe. There all the incentives played positively. International and domestic cooperation provided good outcomes. Policymakers as well as normal citizens became more law abiding. The former were more oriented towards cooperation and problem solving. The latter obtained trust in their politicians and in their institutions. Even the cases, as Spain, that were the most delayed in enjoying the benefits of the new environment strengthen our argument. What was at stake were the huge profits derived from the spectacular gains of productivity – of total factor productivity – attributable to intra-European and international economic cooperation, resulting in constant market expansion. The estimates of western European TFP compared to those of Latin America and the Caribbean are a rough measure of the costs of the lack of intraregional trade integration and international trade openness in the region.

2 ON THE ACCURACY OF LATIN AMERICAN TRADE STATISTICS: A NON-PARAMETRIC TEST FOR 1925[1]

María del Mar Rubio and Mauricio Folchi

Introduction

The issue of the (in)accuracy of foreign trade statistics remains in the economics, development and trade literature to the present day.[2] This chapter proposes a non-parametric test in order to establish the level of accuracy of the Latin American foreign trade statistics when contrasted with the trade statistics of the main trading partners.

The study of Federico and Tena[3] showed that, in historical terms, the accuracy of foreign trade statistics seems to be more robust than previously thought. The results of this chapter also point in such a direction. Nevertheless, this chapter departs from previous exercises regarding the (in)accuracy of foreign trade data in several aspects. First, the chapter focuses in the trade of a particular region in a single year. That is the chapter provides a test for the accuracy of the foreign trade statistics of seventeen Latin American countries for the year 1925. Second, rather than testing for the accuracy of the overall trade figures, the test is performed on data registered for a couple of quite homogeneous products, petroleum products and mineral coal. Third, the test applies to the accuracy of both the volumes and values registered on the official statistics of the exporting and importing countries. Most previous exercises did only test for the accuracy of the values registered, since the aggregate trade figures were used. Most of the previous tests tended to compare figures provided by international bodies (OECD, IMF, League of Nations, etc.), whereas here the foundations of such figures, the official statistics of the individual countries, are contrasted. Fourth, the Wilcoxon Matched-Pairs Signed-Ranks test is used to determine whether the differences between the data registered by exporters and importers are meaningful, and if so, whether the differences are systematic in any direction. At the end of the day, the question addressed is whether the differences observed are statistically meaningful. In other words, whether the story told from the exporters' side is or it is not substantially different from the story told using the importers' figures. The chapter, therefore, is not concerned with the issues of why and from where do the differences arise; these are important questions on their own right, but exceed the aim of this chapter.

The first section of the chapter presents the problem and specifies the issues to be investigated. The second section contemplates the nature of the data proposed for the test and introduces the data set to be used. Section three offers some preliminary contrasts of the data offered by exporters and importers. In section four the choice of a non-parametric test is justified and the workings of the test are revealed. Section five summarizes the results obtained. The conclusions recapitulate the main findings and propose a research agenda.

The Problem

The general mistrust placed on trade statistics, particularly those of underdeveloped countries, represents a heavy burden on economic history research, since trade statistics are one of the oldest and most complete economic series available for analysis. For instance, a research project such as the described in Carreras et al.[4] aimed at estimating the level of economic modernization in Latin American and Caribbean countries before the Second World War making systematic use of the trade statistics of these countries as well as of their principal trading partners in the developed world is immediately under suspicion.

From the seminal work of Morgernstern[5] (1963) to the present day, the users of trade figures are aware of the divergence that exists between exporters' and importers' figures. The impression from the economic literature is that the researcher should be even more suspicious of the data the more underdeveloped the country. Among others, the studies of Naya and Morgan,[6] Yeats,[7] Rozansky and Yeats[8] and Makhoul and Otterstrom[9] show that the accuracy of trade statistics provided by developed countries is higher than that of the developing countries. For instance, Makhoul and Otterstrom[10] found that the quality of the OECD trade statistics is much better than that provided by the non-OECD in a relatively recent period such as 1980 to 1994. Also Rozansky and Yeats[11] found that discrepancies between importers' and exporters' reports appear especially important for the less developed countries.

That underdeveloped countries shall misreport statistics more often than developed nations comes as no much of a surprise. Allegedly many of the causes for misreporting have to do with lack of means for the collection of data, systematic distorted statistics for a specific purpose – improve creditworthiness; collect (or avoid) higher taxes – simple corruption, smuggling, etc., all of which seem to occur more often in low income countries.[12] Following such a line of reasoning the straightforward solution seemed to be to use the statistics of the more developed trade partners instead, which are expected to be of higher quality. However, Yeats[13] concluded that 'the partner country gap filling procedures have little or no potential for improving the general coverage or quality of international trade data'. His final remark points at the need of 'improved procedures for data collection and reporting at the country level'.

In fact, there are a wide array of potential matters that would need to improve in order to reduce the differences between the quantities and, overall, the values, annotated at the port of origin and that registered at destination: different accounting methods (CIF versus FOB, general versus special trade), different times of recording (goods movement versus money movement, fiscal versus calendar years), prices used (declared prices versus official prices), different units of measurement (currencies and exchange rates; units in dozens, weight, volume, length, etc.), misclassification of products (thousands of subcategories versus 'all others' type of categories), geographical misallocation (country of consignment versus country of origin/destination), just to name the most relevant. A detailed explanation of these and more reasons for discrepancies can be found in Allen and Ely[14] and also Federico and Tena.[15] Given the list of issues, the ample pessimism about the accuracy and usefulness of international trade statistics for economic analytical purposes is comprehensible.

In historical terms, the view of Don[16] that the 'comparison of trade statistics, for a historical analysis of economic relations between two countries, must be abandoned', and the cautions of Platt[17] regarding the interpretation of the Latin American trade statistics before the First World War, added to the overall wariness. Also McGreevey[18] insisted in such direction when indicating that the trade data of industrialized countries may offer supplementary and alternative sources, especially for the Latin American countries, which only have incomplete and inexact commercial records.

Few exercises, however, challenge the general distrust on trade statistics. The work of Federico and Tena[19] contested some of the above issues using international foreign trade statistics of the pre-Second World War period and focusing on overcoming errors due to geographical assignment. Their results strengthened the trust on the accuracy of foreign trade statistics, at least at the aggregate level. In addition, they found no significant relationship between the level of development of the countries and the quality of the trade statistics produced.

Given the state of the art, any research based upon Latin American trade statistics first needs to face the challenge of proving that useful and trustworthy interpretations can be extracted from the historical trade figures. This is the challenge of the present chapter. Economic historians cannot hope for improvement of data collected many years ago, but renouncing the use of trade statistics altogether is, to the say the least, inappropriate. The problems associated with trade statistics must be recognized, but also the magnitude of the discrepancies observed must be placed within context. For some purposes a difference that in one metric looks large might in another metric be unimportant. How large is large in the present case depends, as usual, on the question asked. Differences that at the country level may look abysmal, placed in the context of the region will be a minor problem for the analysis at hand. The remainder of the chapter is aimed at proving that the story told from the exporter side is almost identical to the story told using the importers' figures when analysing Latin American countries within the context of the region. The question addressed is whether the differences observed are statistically (and economically) meaningful for the interpretation of the imports of petroleum and coal of the Latin American countries relative to each other.

The Data

Before having a look at the data, let's reflect about the nature of the data proposed for the test. It has been said already that rather than testing for the accuracy of the overall trade figures, the chapter concentrates on the reliability of the data registered for a couple of quite homogeneous products, petroleum products and mineral coal.[20] There are some reasons to believe that specific product comparisons may be more fruitful than overall trade contrasts. To start with, contrasts of homogeneous products had proven to yield better results. As referred by Federico and Tena,[21] the analysis of homogeneous commodities, such as wheat, provides a much less pessimistic view of the quality of the data (see the results of Ricci[22]). Indeed, homogeneous products have some advantages at the time of contrasting figures at port of origin and that of destination. Homogeneous implies simpler standardization and classification. Fewer errors can be attributable to misclassification of products and measurement error. Even when petroleum and coal products were not totally free of such problems the truth is that still the most 'detailed' listings did not go beyond three categories for coal and up to a dozen for petroleum products in 1925. The units of measurement although not completely standardized – long tons, short tons, kilograms, barrels, gallons, litres, cubic metres, were all in use – were straightforward to translate into common units (metric tonnes). In addition, the nature of the products made them difficult to smuggle in sizeable amounts. Finally, there was little incentive to systematically distort the figures in order to avoid taxes. Duties on imports of fossil fuels were small, if any, in the 1920s, according to the report by the US Department of Commerce (by J R Bradley) (1931). As for export taxes, although existing, they were affordable compared to the additional set of taxes paid at origin (production taxes, royalties, handling taxes, etc).

Homogeneity and the nature of the products chosen get rid of some of the problems listed in the previous section, especially when contrasting quantities rather than values traded. Yet some important ones remain on the list. One is the case of the geographical misallocation of trade. Where the final destination was taken to be the port of landing, the trade to all non-seaboard countries (Bolivia and Paraguay) would had been misallocated in the exporters' reports as corresponding to the intermediate countries (Argentina, Chile, Uruguay and Peru). The importance and possible ways of correcting this effect is investigated in Carreras-Marín and Badia-Miró.[23] Another issue, relevant only to the selected products, is the treatment given to bunkering. In some instances coal and petroleum arriving at Latin American ports would be right away loaded as fuel to departing ships. Some countries may record both the import and the export of such amounts, some other countries may record the importation but not the re-export, finally some other countries may not account at all the amounts unloaded and loaded at port for bunkering purposes. Regardless of the treatment given at the port of destination, the amounts were in all instances recorded at the port of origin as exports to the Latin American country.

More crucial to the differences between the values reported by the exporters and those reported by the importers is the so-called 'freight factor'. The 'freight factor' is the ratio between the CIF value of a commodity and the freight rate paid for its carriage, and can be taken as a proxy for the difference between CIF and FOB values. According to Moneta,[24] two main rules apply to the freight factor: (1) commodities of low unit value are relatively more expensive to ship than high-value ones and (2) the longer the distance a given commodity is shipped, the higher the freight rate and the higher the freight factor to be applied. Bulky commodities such as coal, petroleum, wheat, cement etc, are included in the first rule, they have a low unit value and are relatively expensive to ship. A telling illustration of the magnitude of the freight factor for bulky commodities is the method used by GATT still in the 1950s according to which the frequent procedure to adjust values from CIF to FOB was to reduce the value of fuel imports by 50 per cent and that of all other imports by 10 per cent (see Moneta[25]). So in principle, imports of petroleum and coal by Latin America are the worst case scenario for contrasting the values traded according to importers and exporters since both rules apply. The large magnitude of the freight factor should make the values much larger at the port of destination than at port of origin, thus very different.

Having reflected on the nature of the products let's look into the dataset. By 1925, most Latin American countries were net importers of coal and petroleum products, mostly from the United Kingdom, the United States and Germany; Mexico and Peru also supplied petroleum within the region. According to Rubio and Folchi,[26] the United States supplied little more than half of the oil and derivatives imported by Latin American countries in 1925. Mexico, with a share of 40 per cent of the tonnage, and Peru, with 7 per cent, together supplied the remaining half. In the case of coal, the United Kingdom was the main supplier of the larger consumers – Argentina, Brazil and Uruguay – while the United States was the chief supplier, sometimes even the only one, of coal to Central America and the Caribbean. In total, the United Kingdom supplied 68 per cent of the coal, the United States 26 per cent, while Germany and Belgium had much smaller shares (3.4 and 0.05 respectively). Altogether the G4 – United Kingdom, United States, Germany and Belgium – provided 98 per cent of the coal imported by Latin American countries in 1925.

Of the thirty-three countries that constitute Latin America and the Caribbean at the dawn of the twenty-first century eighteen elaborated trade statistics in 1925, although only fifteen offer sufficient detail about the country of origin of the merchandise and the type of products imported.[27] These were Argentina, Bolivia, Brazil, Colombia, Costa Rica, Cuba, Chile, the Dominican Republic, Ecuador, El Salvador, Guatemala, Haiti, Mexico, Nicaragua and Peru. Apparently most of the smaller Caribbean islands and neither Honduras nor Panama elaborated trade statistics in 1925. Paraguay did, but the level of detail made them unusable. From the statistics of Venezuela and Uruguay it was not easy to detect the country of origin of the products but the total amounts imported were collected. According to the Société des Nations[28] most Latin American republics used the Anglo-Saxon system for reporting their imports, that is, they reported 'general trade'.[29] The same source also informs that only Argentina, Guatemala, Paraguay and Uruguay used official prices in the valuation of their imports; the rest applied the declared prices. From the exporters' side the official national trade statistics of the United States, the United Kingdom, Germany and Belgium (referred as G4 hereunder) were used, plus the export statistics of Mexico and Peru in the case of petroleum products. The problems of classification of products and unification of the different units of measurement (volume in some cases, weight in others) were dealt with using the homogeneous criteria described in Folchi and Rubio.[30] Currencies were unified to the US dollar using the exchange rates in US Department of Commerce.[31] The result was a list of pairs of data, in volume and value, consisting of the figures of trade of petroleum products and mineral coal registered both at port of origin and at port of destination. Theoretically, what such lists of data report were cargoes to a specific destination measured at port of origin and the same cargo measured again when it reached its destination. In practice, the measures correspond to different sources, that is, the official publications of the country of origin of the shipment (the amounts exported) and that of the country of destination (the amount imported). From the section above it is clear that the two measures are subject to sufficient hazards to make them differ from each other. Furthermore, exporters (especially the United Kingdom and Germany) did not report minor quantities sold to smallish countries, but these amounts show up in the Latin American home statistics. These cases, where the source was checked but no trade was reported, were accounted as zeros. It may also be the case that amounts reported in the exporter trade statistics could not be verified at destination for lack of sufficient detail in the Latin American country, or mere inexistence of the source. These cases, where the source was unavailable, were accounted as missing values.

Some Preliminary Contrasts

The first impression of the list of data just described is somehow hazy. Take the quantities traded first. In the case of petroleum products there are quite few remarkable matches: Brazil, Cuba, Chile, Haiti, Mexico and Peru report tonnages arriving from the United States that were pretty close to the amounts the United States reported as exported to such destinations; Argentina, Bolivia, Costa Rica, Ecuador and Nicaragua reported imports from Peru only kilos away from the Peruvian exports record. But then, on the contrary, less than half of the weight reported as leaving the United States to destinations such as Colombia, Costa Rica or Ecuador were reported as imports in such countries, while Guatemala and Salvador declare receiving several times over the amount of oil that departed from the United States. Consider now the case of the quantities of coal imported from G4. The contrast of the volume imported according to both types of sources reveals for a first group of countries a very close match: Argentina, Brazil, Colombia, Cuba, Ecuador, Nicaragua and the Dominican Republic. A second group of countries (Chile, Salvador and Peru) exhibits a less satisfactory correspondence, but still plausible. Finally, four countries show what appear to be irreconcilable differences between their statistics and those reported by the exporting countries. These are Bolivia, Costa Rica, Haiti and Mexico. Turning the attention to the values in dollars does not improve matters. There were observable differences of millions of dollars in Argentina and Brazil over the value reported at the ports of origin of the petroleum or coal from the United States, the United Kingdom, Mexico or Peru. A priori these differences could be thought to correspond to the 'freight factor'. Yet a closer look reveals thousands of dollars under valuations found in the same Latin American countries in the trade with Germany and Belgium. Furthermore, Chile and Cuba report values for millions of dollars below the value assigned at the ports of departure. For all the reasons already described differences were expected to be greater in the values than in the quantities, but the swings are not those expected in all occasions. Besides, there are countries where the match comes down to a few hundred dollars in transactions involving several thousands, as it is the case of the United States coal trade with Nicaragua or Ecuador. It is not clear to the naked eye in which cases the quantities and values reported by importers and exporters are close enough to each other's or just the opposite.

Of course, several measures might be deployed to quantify the error. One measure commonly used is the difference between the sources as percentage of either source, although it implies an arbitrary choice of the source that is to serve as denominator. An alternative practical indicator for the measurement of errors in data is the *implicit minimal measurement error*, IMME, defined by van Bergeijk,[32] which here takes the form: {(destination source − origin source)/ (destination source + origin source) × 100}. The IMME-indicator assumes implicitly that both sources are wrong, and offers a conservative estimate (indeed a lower limit only) for the measurement error in the data. It should be considered as an optimistic indicator of accuracy. Even with its help it is difficult to take an informed position over the accuracy of the data as a whole. The indicator ranges from 0 to 100 per cent, and takes both positive and negative swings.

Moreover, it is impossible to find out from this indicator whether the 100 per cent found between say the British exports of coal to Costa Rica is more, less or as relevant as the 78 per cent found for Bolivia in the same trade, or the 30 per cent corresponding to Haiti in its coal trade with the United States. All it responds to is to the fact that there are at least 320 tonnes, 4049 tonnes and 72 tonnes respectively misreported in each of these transactions. Even within the same country it is not clear why the 51 per cent indicator obtained for the value of the petroleum trade from Mexico to Argentina is better or worse than the indicator obtained for the petroleum trade from the United Kingdom (which obtained a minus 69 per cent), when there were US$9 million in excess in the trade with Mexico and not even a quarter of a million mismatch in the trade with the British. Beyond informing of the existence of country-pairs differences, the simple contrast of individual country data does not help much to determine how important the discrepancies are for acquiring an accurate impression of the coal and petroleum trade in Latin America by 1925.

Federico and Tena[33] argued that a better test for the reliability is the comparison between the total of each country's trade (according to its own statistics) and the sum of these flows as registered by its partner countries' statistics. That is rather than using country-pairs contrast, they advocate for comparisons of total trade flows. The trade flows from main trade partners of each country's trade (according to its own statistics) and the sum of these flows as registered by the main partner countries' statistics are reported in Table 2.1 for petroleum and Table 2.2 for mineral coal. Only the countries where sources could be checked at both ends are included in these tables.

Table 2.1: Trade flows from principal partners in 1925, petroleum

Country of origin	Country of destination	Tonnes exported (source: countries of origin)	Tonnes imported (source: country of destination)	US dollars exported (source: countries of origin)	US dollars imported (source: country of destination)	IMME tonnes	IMME value
G3 +Mexico+Peru	Argentina	670,046	677,187	25,388,166	51,569,067	0.5%	34%
G3+Mexico+Peru	Bolivia	7,506	9,768	326,246	481,170	13.1%	19%
G3+Mexico+Peru	Brazil	552,147	505,753	19,591.826	21.019.438	−4.4%	4%
G3+Mexico+Peru	Colombia	11.838	4.189	978.825	408.144	−47.7%	-41%
G3+Mexico+Peru	Costa Rica	36.799	40.298	606.716	614.167	4.5%	1%
G3+Mexico+Peru	Cuba	1.352.397	1.281.949	17.101.243	13.098.023	−2.7%	−13%
G3+Mexico+Peru	Chile	923.112	906.540	12.359.821	10.117.282	−0.9%	−10%
G3+Mexico+Peru	Ecuador	27.838	13.100	628.118	661.074	−36.0%	3%
G3+Mexico+Peru	El Salvador	12.072	22.549	434.678	562.864	30.3%	13%
G3+Mexico+Peru	Guatemala	50.794	68.247	902.237	1.449.398	14.7%	23%
G3+Mexico+Peru	Haiti	5.165	5.446	395.072	419.694	2.6%	3%
G3+Mexico+Peru	Mexico	324.330	361.448	6.237.097	6.241.741	5.4%	0%
G3+Mexico+Peru	Nicaragua	11.639	14.615	705.560	491.826	11.3%	−18%
G3+Mexico+Peru	Peru	6.743	8.006	859.199	996.424	8.6%	7%
G3+Mexico+Peru	Dominican R.	46.908	30.784	1.569.392	1.035.500	−20.8%	−20%
G3+Mexico+Peru	Uruguay	183.684	226.045	5.347.012	7.381.505	10.3%	16%
G3+Mexico+Peru	Venezuela	14.021	8.552	771.165	798.032	−24.2%	2%

Sources and notes: Official publications listed at note 20, below.
G3 refers to United States, United Kingdom and Germany.
IMME = {(destination source − origin source)/ (destination source + origin source) ×100}.

Table 2.2: Trade flows from principal partners in 1925, coal

Country of origin	Country of destination	Tonnes exported (source: countries of origin)	Tonnes imported (source: country of destination)	US dollars exported (source: countries of origin)	US dollars imported (source: country of destination)	IMME tonnes	IMME value
Total G4	Argentina	2,925,091	3,111,979	18,015,876	33,665,568	3%	30%
Total G4	Bolivia	664	6,077	7,402	62,747	80%	79%
Total G4	Brazil	1,814,136	1,715,203	10,198,772	15,159,399	−3%	20%
Total G4	Colombia	3,125	3,252	21,942	27,970	2%	12%
Total G4	Costa Rica	78	808	1,610	7,636	82%	65%
Total G4	Cuba	701,707	659,389	3,513,734	3,114,860	−3%	−6%
Total G4	Chile	195,197	253,554	1,057,486	1,227,050	13%	7%
Total G4	Ecuador	1,131	1,187	7,369	8,462	2%	7%
Total G4	El Salvador	113	154	1,952	7,071	15%	57%
Total G4	Guatemala	3,287	264	18,524	3,279	−85%	−70%
Total G4	Haiti	83	156	1,275	2,771	30%	37%
Total G4	Mexico	118,643	65,746	507,037	566,793	−29%	6%
Total G4	Nicaragua	2,476	2,646	11,238	11,920	3%	3%
Total G4	Peru	32,542	38,389	197,389	281,834	8%	18%
Total G4	Dominican R.	9,484	9,697	69,440	77,157	1%	5%
Total G4	Uruguay	385,457	352,531	2,245,157	3,468,769	−4%	21%
Total G4	Venezuela	20,837	23,816	139,522	156,887	7%	6%
Total 17 countries		6,214,051	6,244,847	36,015,726	57,850,172	**0.2%**	**23%**

Sources and notes: as in Table 2.1 G4 refers to United States, United Kingdom, Germany and Belgium

Indeed, as hypothesized the comparability of the data improves when the aggregated flows are used rather than simply bilateral trade. The range of the IMME indicator improves, since the zeros are not present in the aggregate trade flows, thus it gets rid of the automatic 100 per cent indicators. Nevertheless the variation still goes from 0 per cent, as in the case of the value of the Mexican petroleum imports, to 47 per cent (negative) in the quantity of oil traded by Colombia (which in fact responds to Colombia reporting over 5,000 tonnes of oil coming from Costa Rica, oil that was almost certainly from the United States and so reported at origin, but not accounted here on the Colombian side). In general the gaps are smaller in quantities than in values, but no general rule applies. Only two swings remain negative in the value of coal traded but in petroleum trade five countries report smaller values than the aggregated values at port of origin. But still at the aggregated level there are many millions of dollars over- and underreported at destination. Argentina declared values for oil almost double the values at port of origin, while Cuba and Chile report lower values than their exporter partners.

This repeated issue gives ground to question one of the main assumptions of the literature: the exporters report values FOB, the importers report them CIF. In fact, while the former seems to be generally true, the latter was not in the 1920s. According to the Société des Nations,[34] more than half of the seventeen countries included in Tables 2.1 and 2.2, plus the United States, valued and reported their import figures FOB, at least in the period 1913–26. The list includes Cuba, Chile, Guatemala (if imported by sea however an arbitrary 25 per cent was added to the value), Honduras, Mexico, Nicaragua, Peru (which added 20 per cent to the value), the Dominican Republic and Venezuela. This fact together with the inclusion or exclusion of duties and taxes from the values reported at either end may help to explain the unexpected undervalues at port of destination and that the differences between importers and exporters values were in most cases smaller than the 50 per cent rule generally applied for fuels.

Nevertheless, the most striking feature is the accuracy of the aggregated figures for the region as a whole. The IMME-indicator obtained for the total tonnage comes down to 1 per cent (negative) in the case of petroleum, and 0.2 per cent in the case of coal. In absolute terms the implication is that of the over 4 million tonnes of petroleum and over 6 million tonnes of coal revealed by the exporters as sold to Latin American countries just over 50,000 tonnes of petroleum and 30,000 of coal were somehow misreported. The aggregate values for the region are not so exciting, for the IMME-indicators remain at 11 per cent for petroleum and 23 per cent for coal. In absolute terms the implication is that Latin American countries reported a total value over US$20 million above the values the exporters declared they obtained from their sales to Latin America of each of these products. Most of the difference was solely explained by the Argentinean overvaluation in all cases.

If the analysis were brought to an end at this point, the conclusions could only be pessimistic at the country level. The differences seem irreconcilable for some countries, whichever of the ample list of reasons of the previous section could be blamed for the discrepancies observed. At the aggregate level, however, the results of Federico and Tena still hold, but someone could argue it could be due to mere chance or self-cancellation of errors. Yet as van Bergeijk[35] reminds us 'absolute precision obviously is impossible to achieve and the improvement of the accuracy of economic measurement is in many cases not an optimal solution'. The important question is whether these gaps are sufficient to invalidate any inference extracted from this data. The economic historian would like to be able to take home some lessons from these data that withstand the mistrust on the original data sources. The trust placed on the answer depends very much on the question asked to the data. If the question addressed was about the precise quantity of coal imported by Guatemala, the over 3,000-tonne discrepancy between the importer and the exporters' sources may be a problem (in per capita terms the difference comes down to 0.11 kg per capita versus 1.5 kg, see Rubio and Folchi[36]). If the question, however, referred to the imports of Guatemala relative to the rest of the continent, the difference between sources may be trivial: Guatemala imported very little coal relative to most countries of the region whatever source used.

In fact, the story told from the exporter's side seems to be very similar to the story told using the importers' figures when analysing the Latin American countries within the context of the region. Better than the naked eye or the IMME-indicator this can be grasped graphically. If the importers and exporters were issuing exactly the same reports on the quantities and values traded, when plotted against each other a perfect 45-degree diagonal will appear. A data point below (above) the straight line would indicate that the importer was under-reporting (over-reporting) trade with respect to the partner's data. Our data would match the diagonal line quite nicely. From either source Argentina is the country making the larger expenditure in buying energy inputs. From either source Brazil and Cuba were next, though Uruguay spent just as much as the latter in buying coal. It does not matter the sources used, Argentina bought more coal by weight than any other Latin American country, followed by Brazil, Cuba, Uruguay, Chile and Mexico. In the case of oil, Cuba bought more by weight than any other country, followed by Chile, Argentina, Brazil, Mexico and Uruguay, regardless of whether the exporters or the Latin American nations give the answer. At the other end, Haiti used fewer tonnes of petroleum and coal than any of its neighbours. Bolivia – even admitting than the exporters could not see it as final destination, thus Bolivian statistics reported more tonnes than its trade partners – still remains at the bottom buying little coal and petroleum, and so on and so forth. This is not a complete picture of the energy intakes of the region – alternative suppliers and domestic production must be taken into account as in Rubio and Folchi[37]) – but it is a good indication that useful and trustworthy interpretations can be extracted from the historical trade figures of Latin America. However, the graphical representation is still subject to the observer's interpretation, finding some statistical reassurance confirming that the stories told from either side are sufficiently similar would strengthen the results.

A Non-Parametric Test

It has been already mentioned that is possible to think about the data presented as before and after observations of the same shipment. Theoretically, what the data report are cargoes to a specific destination measured at port of origin and the same cargo measured again when it reached its destination. Before/after matched-pairs tests are widely used in medical, biological, behavioural and engineering experiments, where a choice is to be made between parametric or non-parametric tests of paired data (see, for instance, Bland[38] and Motulsky[39]). Paired data means that the values in the two groups being compared are linked, that is, both samples have some factor in common, it does not matter whether it is geographical location or before/after treatment. That is why they are also known as 'tests for correlated samples'. In studies that gather before and after measurements like this, interest focuses on the difference between each pair.

The choice between a parametric and a non-parametric test derives from the underlying assumptions about the data to be tested. Two assumptions are most relevant here. The parametric tests assume the data to be normally distributed and of equal-interval nature (that is, someone who improved four points improved twice as much compared with someone who improved two points). In a non-parametric test, however, the assumption of being a normal distribution does not have to be met and the data are assumed at an ordinal-metric level (that is, that the original data can be validly ordered and that the difference between the two sets of data can be validly ordered). As stated by Lowry[40] the choice is not simply a question of good manners or good taste. If there is one or more of these assumptions that cannot be reasonably supposed to be satisfied, then the corresponding test for correlated samples cannot be legitimately applied. According to Motulsky[41] a non-parametric test is definitively preferred in situations where either the population is clearly not normal or some values are 'off the scale', that is, too high or too low. To these, most experts add other situations in which non-parametric tests will be preferred: when testing in small samples (<30) and when there are unequal variances across groups.

As it happens, it seems that most of these situations occur in the data presented here. On the one hand, the data presented is skewed. The Shapiro-Wilk normality test applied consecutively to our data rejects they are normally distributed. Neither are there various subgroups of data in the tables or the differences between values and quantities in each table. The differences in volume for the trade originating in the United States and in Mexico are the only series at the edge of a normal distribution, but failed the test. With few data points, however, it is difficult to tell whether the data are Gaussian by inspection, and the formal test has little power to discriminate between normal and non-normal distributions. Nevertheless, non-parametric statistical tests are to be used to assess variables that are skewed or for which normality is doubted as in this case. On the other hand, it is clear that there are values off the scale, million dollars in the larger countries versus few thousands at the bottom end, which also applies to the quantities with millions of tonnes versus a few tonnes. Besides, the equal-interval nature of the parametric tests is difficult to assume here. A country with a US$10,000 gap is not ten times as accurate as one with a gap of US$100,000, while the former may be a huge gap for Haiti, Bolivia or El Salvador, the latter may be a smallish gap for Chile, Uruguay or Argentina. In any event, when the data within two correlated samples fail to meet one or another of the assumptions of the parametric tests, the appropriate non-parametric alternative can be found in the Wilcoxon Matched-Pairs Signed-Ranks test (Wilcoxon-MPSR test, hereafter).

The Wilcoxon-MPSR test, named after the work of the chemist and statistician Frank Wilcoxon,[42] is one of the cornerstones of non-parametric inferential statistics.[43] This test is mostly applied in biological and medical sciences, although it has its foundations on an earlier chapter by the economist Milton Friedman.[44] The assumptions of the Wilcoxon test, according to Lowry[45] are: (a) that the paired values of XA and XB are randomly and independently drawn (that is, each pair is drawn independently of all other pairs); (b) that the measured variable (for eample, a subject's probability estimate) is intrinsically continuous, capable in principle, if not in practice, of producing measures carried out to the nth decimal place; and (c) that the measures of XA and XB have the properties of at least an ordinal scale of measurement, so that it is meaningful to speak of 'greater than', 'less than', and 'equal to'.

The Wilcoxon-MPSR test can be used to determine whether the differences between the data registered by exporters and importers are meaningful, and if so, whether the differences are systematic in any direction. The Wilcoxon-MPSR tests the null hypothesis that there is no systematic difference within pairs against alternatives that assert a systematic difference (either one-sided or two-sided). Ignoring zero differences, the differences between the values in each pair are ranked without regard to sign. Then the sums of the positive ranks (R^+) and of the negative ranks (R^-) are calculated. For a two-tail test, the smaller of

R^+ and R^- is called T. This T is the statistic that may be compared with the critical values in the appropriate statistical table. For one-tailed tests, T will take the value of R^+ or R^-, depending of the specification of the alternative hypothesis. In plain language, if the null hypothesis was true and there was no difference between the two series compared, then we would expect the rank sums for positive and negative ranks to be the same, that is, to have as many large positive as negative differences and as many small positive and negative differences. For the difference to be significant (that is, to reject the null hypothesis) the calculated T must be less than or equal to the tabulated value. Note that the Wilcoxon-MPSR T statistic has a sampling distribution that is approximately normal when the number of pairs is large – say, n ^{3} 15, close enough to allow for the calculation of a z-ratio, which can then be referred to the unit normal distribution, for the approximation formulae see Quang and Hong.[46]

Friedman[47] when pondering non-parametric methods stated that

> it is evident that the method of ranks does not utilize all the information furnished by the data, since it relies solely on the order and makes no use of the quantitative magnitude of the variance. It is this very fact that makes it independent of the assumption of normality. At the same time, it is desirable to obtain some notion about the amount of information lost, that is about the efficiency of the method of ranks.

In the same paper, Friedman concluded that the loss of information in using the method of ranks is not very great. A positive aspect of the Wilcoxon-MPSR test is that it is a very powerful test. If all the assumptions for the parametric tests were met the Wilcoxon-MPSR has about 95 per cent of the power of the parametric alternative. Further detail about the calculation and interpretation of the Wilcoxon-MPSR test can be found in Bland[48] and Conover.[49]

The Results

Two different specifications of the Wilcoxon-MPSR test were designed for the data of Latin American imports of fossil fuels in 1925, one for the quantities and another one for the values. The test for quantities had no prior opinion regarding the direction of the mismatch: the data provided by the importers could either overvalue or undervalue the data registered at the ports of origin. Simply, this test goes along the line that the Latin American statistics are unusable and the errors could go in any direction. Thus in the first test the null hypothesis is *H0: there is no systematic difference between importers' and exporters' tonnage data*, versus an alternative *H1: importers' tonnage records are different (greater or smaller) than exporters' data*. The second test matched the usual assumptions explaining the discrepancies in values: data provided by the importers may be larger in value due to the difference between CIF and FOB registrations. Therefore in the second test, applied to the value data, tests the null hypothesis *H0:*

there is no systematic difference between importers' and exporters' value data, versus an alternative *H2: importers' value records are larger than the values registered by the exporters.*

The results of this first test for the quantities performed over the total flows are very clear: the null hypothesis cannot be rejected either for petroleum or for coal data at the levels of p specified ($p = 0.05$ and $p = 0.01$). That is the Wilcoxon-MPSR test found no compelling evidence that the tonnage data offered by exporters and importers differ when the flows of trade to each country are considered.

Furthermore, we extended the test to the data as it was originally collected. That is testing for individual exporters (for instance, exports of Mexico registered in Mexico contrasted with every country's record of Mexican oil imports). Such a test presumes that the discrepancies among the pairs are independent within exporters, and only tests for those cases where data is known at both ends and sufficient pairs are available ($N > 5$). Again the results are very encouraging, for only in one case, the trade of petroleum from Germany to the Latin American countries, the null hypothesis can be rejected with confidence. Nevertheless, the trade of oil from Germany was insignificant for the region in absolute levels. Actually, it is due to its small magnitude that the data recorded at both ends differ: Germany did not report small trade while small countries did record these imports. In all other cases, for the tonnage of petroleum and coal imported, the null hypothesis cannot be rejected. Therefore, the Wilcoxon-MPSR test concludes that in the contrast of the Latin American imports of fossil fuels with each of the main trading partners, no systematic difference can be found in the tonnage data.

The expectation in the case of values was for rejecting the null hypothesis in most cases due to the assumptions of the literature: data provided by the importers may be larger in value due to the difference between CIF and FOB registrations. The results however point in a different direction. The results for the contrast of the value of petroleum trade are striking. Again as in the case of quantities of petroleum traded, only the German data rejects the null hypothesis. For all the other data, including the total flow and the individual cross-checks for each exporter, the null hypothesis cannot be rejected. According to the Wilcoxon-MPSR test there is no systematic difference between importers' and exporters' reports of value traded in petroleum.

In the case of the value of coal traded, the null hypothesis is rejected in two relevant and related cases: in the aggregated flow of trade and in the trade from the United Kingdom. The rejection on the null hypothesis, thus concluding that importers' value records are larger than the values registered by the exporters in the case of coal trade, seems more in accordance with the expectations of the literature. The issue then is why it is only found in these two cases and neither in the petroleum trade nor in the value of coal traded from the United States or

Germany. The answer may lie on the different compositions of the trade flows and the characteristics of the trade statistics of the destination countries. While almost two-thirds of the coal trade had as destination countries applying CIF valuations and official prices, not even half of the oil trade had such countries as destination. In fact, most of the trade originating in the United States had as destination countries using FOB valuations in their imports and declared prices, which explains the test result of no systematic differences between the United States exports data and the Latin American importing records. On the contrary, over 60 per cent of the trade in coal that originated in the United Kingdom had as destination one single country, Argentina, where imports were valued CIF and official prices were used. In addition, the omission by the British of petty trade added to the overvaluation on the Latin American side.

In summary, the result of the Wilcoxon-MPSP test for the value of coal traded can be explained by the distinct composition of the coal trade flows and the characteristics of the trade statistics of the main destination countries. Nevertheless, these finding do not invalidate the fact that Argentina was the larger importer of coal of the region in 1925, whichever source used. It simply adds a caveat over the value given to such imports at the port of destination, especially if coming from the United Kingdom. As it does for the rest of the imports of coal, which according to these results were overvalued with respect the value at origin.

The conclusion of the several exercises performed in this section is that only in very few cases can we accept the existence of statistically significant differences between the data provided by the exporters and that registered by the importing countries, and these only in value, never in volume. Given the nature of the products traded, the results are not so surprising. It should be pointed out that some works mention the fact that import figures respond better to accuracy tests than export figures, for instance Federico and Tena,[50] Yeats[51] and Kuntz.[52] Nevertheless, it should be noticed that here the exports of petroleum of two Latin American countries, Mexico and Peru, have also passed the test. No significant difference can be found between the export reports of these two countries and the imports reported from them by the rest of the region, either in value or quantities.

Conclusions

The chapter was aimed at proving that the story told from the exporter side is almost identical to the story told using the importers' figures when analysing the Latin American countries within the context of the region. The question addressed, whether the differences observed are statistically (and economically) meaningful for the interpretation of the imports of petroleum and coal to Latin American countries relative to each other found an answer making use of the Wilcoxon-MPSR test. The answer is that in quantities the differences are always unimportant statistically and economically. In values, the several exercises performed showed that only in very few cases can we accept the existence of statistically significant differences between the data provided by the exporters and that registered by the importing countries. The differences found are restricted to the values registered in coal trade, mostly trade from the United Kingdom, where the test rejected the null hypothesis thus concluding that the Latin American values were larger than the values registered at port of origin. It is worth remembering that 'how large is large' always depends on the question asked. Differences that at the country level may look abysmal, placed in the context of the region will be a minor problem for the analysis at hand.

This endorses the view that foreign trade statistics are more robust than previously thought for providing the basis of economic analysis. It is possible to extract some lessons from the Latin American trade data that withstand the mistrust on the original data sources. The results also point to the fact that trade data of industrialized countries are compatible with Latin American trade statistics and may serve as a reasonable supplement and complement to the regions' trade data. The historiography of Latin America describes its foreign trade statistics as mostly unusable. Our research and quantitative results contest this view.

Further research shall expand these results to other products in order to prove whether accuracy was restricted to homogeneous products. The examination shall also extend the time frame in order to explore whether the 1920s were an exceptionally good period for trade reporting. It would also be good to be able to test individual importers with respect to their trade partners (say Argentina's imports of petroleum versus all its suppliers rather than just the main ones) in order to study individual biases of trade. Researchers using historical trade statistics may find useful some of the challenges to the literature that the scrutiny of Latin American trade statistics brings into light: while it seems generally true that exporters report values FOB, not all importers reported their imports CIF in the 1920s, actually less than half of the seventeen countries examined here, plus the United States. Finally, the wider field of economic measurement (in) accuracy may also benefit from the non-parametric test used here, since in most cases, economic data better fit the assumptions of non-parametric inferential statistics than the most widely used parametric ones.

3 LATIN AMERICA AND ITS MAIN TRADE PARTNERS, 1860–1930: DID THE FIRST WORLD WAR AFFECT GEOGRAPHICAL PATTERNS?

Marc Badia-Miró and Anna Carreras-Marín

Introduction

The role of Latin America in international markets has been broadly dealt with by many authors, most of them having emphasized the connections between trade openness of the region and economic development.[1] In that sense, the timing of each growth period has been used, by part of the literature, to show successful stories of international market integration during the so-called first globalization. Such literature has drawn a picture of Latin America growing till the First World War at the same time as it was tightening its connection to international markets. The war has been said to have interrupted that process generating an enormous break through the decline in international trade. The literature of Latin American economic history has explained that break based on the strong decline in total trade volumes but also through the replacement of one main trade partner by another, that is the US replacing the UK.[2]

Such interpretations refer to the whole Latin American region, but they in fact come from data of only few countries, Argentina, Brazil, Uruguay and Chile. Although these few countries have a big role in the region because they are very rich countries, they do not necessarily represent what was going on in the rest of the countries, the majority being smaller or much poorer. When we enlarge the sample of countries by including the rest of Latin America, the area's shared economic history changes a lot.[3] The authors of works on this larger sample have shown an enormous diversity in trade patterns, energy consumption, cement consumption or importation of investment goods, among Latin American countries.

Linked to this is the debate about the area's international trade connections, the dominant idea being that of a Latin America dependent on British trade importation before the First World War, changing to US dependence after the war. But the empirical evidence for the whole region does not support that idea so clearly. Mexico provides a good example of what was going on in many other Latin American countries, where the US replaced the UK well before the First World War. The case of Mexico is well known from Sandra Kuntz,[4] and we enlarge it here to some of the other Latin American countries. Our data show that long before the First World War there were two very different trade patterns in Latin America: those countries importing mainly from the UK and many others from the US. The First World War had a bigger impact on British importers, the US having replaced the UK during the war, but things were not the same for those already importing from the US before the war. The fact that such big countries like Argentina and Brazil were two of the British importers before the war explains why such a phenomenon has been applied to the whole region.

The paper is organized as follows. The first section provides an overview of total Latin American and Caribbean (LA&C) trade with the UK and the US, following a geographical approach. The second section analyses the relationship between dependency on the UK/US coal trade and the First World War. Coal is taken as an example of a bulky homogeneous good for which geography matters a lot when traded and because of that we take trade data in volumes. We used a cluster methodology to identify statistically common share patterns among LA&C countries. We have also included a historical perspective, analysing how such structures changed over time. In the next section we move to total trade values trying to identify the most significant time points of structural changes.[5]

Latin America and Its Main Trade Partners

In a previous paper we noted the high quality of LA&C foreign trade statistics, when compared with those from suppliers.[6] However, if we wish to include as many LA&C countries as possible, we have no alternative but to use statistics from their main suppliers. Neither are foreign trade statistics available for all LA&C countries for the whole of the period (1860–1930). Geographical and historical coverage, therefore, determined our use of British and US sources.

British and US trade data were used as a proxy for total exports of developed countries to the LA&C region. It is necessary to emphasize that not having considered other European countries such as Germany or France hides a not insignificant part of the trade of some particular countries. But as long as we are not interested here in describing the trade patterns of each country as a whole but only in testing the US replacement of the UK after the First World War, our limited sample is sufficient. This is a reasonable assumption, at least for the majority of LA&C countries, and particularly in the case of coal.

Total exports per capita from the US and UK to LA&C countries were marked by highly unequal distribution throughout the region, in line with the enormous intrinsic differences among these countries. Some countries (Argentina, Uruguay, Cuba and Chile) retained a privileged position throughout the period, while others with higher levels of imports in 1890 had fallen by 1913 to lower levels in the context of the region as a whole (as in the case of Haiti or Peru).[7]

An original feature of our analysis is the number of LA&C countries included: thirty states, including the colonies and territories. The larger countries have been broadly treated in many studies, but much remains to be understood about the smaller countries. Indeed, large countries have been used to explain the whole of LA&C history because of the absence of information for the smallest ones. The inclusion of these small countries offers a quite different story about the whole. In 1890, Uruguay imported from the UK and the US US$22,116 per capita meanwhile Bolivia imported only US$95; in 1913, Cuba imported US$33,718 per capita and Bolivia US$1,343; and in 1925 Panama imported US$43,008 per capita but Paraguay only US$1533. As a consequence of such enormous differences among Latin American countries, we seriously question the existence of a unique pattern for the region.

If we focus only on the two main LA&C trade suppliers, we observe the existence of well-defined geographical trade areas, through very different US and British market shares. We have considered the percentage corresponding to each one of the exporters in the importer country as a measure of a country's dependency on each supplier. In the year 1890, the US's importation of Paraguay was non-existent, and the whole trade of that country (only referring to the US and the UK) was British. The UK represented 83 per cent of Argentina's and Chile's importation, 79 per cent of Peru's imports, 76 per cent in the case of Uruguay, 75 per cent of Brazil, 69 per cent of Colombia, 66 per cent of Ecuador, 50 per cent of Venezuela, 42 per cent of Mexico and only 34 per cent of Haiti. In 1913, British percentages were as follows: 100 per cent for Venezuela, 92 per cent for Panama, 71 per cent for Uruguay, 68 per cent for Argentina, 65 per cent for Bolivia and Chile, 59 per cent for Brazil, 56 per cent for Peru, 53 per cent for Colombia, 44 per cent for Ecuador, 35 per cent for Bermuda, 31 per cent for Guatemala, 29 per cent for Nicaragua, 25 per cent for the Dominican Republic and Costa Rica, 18 per cent for Salvador, 17 per cent for Mexico, 16 per cent for Honduras, 13 per cent for Cuba, 12 per cent for Paraguay and 11 per cent for Haiti. In the year 1925 British shares on Latin American trade had changed significantly, being 51 per cent for Paraguay, 49 per cent for Argentina, 47 per cent for Brazil, 43 per cent Chile, 42 per cent for Uruguay, 33 per cent for Peru, Bolivia and Ecuador, 32 per cent for Venezuela, 31 per cent for Colombia, 25 per cent for Salvador, 225 for Guatemala and Costa Rica, 20 per cent for Honduras, 13 per cent for Nicaragua and Haiti, 10 per cent for Mexico, and 6 per cent for Panama, the Dominican Republic and Cuba.

Although the countries with higher British percentages continued to receive imports over time, their shares clearly fell. The highest percentages at the beginning were to be found in the Southern Cone, with Argentina, Chile, Peru, and Uruguay at the top. The 'first globalization' and the entry of these countries into worldwide markets diversified their trade; British imports were still the most important, but with a smaller percentage (corresponding to the beginning of US trade expansion in the area).

At the same time, the importance of US foreign trade in Central America and the Caribbean was reinforced. The impact of the First World War, which meant the disappearance of European competition, together with the opening of the Panama Canal, which meant a significant fall in transport costs, had an important effect on the diminishing total amount of British exports.

The British percentage of the top countries (with the exception of Paraguay) decreased, and the US became the clear leader in the region, as Great Britain had been before. The finding has been widely reported in LA&C studies. Nevertheless, there were notable differences between areas. Whereas in the southern cone British exports accounted for more than one-third of the total, in Central America and the Caribbean this percentage was less than 20 per cent in most countries, and even lower in places such as Panama, Mexico or Cuba.

We have stated that there were important differences in the global trade substitution process after the First World War, but we also found differential patterns in the geographical coverage of each LA&C supplier. The distribution of British exports was generally much more concentrated than the US's.

In the British zone, three main destinations (Argentina, Brazil and Chile) accounted for 60–70 per cent of total exports throughout the period. In the US zone, three main destinations (Cuba, Mexico and Argentina (and Brazil instead of Argentina in 1890 only)) accounted for a smaller share, between 43 and 57 per cent of the total. Certainly, the large countries like Argentina, Brazil or Mexico appeared to be the main destinations for both exporter countries, as expected by their size, but in both cases other countries also appeared: Cuba for US exports and Chile and Uruguay for British exports.

The trend in British exports across the period shows an increased concentration in the 'first globalization', and a decrease in the later period. The same happened for the US, although a greater diversification is observed across the whole period. The only Caribbean country of certain relevance for British exports was Cuba, due to the importance of this country across Latin America. In contrast, US imports had already reached the smaller South American countries – like Peru, Chile and Uruguay – by 1913.

Latin American Coal Trade Geography

The LA&C coal trade began at the end of the nineteenth century. The almost complete absence of this resource in the region made importation necessary, despite the fact that some coal had been produced in Chile and Mexico since

1890, in Peru since 1900, in Brazil since 1912 and in Venezuela in 1913. At all events, LA&C coal production had a clearly secondary role across the region, and accounted for only 15–29 per cent of total consumption. These percentages are obviously greater for the few coal producers, but even so, shares varied a lot.

Chile was the only country to export coal, mainly to Bolivia, and in 1900 produced 98 per cent of its coal consumption, the maximum level reached for the period under study. Peru reached its maximum at the end of the period, with 87.7 per cent. Mexico only achieved 90 per cent in the 1920s, whereas for the period before the First World War its share was quite low (below 50 per cent). Brazilian post-war coal production only accounted for 14–17 per cent of its consumption, while the figure for Venezuela was even worse (around 2 per cent). Even considering the coal producer figures, dependency on coal importation was a common feature and clearly influenced the opportunities for modernization.

Although coal importation was imposed by the absence of the resource, there was some choice over coal suppliers. In the international markets there were only three large coal exporters: the US, Great Britain, and Germany. Although German coal had a marginal presence in the region, a huge amount came from UK. Indeed, British coal accounted for more than 50 per cent of supplies across the period, if the war years are not taken into account. If we look at the 1920s, the war does not seem to have caused dramatic changes in LA&C coal suppliers.

However, the high British figure refers exclusively to a minority of countries: Argentina, Uruguay, Brazil and the British colonies. For the other LA&C countries the big supplier was the US, even before the First World War. The higher concentration in British coal trade was the same as that observed for total trade in the previous section. What is different in the case of coal is the absence of a dramatic UK/US trade substitution after the war. Although the British coal share persisted well beyond the war years, a gradual decreasing tendency in the long run shows the substitution process taking place, even before the conflict.

A Cluster Analysis on Coal Trade Market Shares in Volumes

The First World War had a big impact on total coal imports in the region, there being a shift from an upward trend to stagnation in the 1920s. After the war, Great Britain almost managed to recover its market shares, while the US and Germany also increased their shares significantly. However, while this may be true for all the countries as a whole, the situation is quite different for each one in particular.

We thus developed a country classification method using statistical criteria based on market shares. Looking for common patterns we studied the share of each supplier, country by country, and its variation over time; we used a cluster methodology to identify these patterns, in which similarities are defined statistically.[8] The war years were excluded from the sample, because we were interested in testing structural changes before and after it.

A first group of countries shows a clear dependency on British trade in the two periods. Argentina, Brazil and Uruguay imported around 90 per cent from Great Britain before 1914, and only a little less in the 1920s. A common feature of these three countries is that they were not coal producers. Although it is an exceptional situation, we can also observe the disappearance of British imports during the war years. It is well known that the US entered LA&C markets at that time, partly because of the absence of European competitors and also as a result of increasing transport costs. What is more surprising is the relative recovery of the UK subsequently.

A second group of countries started the period being dependent on British imports and finished it as US dependents. The effect of the war proved lasting for this sample of LA&C countries, although for some of them the country substitution had begun even before 1914. Their small size, compared to the countries of the previous group, explains the greater instability of the results. It is somewhat surprising to find the British colonies in that group, as this would suggest, a priori, that Great Britain would be able to maintain its predominance. However, it seems that geographical proximity was a stronger factor than political ties.

A third group is defined by its high dependence on the US from the beginning of the period. All these countries were non-coal producers, and for most of them the US was the only coal supplier, providing 100 per cent of their imports for almost the whole period. These countries were Barbados, the Dominican Republic, French Guiana, Honduras, Jamaica, Nicaragua, Trinidad and Tobago, Panama and Paraguay. The First World War had no influence on them, as US predominance was already a reality prior to 1914.

For a fourth group of LA&C countries the US was the main supplier but its predominance was less stable than in the preceding group. The First World War appears here as a joint influence along with the opening of the Panama Canal in 1914. This enormous feat of engineering enabled distances to be crucially shortened, and ships no longer had to travel the long and treacherous route via the Drake Passage and Cape Horn. For example, shipping British coal to Ecuador entailed a journey of around 11,000 km prior to 1914 and only 5,000 km once the canal was open.

The fifth group comprises the coal producers: Mexico, Peru and Chile. A country's own production increasingly determined its consumption, whereas their main import trade partner remained unaltered: Great Britain for Chile and Peru, and the US for Mexico. What can be clearly seen in these countries is an import substitution process, which became more noticeable after the war.

All these results illustrate the geographical nature of these classifications. Proximity and trade areas seem to explain most of the common features identified in this section.

A Structural Change Test on Latin American Trade Values

The understanding of the different patterns of trade between countries requires a more detailed analysis, especially to test the importance of the First World War as a turning point in the relations between the US and Latin America. To do that we consider a structural change analysis to determine the existence of changes in trend in the series of foreign trade. In particular, we have analysed the structural change of the series of percentage of US exports on the sum of total exports of the US and Latin America. With this exercise we were able to determine the changes in the relative weight of these two countries.

The analysis examines the structural change of the parameters that arise from an analysis of time series by OLS.[9]

$$y_t = x_t^T \beta + \varepsilon_t$$

To do this we assume that for the time series we consider the existence of n points of structural change where the coefficients change, thus the model become

$$y_t = x_t^T \beta_j + \varepsilon_t \; (i = i_{j-1} + 1,..., i_j, j = 1,..., m+1)$$

where j is the turning point. At the same time, this point j must be estimated endogenously, minimizing the sum of the squares of the residues of the estimates. The procedure that we follow to find the breakpoints in the time series is given by the initial work of Bai[10] and their following works which are focused on finding the existence of multiple optimal breakpoints.[11]

The resulting breakpoints of the structural change analysis of the time series of the percentage of the US exports over the exports of the US and UK for all the countries and regions considered can be seen below. Since we have obtained the breakpoints endogenously, the number of years varies in each observation. In eight cases we have found three breaks, one break in two cases and in one case, four breaks. The breaking points have been for each country: in the case of Bahamas, the British West Indies and Guyana, 1896, 1916 and 1923; for Brazil, 1890 and 1913; for British Honduras, 1891, 1898, 1913 and 1921; for Argentina, 1898, 1908 and 1915; for the Central American republics, 1888, 1896 and 1913; for Chile, 1900 and 1913; for Colombia, 1888, 1897 and 1915; for Cuba 1892, 1904 and 1913; for the Danish West Indies 1900, for the Dutch West Indies 1896, 1914 and 1920; for Ecuador 1899 and 1914; for the French West Indies 1896, 1916 and 1923; for Haiti and Santo Domingo, 1911; for Mexico, 1899; for Peru 1900, 1907, 1914; for Uruguay 1908 and 1915; and finally, for Venezuela, 1913.

Instead of the search for structural change breakpoints endogenously obtained (with a non-fixed number of them), we would like to rank them to identify the most important ones, and we have to consider, a priori, a single break for every country or region. The results are as expected. In most of the countries, the first breakpoint is found around the First World War, except in British Honduras (1896), Central American States (1896), Cuba (1897), the Danish West Indies (1900), the Dutch West Indies (1896), the French West Indies (1896), Haiti (1911) and Mexico (1899). This result reinforces the idea about the need to observe what happened with the trade between the US and the region during the end of the nineteenth century and the beginnings of the twentieth century.

We observe a break around the war years in all Latin American countries, except Mexico, Haiti and Santo Domingo and the Dutch West Indies[12] where the US's exports had already overtaken those of the UK during the nineteenth century (in Mexico and Haiti it was in 1860 although in the Mexican case this was not constant until 1890). But we also observe a break in every Latin American country long before the war. As a result, something happened around 1890 that had the same or even more impact on Latin American trade as the outbreak of the First World War. Where can we find the explanation for this finding of the US as a main trade supplier before the First World War?

At first sight this should be an economic geography story caused simply by trade costs. But facts don't match this view because the more distant country in geographical terms (the UK) was nearer in an economic sense just at the beginning of the period, that is, when trade costs were higher, at the same time as the closest country (the US) in geography was more distant in economics. The fall of trade costs, which was the main figure of the first globalization, should have produced an increase of trade with distant countries related to nearer ones. But surprising facts work exactly in the opposite way: the closest country (the US) increased its presence while the distant country (the UK) lost trade shares. That astonishing result makes us look in other directions. At that point, Mexico, following the work of Kuntz[13], can give some clues. Was railway investment causing trade path dependence?[14] Did the US have smaller trade costs with Latin America at the beginning of the period? Should we measure the fall in trade costs in a different manner? Or it is all simply the US political determination from the end of civil war to expand its economic influence over its neighbours? Anyway, whether caused by railways, geography or politics, the common view of the US's changing relationship in the trade of industrial goods with Latin America before the First World War should be revisited.

Conclusions

The main contribution of this paper has been the evidence of the irruption of US trade in many countries of Latin America before the outbreak of the First World War. Only for a few South American countries (Chile, Brazil, Argentina and Uruguay), British exports were higher than that of the US in 1913. This finding differs substantially from the common idea about the war causing the replacement of trade partners in Latin America. Of course, this doesn't means that war was not a big shock in trade, especially for Latin American countries so dependent on external trade. But the US had already overtaken the UK before that big change in trade volumes. War had only increased something that had started before, at least for many countries in Latin America.

4 THE STRUCTURE OF LATIN AMERICAN INVESTMENT IN EQUIPMENT GOODS DURING THE MATURE PERIOD OF THE FIRST GLOBALIZATION

Xavier Tafunell

Introduction

Specialist literature on the Latin American economies during the mature period of the first globalization (1890–1929) has to date not studied the characteristics of the process of capital formation in these countries. This study presents a global while also detailed quantification of their investment in equipment goods, which helps to better understand the growth dynamic of these economies during this historical period, which was of vital importance in the race for economic development.

The first contribution of this study is the homogeneous annual series for spending on different types of equipment goods for a wide and representative sample of Latin American countries. This essay does not shirk the discussion of methodological problems of calculation which severely limit the overall results obtained from the sources. If reservations about methodology invite caution when dealing with the data, the results obtained advocate a revision of historiography. The most important contribution of this quantitative elaboration is that the results support the traditional view on the characterization of the productive systems of the Latin American nations as primary export economies. This, then, refutes the revisionist thesis which proposes that some nations made significant industrial progress during this period. The investment structure did not undergo any relevant change. Investment efforts focused on goods typical of the agro-export model: agricultural machinery and means of transport. The only element that apparently altered the investment model arose from the process of electrification. Those countries which channelled a greater proportion of resources into the acquisition of electrical equipment were those which invested most per capita and stood out for their relative level of economic development.

Over the past twenty years, economic history studies of the Latin American economies during the half century before the Great Depression have uncovered the key elements of the economic growth pattern of these economies.[1] However, the absence of sufficiently reliable GDP estimations for most of the countries in the region up to 1920 means there is still a knowledge deficit about their macro-economic evolution.[2] From a quantitative viewpoint, specialists still tend to overly base their interpretations on the magnitude of foreign trade, on the premise that the course of foreign trade determined the progress of the entire economy in these countries – the advanced and backward ones alike.[3] Data on productive investment may be indispensable as a complement to trade data. Is there any doubt that a quantitative reconstruction of productive investment would be extremely helpful in this sense? There are at least two good reasons why it would. The first is that, as historical experience shows, there is a relationship between fixed capital formation and total production in such a way that their behaviour tends to be analogous – to be more precise, the movements of the former are usually far more intense and occur slightly before those of the latter. The second reason lies in the insight that the composition of investment can provide us with the keys to decipher or better understand certain distinctive features of the growth model of the Latin American republics. It is common knowledge that some gave preference to the exploitation of their abundant mining resources, while others specialized in the exportation of certain agricultural products, whether processed or totally unprocessed. But, generally, the weight of the dominant activity is unknown, as well as the importance of the sectors that dealt with domestic demand.

In recent studies, the author has made known his quantitative elaborations on investment in machinery and other equipment goods.[4] This paper attempts to go further in this direction, and the point of departure of the analysis is the main components of investment in equipment goods. This quantitative study presents, for the first time, homogenous annual series for spending on the different categories of equipment goods by Latin American countries between 1890 and 1930. The systematic comparison of these series enables us to identify the similarities and differences in the investment structure among the countries as well as over time. This is substantial breakthrough in Latin American economic literature which takes us into totally unexplored territory. An examination of the data yields valuable insights about the economic dynamics of the countries studied, while at the same time innumerable enigmas come to light, begging clarification from national experts. Due to constraints of space and the considerable volume of the empirical material presented here, it is inevitable that many of the questions emerging from the data will be left unanswered.

The Decomposition of Investment in Equipment Goods: A Note on Methodology

Fixed capital formation has two basic components. One is the acquisition of machinery and other equipment goods and the other is expenditure on building and other structures.[5] This study concentrates only on the former, that is, according to economic literature, the one with the strongest link to long run growth – at least for economies at a low or intermediate level of development.[6] Ideally, within the division of capital formation into machinery and other equipment goods for the Latin American countries of this period, at least five groups should be defined: equipment for agriculture, for mining, for the manufacturing industry, electrical goods and, finally, means of transport. Given the importance of food processing, it would be highly advisable to distinguish between investment in this activity and investment for industry overall. Unfortunately, the sources used have their limitations which are, to an extent, insurmountable.

My quantitative elaboration is based exclusively on the official foreign trade statistics of the three major suppliers of capital goods: Germany, the United States and the United Kingdom (G-3 for short), on the premise that industry in these three countries supplied an extremely large (and stable) proportion of the equipment goods of these Latin American economies.[7] The virtues of this source compared with those of official import statistics of the Latin American countries have been explained in previous studies.[8] These prior studies also describe the shortcomings of the source, as well as the procedures followed to compensate for these so as to be able estimate investment in a sufficiently reliable manner. It is worth adding that when using the statistics of the G-3, we encountered great difficulties when trying to decompose investment into different types of machinery. Before 1900 German statistics made no distinction in this regard, and hence the calculation was based only on British and American statistics. For the entire period, British statistics provide only enough information to determine the agricultural machinery exported to nine countries in the region: Argentina, Brazil, Chile, Colombia, Cuba, Guatemala, Mexico, Peru and Venezuela. For the rest, we only know with complete certainty the magnitude of all the machinery exported by the United Kingdom, which has obliged me, very reluctantly, to limit this study to the above-mentioned countries. I have found no other way of ascertaining the approximate magnitude of industrial machinery for these countries, other than by calculating the difference between total machinery and that destined for agriculture. Naturally, the resulting residual value encompasses a wider range of activities than the purely industrial. We can assume that devices for the service sector, such as typewriters, calculators and cash registers were of little relevance. What were important however, were machines and large tools for mining. Accordingly, investment in industrial machinery comprises the manufacturing and mining industries, and to a lesser extent activities outside of the secondary sector.[9]

Table 4.1 contains four annual series of investment for each of the given countries as well as aggregate investment (AL-9). The series for transport equipment and machinery differ from those previously published because here I have opted not to make any extrapolations to estimate the total value of imported goods. Also, in the case of transport equipment I have deducted family cars since these are chiefly a consumer good. I have not applied the same criteria to electrical goods since the sources used made it impossible to distinguish consumer goods.[10] Given the calculation method used, the sum of agricultural machinery, industrial machinery, and electrical equipment equals total machinery. The addition of transport equipment gives as a result the aggregate of machinery and other equipment goods.

Table 4.1: Investment in equipment goods, by categories, in thousands of pounds sterling at 1913 prices*

	Argentina				Brazil				Chile				Colombia				Cuba			
	Agricultural machinery	Industrial machinery	Electrical equipment	Transport equipment	Agricultural machinery	Industrial machinery	Electrical equipment	Transport equipment	Agricultural machinery	Industrial machinery	Electrical equipment	Transport equipment	Agricultural machinery	Industrial machinery	Electrical equipment	Transport equipment	Agricultural machinery	Industrial machinery	Electrical equipment	Transport equipment
1890	263	580		2,344	124	771		649	106	218		649	7	89		7	41	459		226
1891	175	173	15	1,022	199	1,383	293	1,719	57	166	21	252	8	95	12	10	31	613	33	284
1892	498	280	44	188	156	920	145	1,494	126	212	27	334	9	81	10	21	48	824	40	264
1893	950	253	21	356	208	1.044	44	1,519	157	234	46	244	8	82	9	26	57	705	36	230
1894	919	202	28	225	199	937	63	1,044	84	228	21	407	9	72	8	14	37	503	34	214
1895	523	264	44	330	201	982	343	1,169	91	338	19	329	9	82	8	9	18	269	25	97
1896	305	340	61	435	226	947	113	1,213	60	249	20	235	12	108	13	17	11	100	14	26
1897	180	452	80	337	145	618	123	927	44	208	16	66	11	116	14	26	6	50	8	25
1898	444	430	291	536	149	549	67	608	42	140	21	99	8	104	12	25	8	73	15	40
1899	670	488	199	473	117	657	95	417	54	218	76	210	3	56	9	12	41	188	38	85
1900	520	598	151	540	98	627	477	448	42	291	32	320	1	32	7	6	40	269	52	149
1901	512	587	131	857	108	442	82	205	33	321	20	786	1	39	6	33	25	338	44	371
1902	613	607	93	648	115	560	129	139	37	360	19	408	2	39	6	56	51	306	33	186
1903	974	978	119	666	108	675	110	186	77	445	37	188	5	90	8	79	64	298	33	178
1904	1,397	1,265	142	1,585	128	885	166	297	78	540	44	577	7	111	7	39	48	570	95	222
1905	1,799	1,734	280	2,797	151	1,051	205	687	149	882	242	650	6	115	13	34	55	948	126	386
1906	1,544	2,593	694	5,144	177	1,328	369	854	204	1,038	173	1,059	8	93	8	27	40	840	134	460
1907	1,159	2,084	796	4,986	230	1,950	453	1,419	198	1,171	205	1,010	11	116	16	39	41	755	158	419
1908	1,601	2,002	705	3,044	213	1,782	420	1,458	72	769	371	968	12	138	11	61	38	558	132	289
1909	1,728	2,223	828	3,670	203	1,807	638	1,645	122	636	165	367	15	133	20	58	56	712	143	271
1910	2,011	2,480	1,312	3,464	292	2,250	1,142	6,622	234	710	258	328	15	164	33	70	77	1,054	247	465
1911	1,768	2,663	1,076	3,579	330	2,821	1,089	1,893	324	954	255	751	20	181	30	75	73	1,115	225	582
1912	1,796	2,801	1,265	3,591	358	3,369	1,225	2,832	301	1,002	382	800	29	236	39	60	68	1,096	275	542
1913	1,398	2,694	1,444	3,717	337	3,408	1,154	2,326	225	1,065	417	774	37	270	59	95	68	1,017	294	657
1914	690	1.665	898	2,540	182	1,683	565	974	89	691	224	682	21	239	62	92	56	762	260	622
1915	504	762	302	796	111	447	258	228	27	235	107	87	11	160	47	45	87	1,186	292	701
1916	508	621	287	423	154	555	364	240	39	392	226	159	12	128	50	32	112	2,123	413	994
1917	344	484	392	148	138	694	438	153	35	374	307	195	13	130	49	36	109	2,371	474	940
1918	509	418	321	148	108	575	322	126	24	575	338	235	11	73	31	44	100	1,514	352	911
1919	493	850	409	456	209	1,015	577	454	55	534	242	218	22	120	53	52	70	1,733	359	1,255
1920	739	1,705	771	1,367	422	1,975	852	1.331	108	605	257	318	74	397	109	203	198	3,558	899	3,792
1921	1,277	2,214	999	1,853	258	2,254	753	1.136	75	807	414	315	66	374	203	142	142	2,901	704	1,821
1922	1,006	1,990	814	3,195	349	2,239	397	795	48	609	462	1,095	59	359	59	100	77	1,019	248	258
1923	2,485	2,457	1,360	1,130	354	2,024	590	331	102	870	740	904	92	420	93	251	279	1,706	434	921
1924	3,188	2,691	1,134	1,447	533	3,118	811	913	133	1,032	492	731	90	511	115	293	348	2,176	669	1,339
1925	3,233	3,407	1,441	2,859	551	4,215	911	2,422	199	1,363	453	923	170	731	134	448	187	2,095	723	1,621
1926	3,138	3,522	2,117	2,772	279	3,304	1,007	2,482	210	1,636	1,058	1,228	113	990	217	1,032	133	1,081	522	1,269
1927	2,928	4,007	2,387	4,607	343	3,087	1,148	3,451	165	1,180	606	1,067	101	1,136	329	1,301	189	1,500	546	1,270
1928	3,609	4,888	3,042	7,019	525	3,534	1,336	3,759	171	982	674	900	92	1,059	438	1,491	149	952	487	649
1929	5,868	4,560	2,964	7,435	500	4,014	1,681	4,260	203	1,672	811	4,227	85	1,095	424	968	205	828	588	784
1930	3,230	4,277	3,273	5,980	233	2,329	1,198	1,103	149	2,099	1,146	2,182	48	366	307	168	110	503	563	474

*   G-3 exportations (Germany, the United States and the United Kingdom). See text.

Source: See table 4.2

	Guatemala				Mexico				Peru				Venezuela				AL-9			
	Agricultural machinery	Industrial machinery	Electrical equipment	Transport equipment	Agricultural machinery	Industrial machinery	Electrical equipment	Transport equipment	Agricultural machinery	Industrial machinery	Electrical equipment	Transport equipment	Agricultural machinery	Industrial machinery	Electrical equipment	Transport equipment	Agricultural machinery	Industrial machinery	Electrical equipment	Transport equipment
1890	1	42		10	102	378		476	8	95		20	3	48		14	656	2,681		4,397
1891	1	49	12	14	69	464	60	428	10	127	15	36	3	95	11	21	553	3,164	472	3,786
1892	2	57	8	11	64	361	41	246	6	66	7	38	4	70	11	48	912	2,872	334	2,643
1893	3	69	6	14	71	322	31	184	4	68	5	26	4	77	11	39	1,462	2,853	210	2,638
1894	2	80	7	29	63	367	47	159	8	51	3	19	5	83	13	19	1,326	2,524	224	2,131
1895	12	97	13	50	99	482	68	251	8	74	7	19	6	97	17	17	968	2,686	544	2,272
1896	14	139	15	48	102	510	76	355	12	112	11	30	6	71	17	12	749	2,577	341	2,371
1897	9	93	14	20	89	639	120	389	9	96	9	26	4	63	19	12	496	2,336	404	1,828
1898	2	39	6	5	116	850	99	339	10	104	5	28	3	51	10	8	783	2,340	527	1,688
1899	4	20	4	1	152	1,107	112	365	12	101	13	30	3	46	5	7	1,054	2,881	553	1,600
1900	4	19	5	7	146	1,145	116	481	10	155	39	57	4	38	5	10	866	3,174	884	2,019
1901	8	21	4	11	104	907	84	570	10	167	14	57	4	44	6	12	806	2,865	390	2,902
1902	7	24	3	5	102	887	156	610	7	158	21	66	2	25	6	9	935	2,966	466	2,126
1903	2	17	3	2	133	882	147	967	10	184	37	113	3	41	10	9	1,375	3,610	504	2,387
1904	5	30	4	8	127	949	147	766	12	235	33	104	3	73	19	12	1,805	4,657	656	3,610
1905	9	42	5	30	150	964	244	643	14	230	43	125	3	66	22	17	2,336	6,032	1,181	5,370
1906	9	39	6	27	187	1,275	309	898	17	234	70	184	5	62	30	13	2,190	7,504	1,792	8,667
1907	8	39	10	17	182	1,432	334	1,099	22	238	95	169	7	58	38	7	1,857	7,844	2,104	9,164
1908	11	30	6	13	157	1,277	251	773	23	198	39	95	9	67	21	9	2,136	6,820	1,955	6,710
1909	8	47	8	19	145	1,113	454	546	19	166	48	68	12	77	21	10	2,308	6,915	2,325	6,654
1910	10	41	9	32	192	1,271	744	803	31	241	50	72	11	98	28	17	2,873	8,309	3,824	11,873
1911	12	50	8	22	220	1,272	543	767	28	249	43	134	12	131	29	24	2,788	9,437	3,296	7,826
1912	15	65	14	18	217	1,204	504	528	24	267	66	90	15	171	27	32	2,823	10,210	3,795	8,492
1913	13	76	17	40	168	1,097	439	430	22	355	96	140	13	220	38	65	2,282	10,202	3,958	8,244
1914	7	53	11	42	42	472	235	221	15	278	62	93	8	146	34	52	1,112	5,987	2,351	5,319
1915	2	20	6	18	24	231	128	136	10	125	50	43	5	114	38	19	781	3,280	1,229	2,074
1916	3	24	9	8	36	316	164	221	16	209	58	67	5	106	43	25	885	4,473	1,614	2,169
1917	4	20	9	8	83	415	213	304	23	206	97	76	6	85	39	22	756	4,779	2,017	1,883
1918	4	17	6	10	119	475	207	386	36	249	77	132	8	54	24	16	919	3,949	1,678	2,010
1919	5	25	13	13	170	717	268	519	46	287	143	174	13	71	29	27	1,082	5,351	2,094	3,169
1920	17	35	19	28	222	1,431	490	1,049	65	509	290	442	31	180	55	82	1,877	10,396	3,742	8,612
1921	24	97	28	20	231	2,694	774	2,206	48	722	189	235	21	181	67	56	2,142	12,244	4,131	7,874
1922	30	70	15	15	208	1,546	420	474	29	311	71	146	31	208	45	47	1,836	8,351	2,531	6,125
1923	30	99	38	24	245	1,564	470	537	65	452	137	192	47	219	55	73	3,699	9,810	3,916	4,363
1924	29	120	73	71	338	1,667	914	1,711	117	555	156	418	48	376	80	164	4,825	12,247	4,444	7,086
1925	36	156	46	187	433	1,931	723	1,436	137	656	154	528	57	505	112	315	5,004	15,059	4,696	10,738
1926	39	128	87	169	476	1,839	776	1,094	86	565	138	442	63	811	200	674	4,538	13,874	6,121	11,161
1927	41	140	80	111	306	1,778	881	1,144	52	629	186	500	51	722	217	689	4,176	14,178	6,381	14,140
1928	30	143	92	189	382	1,964	895	1,203	63	526	140	443	38	609	236	575	5,059	14,655	7,340	16,228
1929	25	160	85	150	370	2,111	996	2,049	80	537	205	490	70	883	267	508	7,406	15,860	8,020	20,870
1930	16	52	51	127	469	2,399	1,344	1,822	46	404	164	428	55	651	404	406	4,356	13,080	8,448	12,690

Before examining the results, it is worth pointing out that the sample of countries we worked with is highly representative of the group. This is easily demonstrated by contrasting the magnitude of those investment variables from which we can extract values corresponding to the AL-9 and to the twenty Latin American republics (AL-20). The discrepancies in the respective growth rates are of no relevance.[11]

The Prevalence of Continuities in the Investment Structure

A good starting point for an analytical examination of the subject is to consider the relative weight of investment in different types of goods in each of the countries, for the entire period of 1890–1930. These data are compiled in Table 4.2. There are two features that stand out strongly. The first is that industrial machinery purchases easily triple those of agricultural machinery. As we observe in the last line of AL-9, the former absorbed 39.5 per cent of total expenditure on equipment goods, whereas the latter barely reached 12 per cent. This overwhelming predominance of industry and mining as opposed to agriculture is, at first glance, very surprising, since within historiography there is consensus on the characterization of these economies as producers of primary commodities destined for domestic consumption and export. Several hypotheses can be formulated to try to explain this. One of them is that, in effect, activities of resource extraction and industrial transformation demanded considerable capital endowment, whereas the capitalization of agricultural activities remained low. Another more convincing hypothesis advocates that the capitalization of agriculture appears strongly underestimated in my figures due to the fact that farmers preferred to use agricultural implements that were simple and locally or nationally produced.[12] According to a third, more plausible hypothesis this disproportion is simply due to the fact that machines and instruments used in the processing of agricultural products are not counted as agricultural machinery but rather as industrial machinery. This clears up the mystery at least in those cases where the agri-food industry was very important, as was the case with sugar production in Cuba.[13] Finally, an alternative hypothesis claims that the industrial sector was indeed preponderant over the agricultural: the investment effort both reflected and contributed to the progress towards industrialization made by some economies in the region. But, the data itself in Table 4.2 raise serious questions about this last hypothesis. Let us consider this.

Table 4.2: Composition of investment in percentage of the total, 1890–1930 (%)

	Agricultural machinery	Industrial machinery	Electrical equipment	Transport equipment
Argentina	22.3	30.5	12.9	34.4
Brazil	6.1	45.7	13.8	34.5
Chile	6.4	41.1	15.7	37.0
Colombia	5.7	48.0	13.5	32.8
Cuba	4.3	51.0	13.1	31.7
Guatemala	9.0	47.2	15.1	28.8
Mexico	7.5	46.6	15.6	30.4
Peru	5.6	52.0	13.6	28.9
Venezuela	4.7	52.0	15.7	27.8
AL-9	12.0	39.5	14.2	34.4

Source: Official foreign trade statistics of Germany, the United States and United Kingdom:
Germany. Kaiserlichen Statistischen Amt. *Statistik des Deutschen Reiches. Auswärtiger Handel* (Berlin, various years), *Statistik des Deutschen Zollgebiets* (Berlin., various years).
Germany. Reichsamt des Innern. *Auswärtiger Handel des Deutschen Zollgebiets* (Berlin., various years).
Germany. Statistischen Reichsmat. *Statistik des Deutschen Reiches. Der Auswärtiger Handel Deutschlands* (Berlin., various years).
United Kingdom. Statistical Office of the Customs and Excise Department, *Annual Statement of the Trade of the United Kingdom with Foreign Countries and British Possessions* (London: His Majesty's Stationery Office, various years).
US Treasury Department. Bureau of Statistics, *The Foreign Commerce and Navigation of the United States* (Washington, DC: Government Printing Office, various years).
US Department of Commerce. Bureau of Statistics, *The Foreign Commerce and Navigation of the United States* (Washington, DC: Government Printing Office., various years).

The second striking aspect about the table is the miniscule differentiation among countries with regards investment composition. Argentina is a notable exception. Its productive model appears different from the rest owing to the decisive weight of cereal cultivation.[14] However, what is most noteworthy is that the investment structure of the other countries is so similar. Moreover, a thorough examination of the figures is increasingly disconcerting, since the national differences we find are not those expected. In fact, they do not fit in with the view held by the most recent economic literature on the industrial progress made by the region in the decades before the Great Depression.[15] According to this viewpoint, a handful of countries spearheaded industrial progress: Argentina, Brazil, Chile and Mexico.[16] Table 4.2 suggests that not only Argentina set itself apart from the rest, directing investment so manifestly towards the agricultural sector. Chile directed proportionally the same capital resources to industry as the group of Latin American countries (AL-9). Brazil and Mexico dedicated relatively more resources, but were far from pouring a major part of their capital into the industrial sector. The countries which showed a greater inclination towards industrialization were Peru,

Venezuela, Cuba, Colombia and ... Guatemala! It is true that the differences observed are not great (excepting Argentina), but it is also true that these differences are greater than those among the other types of investment goods. How to explain such a paradox? The answer surely lies in the dynamism of both the agro-industry and mining. Bear in mind that oil drilling experienced explosive growth from the 1920s onwards in Colombia, Peru and Venezuela.[17]

Note how investment in the different types of goods developed over time. Table 4.3 shows the contribution of each category of capital to aggregate investment in seven sub periods. Table 4.4 proposes a different perspective on the issue by providing a comparison of the growth rates of the different categories of investment.

Table 4.3: Composition of the AL-9 investment in percentage of the total, in periods (%)

	Agricultural machinery	Industrial machinery	Electrical equipment	Transport equipment
1890–4	13.7	39.3	4.4	42.2
1895–9	14.0	44.2	8.2	33.7
1900–7	12.8	40.7	8.4	38.1
1908–13	11.2	38.1	14.1	36.6
1914–19	9.1	45.6	18.0	27.3
1920–4	12.0	44.1	15.6	28.3
1925–30	12.5	35.5	16.8	35.2
1890–1930	12.0	39.5	14.2	34.4

Source: See table 4.2

There are some more surprising discoveries in table 4.3, which fit badly with the hypothesis of early industrialization propounded by recent literature. There are two types of goods whose relative importance declines over time, though in a very gradual manner. These are agricultural machinery and transport equipment. They followed the same path: decline until the end of the First World War, and partial recovery in the 1920s. Electrical equipment evolved in the opposite way, and much more intensely. Its rise was so decisive that its relative weight increased fourfold in the first quarter century (until 1914–19), subsequently falling back slightly. With regards industrial machinery, there is no definite long-run trend observable, which does not support the optimistic thesis on industrial development of the Latin American economies in the mature period of globalization.

Table 4.4: Compound annual growth rates of different types of investment of the AL-9 in historical periods (%)

	Agricultural machinery	Industrial machinery	Electrical equipment	Total machinery	Transport equipment	Total equipment goods
1890–1929	6.4	4.7	7.7	5.8	4.1	5.0
1890–1913	5.6	6.0	10.2	6.8	2.8	5.2
1913–29	7.6	2.8	4.5	4.4	6.0	4.8
1890–1900	2.8	1.7	7.2	3.9	-7.5	-1.1
1901–13	7.7	9.4	21.3	11.4	9.1	11.1
1913–20	-2.8	0.3	-0.8	0.4	0.6	0.0
1921–9	16.8	3.3	8.6	5.9	13.0	8.9

Source: see table 4.2

If we consider the growth rates according to historical periods (see Table 4.4), we need to qualify the above statements. If we take the entire period (1890–1929), we find that transport was the least capitalized sector. This can be partially explained by the level of development reached in a previous phase, in the 1870s and 1880s. This was also due to the investment collapse following the financial crisis of 1890, the Baring crisis.[18] The strong boost of the 1920s did not make up for the paralysis of the previous phases.

Investment in the industrial sector (which we should not forget was mining-industrial) also expanded at a rate below that of the remaining group of activities. Interestingly, in 1890–1913 the stock of industrial equipment increased more than total stock. The jump ahead occurred in the long decade before the Great War, in a context of highly accelerated investment expansion, although not even at this juncture did industry stand out above the rest. The problem arose in the final stage, when it suffered an unexpected loss of buoyancy. It is noteworthy that the very modest expansion and renovation of industrial equipment occurred simultaneously to the extraordinary capitalization of agriculture, in the period 1921–29. During this decade agricultural machinery was the most dynamic component of capital formation. This suggests that Latin America redoubled its investment efforts in agriculture with the aim of deepening its specialization in the production of primary products, taking advantage of the opportunities offered to this sector by the world economy.

The clearest sign of economic modernization is not to be found in industry, but rather in electrical goods, the acquisition of which grew more than that of other equipment goods, particularly in the period before 1914. It grew in leaps and bounds in the initial decade (1890–1900), when investment in machinery progressed very moderately and investment in transport collapsed. The powerful initial take-off of electricity turned into explosive growth in the peak phase of globalization, the Belle Époque (1901–13). But the European war altered investment dynamics in this field too. Investment in goods typical of the agro-export model (agricultural machinery and transport material) absorbed such an enormous quantity of resources that it was, it seems, impossible to resume the vigorous pace of electrification of the pre-war years.

Table 4.2 led us to an enigmatic conclusion: that all the Latin American economies, with the exception of Argentina, apparently had very similar investment paths. This is difficult to reconcile with recent literature, which has highlighted the differences existing in the region.[19] A fresh look at the growth rates of the different types of capital goods, now with reference to each country, may help to resolve this. If, instead of focusing our attention directly on the rates in question, we express these as the difference from the growth rate of investment for total equipment goods, we will easily grasp what we could call the 'revealed specialization'. A higher rate of investment – sustained positive value – in a particular type of goods gives us a simple indication of the national economic model. Table 4.5 shows the results of this calculation for the nine countries studied and also for the AL-9, by way of a reference. In the table we can identify two fundamental historical sub-periods, with a view to distinguishing between transitory and permanent (long-run) specializations.

Table 4.5: Differentials between the compound annual growth rates of investment in total equipment goods and in each type of goods, by countries and in historical periods (in percentage points)

Country – period	Agricultural machinery	Industrial machinery	Electrical equipment	Total machinery	Transport equipment
Argentina					
1890–1929	3.4	0.5	10.1	2.3	−1.9
1890–1913	2.8	2.2	18.4	3.5	−2.7
1913–29	4.2	−1.9	−0.6	0.5	−0.8
Brazil					
1890–1929	−1.4	−0.7	−0.3	−0.1	−0.1
1890–1913	−2.5	−0.3	−0.5	0.2	−1.2
1913–29	0.2	−1.3	0.0	−0.7	1.5
Chile					
1890–1929	−3.5	0.2	5.0	0.5	−0.2
1890–1913	−0.8	3.0	10.5	3.0	−3.4
1913–29	−7.3	−3.8	−2.4	−3.2	4.6
Colombia					
1890–1929	−1.9	−1.9	1.3	−1.4	4.7
1890–1913	1.0	−1.8	0.8	−1.5	5.0
1913–29	−6.0	−2.2	1.8	−1.3	4.3
Cuba					
1890–1929	1.1	−1.6	4.8	0.2	0.1
1890–1913	−2.4	−1.1	5.9	0.1	0.2
1913–29	6.1	−2.3	3.4	0.3	0.1

Country – period	Agricultural machinery	Industrial machinery	Electrical equipment	Total machinery	Transport equipment
Guatemala					
1890–1929	2.2	−1.9	−0.2	−1.1	1.7
1890–1913	5.9	−1.8	−2.9	−1.3	1.6
1913–29	−2.9	−2.0	3.8	−0.8	1.8
Mexico					
1890–1929	−1.3	−0.1	3.1	0.3	−0.8
1890–1913	−1.4	1.2	5.9	1.7	−4.0
1913–29	−1.1	−1.9	−0.9	−1.7	4.1
Peru					
1890–1929	−0.2	−1.7	0.8	−0.6	2.3
1890–1913	−2.7	−1.3	1.5	−0.3	1.5
1913–29	3.5	−2.3	0.0	−0.9	3.3
Venezuela					
1890–1929	−0.2	−1.0	−0.1	−0.9	0.9
1890–1913	−0.6	−0.6	−1.7	−3.0	−0.5
1913–29	0.4	−1.7	2.1	2.4	2.9
AL-9					
1890–1929	1.4	−0.4	2.7	0.8	−0.9
1890–1913	0.4	0.8	5.0	1.6	−2.4
1913–29	2.8	−2.0	−0.3	−0.4	1.2

Source: See table 4.2

Table 4.5 makes manifest the general absence of industrial specialization, that is, the relatively weak impulse of industrial investment. Only in two countries, Argentina and Chile, did the purchase of industrial machinery grow faster than that of all equipment goods during the entire period (1890–1929). But in both the push was weak or rather, unsustained: in 1913–29 virtually everything gained in 1890–1913 was lost. All the remaining countries, except Mexico, registered a negative differential in both sub-periods. The Mexican economy is similar in this sense to the Argentinean and Chilean ones, with the peculiarity that the relative growth of industrial investment was lower in the period 1890–1913 which was subsequently more than offset by the inferior relative growth in the later period.[20] The joint industrial investment of these three aforementioned economies weighed significantly within the group of the AL-9 which is why it registered a positive differential (0.8 percentage points) in the period before the First World War. But in the following period the opposite occurred, and in a more decisive manner. In short, this corroborates what we deduced from the previous table: that Latin America showed a tendency to invest less in industrial machinery than in other equipment goods.

Argentina is the only economy to demonstrate clear and consistent agricultural specialization. In all of the historical periods studied, Argentinean investment in agricultural machinery grew at annual rates of between 3 and 4 percentage points above the growth rates of aggregate investment. And since this represented an astonishingly large proportion of the AL-9's investment in agricultural machinery,[21] it carried along the entire region to demonstrate a specialization in agriculture, albeit considerably less vigorous than that of Argentina. We can deduce from the table that, in reality, no other country showed this pattern of specialization. Cuba and Guatemala recorded extremely high positive growth differentials in a given period (around 6 percentage points) but these were largely cancelled out by resoundingly negative differentials in another period. In Chile and Mexico investment in agricultural machinery always grew at a rate below that of total investment, whereas Colombia seems to have turned its back on agriculture from 1913. Brazil and Peru (and Cuba) did the same before 1913, though more moderately.

What insights can be drawn from the table about other capital goods? With regards transport, it is worth highlighting the investment effort made by Colombia, Guatemala and Peru. All three show positive differentials in both sub-periods, which in the case of Colombia are very large. This must be attributed to their extremely delayed development of modern transport systems.[22] However, Venezuela, though in a similar situation, followed a path that demonstrates that the scant capitalization of this strategic sector did not lead automatically to investment in the sector.[23] Argentina is striking in the opposite sense, in that it neglected the transport sector because it had overinvested in it during the 1870s and 1880s.[24]

The data examined also gives a very clear picture of the situation of electrical equipment. Cuba, having concentrated its investment efforts in electrical equipment for four decades, stands out with the highest level of electrification in the region in around 1930.[25] For their part, Argentina and Chile dedicated such a huge quantity of resources between 1890 and 1913 that they recorded enormous positive differentials (from 10 to 15 percentage points respectively) over the entire period of 1890–1929. The electrification drive in Argentina in 1890–1913 (which in reality was far more in 1890–1900 than in 1901–13) was resolved in an unprecedented investment boom. Chile followed suit in 1901–13 (in Table 4.5, 1890–1913). Because this was a practically new activity, starting off from minimal levels, expansion in the initial phases easily translated into extremely high growth rates, and hence marked differences between the growth rate of electrical goods and those of other types of goods. However, the other countries did not experience the relatively intense bursts of electrification (in relation with the rest of their productive investments) comparable to those experienced early on by Argentina and Chile.[26] The Mexican experience was similar, though of much lower intensity. In Guatemala and Venezuela the electrical sector was neglected until the First World War. Subsequently, investment in the electrical sector grew at a higher rate than for general equipment goods, although not enough to compensate for the underinvestment of the previous period. In the remaining countries – Brazil, Colombia and Peru – electrical investment did not differ significantly from that of global investment. It is no coincidence that around 1929 all of these economies, including Mexico, had levels of capital formation that were far below those of Argentina, Chile and Cuba.[27]

Conclusion

The aim of this quantitative study is to show the results of an estimation of the basic components of investment in equipment goods for a sample of countries which are highly representative of Latin America. The series of the three categories of these products – machinery in general, means of transport and electrical equipment – have been presented in previous studies, which is why this paper does not focus on a description and analysis of the movements of the series of expenditure on investment goods. Apart from making known for the first time the complete quantitative elaboration, the text pursues the study of the investment structure. The exercise carried out on the previous pages aimed at unravelling the defining features of this investment structure, the continuities and discontinuities between the period before the First World War and the period from the outbreak of the war, as well as existing national differences in this regard.

The statistical reconstruction carried out revealed some surprising phenomena. One of these is the secondary importance of investment in agricultural machinery in relation to industrial machinery. Only in Argentina was the former not remarkably lower than the latter. In the other countries agricultural machinery represented no more than 10 per cent, or at the very most, 20 per cent of industrial machinery. At first glance, these results appear paradoxical, even implausible. The paradox is resolved when we cease to identify the second group with the manufacturing industry. Mining, in some cases, and the agrifood industry, in virtually all, explain the preponderance of industrial machinery within equipment goods. Unfortunately, the sources make it impossible to isolate investment in mining and in the food industry.

When we move from a static analysis to a dynamic one, we discover that investment structure did not undergo any significant change in the long run concerning agricultural machinery, industrial machinery and means of transport. The only really substantial change recorded had to do with electrical material, which became increasingly important until the First World War. Electricity proves to have been the engine of change for the investment model in those countries in the mature period of the first economic globalization.

A comparative examination of the growth rates of the different types of investment goods across historical periods leads us to the conclusion that mining-industrial capital stock grew less than agricultural and total capital stock. In the post-war period Latin America redoubled its investment efforts in primary industry, whereas industrial investment clearly decelerated. This leads one to believe that the economies in the region deepened the traditional productive model based on the exportation of primary products. If this were true, it would refute, or at least question, the optimistic thesis advanced by recent authors, myself included, which claims that industry progressed significantly in some Latin American countries during the era of globalization.[28]

The differences among the growth rates of the different types of goods, at a national level, reveal that only Argentina and Chile showed a propensity towards industrialization – and even this was moderate. Colombia, Guatemala and Peru concentrated their capital resources on improving stock in the transport sector in order to better their extremely backward infrastructures. Brazil and Venezuela followed a process of capitalization which was undefined, or unbalanced, since precedence was not given to investment in any type of goods in particular. Cuba, on the other hand, promoted electrical goods above all other types of fixed capital.[29] This assured it of a pre-eminent position in the process of the adoption and diffusion of electricity. In the same manner, Argentina and Chile became the most advanced Latin American countries in the race for electrification. These three countries enjoyed a far higher level of economic modernization and of capital formation per inhabitant than the other members of the AL-9, thanks (at least in part) to their decision to invest decisively in electrical development.

5 FACTORIAL DISTRIBUTION OF INCOME IN LATIN AMERICA, 1950–2000: NEW SERIES FROM THE NATIONAL ACCOUNT DATA

Vicente Neira Barría

Introduction

The income factorial distribution (IFD) is a decomposition that shows the contribution of each factor, capital and labour, to total income. Based on the identities of the national accounts system, we assume the following identity:

$$Y = Y_L + Y_K$$

Where Y is the GDP at factor cost, and YL and YK represent the total amount retained by labour and capital, respectively. We can also express the identity as:

$$Y = Y \times (LSh + KSh)$$

Where LSh and KSh denote the share of total income retained by each productive factor.

The IFD has recently received a great deal of attention from economists and economic historians alike for two reasons. One is that the IFD provides a long-term approximation of the distribution of income (hence, revealing issues of inequality), which complements analyses based on individual or household income. IFD can also be useful in providing information about trends in inequality when indicators of individual income are unavailable. More generally, the IFD relates directly to a number of areas of interest in macroeconomics – for instance, growth accounting.

New efforts to study the IFD in Latin American (LA) countries, using various methodological approaches, have been seen in national[1] as well as comparative analyses.[2] There are many reasons for this surge of interest.

First, global efforts of economic historians to provide earlier and spatially broader estimations of inequality have focused mainly on income distribution,[3] and this work has provided useful estimates of IFD for a number of Latin-American countries.[4] Second, the relative statistical wealth of Latin-American countries among peripheral economies encourages their inclusion in global data sets. Third, the persistence of enormous inequality in Latin America has spurred a great deal of academic discussion about the region.[5] Finally, some current macroeconomic and historic debates have indirectly contributed to improving the study of IFD. Among them is the discussion of the links between inequality and growth. Some investigations in this field have produced useful information for the study of the IFD,[6] along with other studies which focus on the impacts of the economic crises,[7] or those of economic policies and globalization.[8]

These debates, which directly or indirectly address the issue of the IFD, have been influenced by a more technical discussion of methodology. Gollin[9] suggests that the *LSh* extracted from national account statistics are understated because they exclude the income of own-account workers. While the definitions in national statistical accounting systems have since changed – the Fourth Revision introduced mixed income data – the importance of the exclusion of self-employed workers' wages has been stressed in past works by a number of authors.[10] Gollin's most important contribution is the three methodologies he proposes to calculate the 'shadow wage' of the own-account workers. He concludes that when *LSh* is corrected, the correlation between *LSh* and GDP per capita, identified by some authors,[11] disappears and the commonly held view of stability – both temporal and spatial – is reaffirmed. Using Gollin's methodology, Bernanke and Gürkaynak[12] arrive at the same conclusion. Some authors, however, argue that the observed difference between the *LSh* of developed and poor nations cannot entirely be considered a methodological illusion,[13] and that even when adjustments are made, significant trends in IFD can be seen over time.[14] The aim of this paper is to contribute with some new perspectives to this discussion.

In section 1, I briefly review some relevant methodological issues. In section 2, I present comparable IFD series extracted from the national accounts statistics of eleven Latin-American countries between 1950 and 2000, which have not been corrected for the 'shadow wage'. The aim of this section is to provide a reliable baseline IFD data set to consult when addressing inconsistencies observed among data sources. In the third section, I present corrected series of IFD (that is, with a correction of the shadow wage) for eleven Latin-American countries. To do this I apply a methodology whereby own-account workers are assigned a wage that is equal to the average wage of employees. This corrected series is the first long-term estimation of IFD for Latin American countries. In the fourth section I analyse the potential impacts of these results in furthering the debate initiated by Gollin. I will discuss whether the differences in *LSh* observed between countries can be attributed to methodological illusion. In the last section I present some brief conclusions and describe my research agenda.

Methodological Approaches

There are three levels and corresponding methodologies used to study the IFD.

First, there are sectorial studies, which are usually focused in the industrial sector. The advantage of this approach is that it considerably reduces the weight of the own-account workers (hence reducing the effect of 'shadow wages') and therefore the impact of the adjustment choice.[15] The results of these studies can however be limited as they are difficult to extend to other sectors and differences between industrial surveys can reduce their comparability.

Secondly, the IFD can be estimated from indirect data, outside the framework of the national accounts. Based on the occupational structure of populations and nominal wages within sectors (extracted from census or employment surveys), it is possible to obtain estimations of workers' wages.[16] The accuracy of such estimations varies significantly depending on the availability and quality of the data used. When household and workplace surveys of sufficient quality exist, providing data about wage gaps by qualification, gender, economic sector and status, it is possible to obtain estimations that rival, or even surpass, the data available from national accounts.[17] Unfortunately, in the majority of cases, obtaining such data is unlikely in Latin America where it is often difficult even to obtain complete data sets of real wages throughout the twentieth century. For these reasons, the construction of IFD estimates using this methodology necessitates making assumptions that limit the reliability of the results.

The third option is to compute the IFD from national accounts sources. The IFD estimations using these data are temporally limited depending on the coverage of national accounting in Latin America, where, in the best of cases, data do not extend beyond the second half of the twentieth century. The advantage of this approach is that the IFD estimates obtained are more consistent and comparable since national accounting sources must comply with UN statistics guidelines. The reliability of these data is ensured through the publication of annual issues of the Yearbook of National Accounts Statistics (YNAS), where revisions of national accounts data are reported and any deviations from the established data reporting standards are identified.

However, the construction of the IFD from the national accounts data leads to two important problems.

First, even when data are taken from official UN sources, an initial process of analysis and revision is necessary since values of LSh for any given year vary from edition to edition. Furthermore, most countries have breaks in their annual data series due to changes in base years and changes between revisions of the account system. Thus, in order to obtain comparable and reliable data, a coherent revision methodology must be employed.

Secondly, employee remuneration data reported in national accounts exclude the 'shadow wage', the remuneration to the labour factor of the own-account worker's which are included in gross operating surplus data.[18] Using employees' remuneration as an indicator of labour remuneration leads to a serious underestimation of IFD. It is therefore necessary to obtain an estimation of this 'shadow wage'. This correction is especially important in the case of underdeveloped countries, since the ratio of own-account workers to the total economically active population is consistently higher than in developed countries.[19] In the next section the implications of methodology choice for estimating 'shadow wage' will be examined. At this point, it is important to note that the comparability of corrected IFD series strongly depends on using consistent estimation methods.

To my knowledge, of the two issues mentioned above, revision of data sets from official sources and obtaining an estimate of 'shadow wages', the former has not been discussed in the literature, while the latter has been the topic of much debate.

The Factorial Distribution of Income in Latin-America from National Accounts Data

Labour share was calculated from national accounts data by computing the ratio of total employees' remuneration over GDP or the national income. This data can be found in the primary distribution of income account, or in the relationships among main national accounts aggregates tables, depending on the source.

We calculate the shares of each factor as follows:

$LSh = Y_L/Y$
$PSh = Y_K/Y = 1\text{-}LSh$

As noted earlier, Y is the GDP at factor cost since the exclusion of net indirect taxes facilitates the distributional interpretation of the results. LSh is the share of the remuneration to employees' workers – which includes payments in kind and employers' contributions to social security. PSh is the share of the gross operating surplus, which includes remuneration to labour factor of own-account workers.[20]

To obtain a broad view of the existing data, employees' wages (Y_L) and GDP data at factor cost (Y) were collected from different sources. The main sources used here are Yearbook of National Accounts Statistics of the UN (YNAS) and Statistical Yearbook for Latin America and the Caribbean (SYLA) of the Economic Commission for Latin-America and the Caribbean (ECLAC) since they provide a greater breadth of spatial and temporal coverage, and because they are the most consistent data sets available within the national accounts. When necessary, the Common Database of UNSTAT, the Statistical Bulletin for Latin America from ECLAC, the Statistical Abstract for Latin America edited by

UCLA and the Yearbook of Labor Statistics and the LABORSTA from ILO. In some cases national data were used as complementary sources.[21]

Naturally, previous global and regional studies have also used the sources cited, especially the first two. However, it has not been noted that in computing annual data, strong disagreement exists among the various sources, and even among different issues of a single source. For example, if we calculate the *LSh* of Colombia in 1955 we obtain a value of 0.435 from YNAS 1958, a value of 0.336 from YNAS 1960, and from YNAS 1961 the value obtained is 0.372. Hence, the measurement from the 1958 issue is 10 points (30 per cent) higher than the 1960 result. While this gap is illustrative, it is not extreme, since it is possible to find greater discrepancies between sources. If we analyse the differences between sources, the gap can be as high as 35 per cent. Discrepancies within and between sources oblige us to perform a comprehensive survey of data sources in order to assess their differences. In other words, extracting data from official sources which should be reliable in theory does not guarantee reliability of the data because strong annual variations could be noise resulting from disagreements within or between sources.

Once a thorough survey of the sources has been performed, general criteria for harmonizing the annual series must be defined. Inevitably, this process involves a subjective element since the reliability of different data sets is deduced contextually or according to certain criteria with no first-hand knowledge of the actual quality of the data published in the statistical issues.[22] Some gaps in the times series have been filled, especially those in the SYLA source where they are clearly marked.[23] In an effort to permit criticism and further improvements, in earlier versions of this work considerable efforts have been made to provide an explicit description of the methodological decisions.[24] In cases where temporal hiatuses exist in the data sets, we present the geometrical interpolations of the values.

In Table 5.1, the uncorrected values of the *LSh* and regionally weighted averages are presented for eleven Latin American countries.

Table 5.1: Latin American labour shares, corrected and uncorrected, 1950–2000

	ARG	BOL	BRA	CHI	COL	CRI	ECU	MEX	PER	URU	VEN	Average
	Labour share without correction											
1950–4	0.46		0.40	0.40	0.37	0.55	0.29		0.37		0.38	0.39
1955–9	0.42		0.44	0.43	0.36	0.56	0.30		0.38	0.53	0.38	0.39
1960–4	0.39	0.40	0.47	0.42	0.39	0.53	0.31	0.33	0.39	0.55	0.41	0.40
1965–9	0.44	0.40	0.46	0.44	0.41	0.53	0.31	0.35	0.40	0.54	0.41	0.41
1970–4	0.46	0.37	0.39	0.50	0.41	0.53	0.33	0.38	0.42	0.52	0.40	0.41
1975–9	0.41	0.39	0.37	0.47	0.41	0.54	0.32	0.41	0.41	0.44	0.41	0.40
1980–4	0.31	0.40	0.40	0.49	0.43	0.51	0.30	0.37	0.41	0.42	0.40	0.39
1985–9	0.34	0.39	0.47	0.38	0.39	0.55	0.22	0.33	0.40	0.46	0.39	0.40
1990–4	0.41	0.39	0.50	0.40	0.37	0.51	0.15	0.36	0.31		0.37	0.42
1995–9	0.39	0.39	0.45	0.44	0.40	0.49	0.17	0.33	0.28		0.37	0.39
1950–99	0.40	0.39	0.43	0.44	0.39	0.53	0.28	0.36	0.38	0.49	0.39	0.40

	ARG	BOL	BRA	CHI	COL	CRI	ECU	MEX	PER	URU	VEN	Average
						Corrected labour share						
1950–4	0.62		0.70	0.53	0.60	0.72	0.49		0.72		0.61	0.60
1955–9	0.57		0.78	0.55	0.59	0.74	0.54		0.71	0.71	0.59	0.61
1960–4	0.53	0.72	0.81	0.55	0.63	0.70	0.58	0.51	0.72	0.73	0.64	0.63
1965–9	0.59	0.78	0.78	0.57	0.62	0.69	0.58	0.53	0.75	0.72	0.62	0.64
1970–4	0.62	0.79	0.62	0.67	0.58	0.68	0.61	0.58	0.80	0.70	0.59	0.62
1975–9	0.55	0.86	0.55	0.65	0.57	0.68	0.57	0.64	0.80	0.59	0.59	0.60
1980–4	0.42	0.80	0.57	0.71	0.62	0.64	0.53	0.58	0.79	0.56	0.57	0.57
1985–9	0.47	0.70	0.68	0.55	0.56	0.73	0.36	0.48	0.76	0.62	0.55	0.58
1990–4	0.57	0.66	0.74	0.57	0.54	0.70	0.26	0.52	0.59		0.54	0.61
1995–9	0.53	0.72	0.65	0.62	0.62	0.67	0.29	0.49	0.52		0.55	0.58
1950–99	0.54	0.75	0.69	0.60	0.59	0.69	0.49	0.54	0.72	0.66	0.59	0.60

'Shadow Wage' Estimation and Corrected Factorial Distribution

A number of different methodologies exist for correcting Y_L so that it includes labour remuneration of own-account workers', which in turn allow corrected *LSh* (*CLSh*) and IFD values to be calculated.

Some methodologies add a part of the mixed income to Y_L. Most frequently, *YL* is summed with all the mixed income (over-rating the *LSh*), or with a supposedly observed fixed share of the mixed income (commonly two-thirds of extracted 1950s observations are used), or, in other cases, Y_L is summed with the same share of the mixed income observed in the corporate sector. All these options employ mixed income data, which can restrict the temporal span of the sample since the disaggregation required are, if at all, only available for a few recent years within the national accounts of LA countries.[25]

The correction applied in this paper, most suitable for LA countries, is to assign own-account workers the average wage received by employees using the following equation:

$$LSh = \frac{Y_L C}{Y} = \frac{Y_L/T_{AS} \times T_T}{Y}$$

Where T_{AS} is the number of employees, and T_T is the economically active population.

This is the formula used by the European Commission (Annual Macro-Economic Database, AMECO), as well as one of the methodologies employed by Gollin.[26] It requires EAP by Status in employment data, which can be found in the Yearbook of Labor Statistics (YLS), and usually intercensal data must be interpolated.[27] This author notes that even though this methodology could theoretically produce *LSh* values greater than 1 (an impossible value and a clear sign of overestimation), it does not occur in his sample. However, applying this methodology to our series we obtain many *LSh* values greater than 1 (for example, for Bolivia – which, along with Ecuador is one of the two LA countries included in Gollin's study – reach values higher than 1.1 in the 1960s). While the causes of the failure of this methodology may be diverse, the most probable cause involves assigning all own account workers the average salary earned by employees. The own-account workers category includes members of agrarian cooperatives who may not receive monetary payment. The same could be said about assigning average income to contributing family members. It would result in an overestimated *LSh* value.

For these reasons, *LSh* was finally calculated in the following way:

$$LShC = \underset{Y}{\underline{Y_L C}} = \underset{Y}{\underline{Y_L/T_{AS} \times (T_{AS} + T_{AU})}}$$

Where T_{AU} is the number of employers and own-account workers, excluding cooperative members and auxiliary family workers. In this way the principal cause of overrating present in the previous methodology is eliminated, while indirectly including part of the informal sector of the economy.

It is possible to improve this methodology to obtain wage estimations for own-account workers per economic sector, employment status gender, informality, and so on, but the availability of this kind of data is extremely limited.[28]

The *CLSh* series seem, in some cases, to amplify the cyclic element. This could be because our EAP series includes intercensal interpolations, which eliminates adjustments for contracting activity rates during crisis periods. At the same time, own-account workers can suffer greater losses in income than employees during these periods, but the data to include these variations in the calculations are not reliable. It had been mentioned that during periods of economic crisis, there is generally an increase in the informal sector, but the data do not permit us to properly include this and this further amplifies the cycle. In some countries, the increase in informal economic activity during crisis periods can reach striking levels, challenging the assumption that own-account workers and employees earn equivalent incomes. Thus, these results demand further evidence to prove the reliability of the methodology used during these periods. Nevertheless, we believe our methodology is more robust than methodologies used in past studies[29] that fail to address the issues discussed above. In addition, one of the principal advantages of this estimation method is that it allows a large number of countries to be included, since it uses available data, and thus avoids the distortions that result in smaller sample sizes.[30]

The levels of *LSh* and *CLSh* for eleven LA countries (Argentina, Bolivia, Brazil, Chile, Colombia, Costa Rica, Ecuador, México, Peru, Uruguay and Venezuela), as well as the regional weighted averages for both indicators, are presented in Table 5.1.

Results Analysis

As expected, the results are consistent with the argument that correcting IFD to include the earnings of own-account workers significantly increases the value of *LSh* obtained. This is most evident when the data are viewed at the regional level (Figure 5.1), although caution is needed when drawing conclusions from aggregates like this. The figure clearly illustrates the impact of the correction (the average for the period 1950–2000 is 20.3 points of the *LSh* percentage), supporting the views of the authors that emphasize the importance of correcting the original series of factorial distribution.

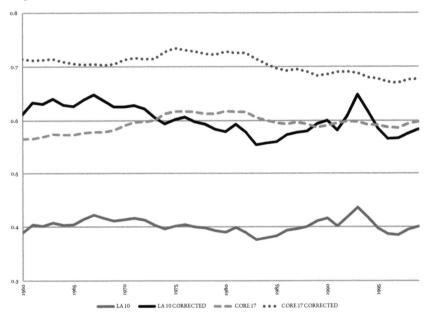

Figure 1: Labour share, LA and CORE, 1960–2000

As seen above, one of the questions arising from the debate initiated in Gollin is whether the correction reinforces the view that IFD is temporally stable. The results are conclusive that over time the IFD varies significantly within countries, with strong cycles, and in some cases long-term trends. In addition, the important differences in the level of *CLSh* between LA countries do not support the view that factor share values are similar across most or all these nations. Hence, our results reject the assumption that IFD is stable over the long run between or within countries.

Having rejected the assumption of temporal and spatial stability of IFD, the next question is whether our results support the hypothesis that there is a relationship between the levels of *LSh* and the wealth of the countries.

The moment we compare our results with results from previous long-run studies for countries at the core of the world economy, we encounter methodological variations such as those mentioned above. To perform such a comparison it is simplest to construct similar series of *LSh* for a group of developed countries. A weighted average of the EU-15, Japan and the US between 1960 and 2000, covering the bulk of the core economies, has been constructed using the AMECO database (CORE 17 in Figure 5.1). The AMECO database offers a *CLSh* based on the same methodology as used in this paper, although it assigns an implicit wage for all workers who are not employed (including producer's cooperative members and auxiliary family workers). In the case of these countries, the impact of this difference in the correction methodology is extremely low – since there are very few people in these categories – which facilitates this comparison. [31]

As is clearly shown in Figure 5.1, even if the correction of the *LSh* reduces the gap between core countries and LA, it is still significant. Our results indicate that the difference in *LSh* levels cannot be explained only by methodological adjustment.

The *CLSh* offers a general view of inequality trends in LA. Two cycles can be identified in the region: in the first we see a rise in *CLSh* up until the mid-1960s, followed by a drop until 1983; the second peaks in the mid-1990s, and seems to decline at least until 2005. National differences aside, the regional results only partially support the arguments of Sáinz and Calcagno,[32] because these authors attribute the drop of the *LSh* to the crisis in the 1980s, whereas our results show an earlier decline. The *CLSh* shows a negative trend in the whole period, which is not apparent in the uncorrected series. It is important to be prudent when interpreting regional data that includes countries which differ significantly because such aggregations can be misleading due to the weight of the major economies. In future analyses I will explore these results in more depth, paying closer attention to national differences.

Conclusions and Research Agenda

These results, obtained through a comprehensive process of data collection from national accounts, harmonization of the series and estimation of the shadow wages of the own-account workers, do not support the view held by Gollin and Bernanke and Gürkaynak,[33] that the *LSh*, once corrected, presents a stable pattern which is similar between core and peripheral countries. On the contrary, we find that the corrected *LSh* shows important variations between and within countries. On the whole, the *LSh* of LA countries is lower than in the core countries of the world economy.

But beyond this debate, the IFD series allow for a great depth of exploration in future works. First, we must analyse, for each country, the trends in inequality of IFD in light of a nation's economic and social history and compare the factorial inequality with the available personal inequality indicators. This approach, more sensitive to national history, complements the regional picture and avoids excessive generalization.

These results also allow a study of the determinants of the IFD, as addressed in other works.[34] A broad study of these determinants must include the evolution of the GDP, real wages, inflation, unemployment, changes in EAP and employment status,[35] technological change and capital–output ratio,[36] openness of trade, liberalization policies and political bargaining of workers,[37] as well as the accumulation patterns of human and physical capital.[38]

The inclusion of these elements in the framework of an econometric study which analyses their effect on the IFD will provide a better picture of how broad economic processes such as globalization or development policies impact Latin America.

6 THE INFLUENCE OF THE FIRST WORLD WAR ON THE ECONOMIES OF CENTRAL AMERICA, 1900–29: AN ANALYSIS FROM A FOREIGN TRADE PERSPECTIVE[1]

Frank Notten

Introduction

In current Central American historiography not much attention is paid to what happened to the region's economy during the First World War. The impact of the war is virtually unknown, other than that Central American trade temporarily shifted from Europe to the United States because of the naval blockades of the former during the conflict.[2] For the period before the 1920s, no yearly GDP estimates exist, so in order to find out about the economic impact of the war, we need to consult other economic indicators. Fortunately, the five Central American republics published foreign trade statistics on a regular basis from the first decade of the twentieth century onwards. As the Central American countries depended exclusively on imported capital goods and fossil energy, we can find out the levels of apparent consumption of these products per country by studying their yearly import statistics.[3] I will analyse the import statistics of machinery, energy, cement and foodstuffs. The behaviour of these different import cycles can give us indications about the economic performance of each Central American country, before, during and after the First World War. The aim of this paper is to measure the impact of the war and explain why some countries suffered a serious economic setback during the conflict, while others managed to benefit from its consequences.

During the nineteenth century, the Central American countries opened their economies to the rest of the world. Costa Rica started first with the export of coffee, followed by Guatemala, El Salvador and Nicaragua. Towards the end of the century, big American companies, like the United Fruit Company, started to build railroads in the Atlantic regions of the isthmus and exported bananas to the US and, later, Europe. After the conversion to economies based on agro-industrial mono-exportation, Central America used its best located and most fertile soils for the cultivation of coffee and bananas, while most of its export income was used to pay for the imports of textiles, capital goods, energy and also foodstuffs. Depending heavily on the income generated by its exports, the region almost never imported for more value than the worth of its exports, resulting in structural surpluses in their trade balance which were used to pay for dividends and interests on foreign debts. The strong dependence on banana and coffee exports was no problem at all as long as the net barter terms of trade (NBTT) of Central America kept on rising, which is exactly what happened from the late nineteenth century till the outbreak of the First World War.[4]

However, during the First World War, coffee (and other) exports to Europe were partially interrupted and Central American merchants had to sell a considerable segment of their coffee in the United States, whose markets were used to cheaper coffee, and refused to pay high prices for the high quality Central American coffee. At the same time, because of the war, prices of iron and steel products and freight rates rose, resulting in rapidly decreasing terms of trade for Central America.[5] As mentioned before, the Central American countries rarely spent more on imports than the income of their exports, so total imports in absolute terms decreased dramatically, especially because total exports did not compensate the decline in NBTT. These import falls were not as extreme in every country in the region, nor in every economic sector, depending on their particular economic and political situation at the outbreak of the war.

In the first part of this paper I will identify the different performances of the import curves of Central American countries, divided by groups of products and countries.[6] In the second part I will explain these differences by analysing them in a national historical economic context. To achieve these goals, I have used Central American trade statistics converted to FOB prices, expressed in US dollars.[7]

Measuring the Impact of the War

Imports of Capital Goods: Machinery

Following the line of arguments developed by Albert Carreras and Xavier Tafunell,[8] in this article I will use machinery imports as an indicator for capital investment in the region, assuming that the Central American republics did not produce their own machinery before 1929, and accepting that the apparent consumption of these capital goods reflects economic growth in the middle and long run. Analysing index numbers is the best way to see at a glance the different impact of the war on the five countries. However, it should be clear that these countries did not depart from the same levels: in the base year 1913, Costa Rica, the leading country of the region, imported machinery for US$0.79 per capita, while El Salvador and Guatemala only imported US$0.40 and US$0.30 dollars per capita. Nicaragua and Honduras imported a bit more machinery: US$0.58 and US$0.60 dollars per capita.

Analysing machinery imports in index numbers,[9] we obtain a general idea of the magnitude of the impact of the First World War on the economies of Central America and of the time that these economies needed to recover from this external shock. The First World War had similar effects on investment in machinery in Costa Rica, Guatemala and El Salvador. The imports of machinery in these countries fell in 1915 to only a third of the level in the base year 1913 and, after a small break in 1916, continued to decrease till 1918, reaching index numbers of 15 in the cases of El Salvador and Costa Rica and 22 for Guatemala. The exception was Nicaragua, where machinery imports also fell in 1915, but then increased till 1917, and after a dip in 1918–19, this country imported more machinery in 1920 than before the war. Because of Honduras's incomplete annual statistics, we only know that the machinery imports of this country went down in 1915, just like in the rest of the region, but had already completely recovered by 1922.

The recovery of machinery imports in the rest of the region after the war was more heterogeneous than their fall during the conflict. Costa Rica recovered initially at a slow rate without much volatility, reaching the pre-war level of machinery imports only in 1927, enjoying faster growth rates in the late 1920s. El Salvador seemed completely recovered in 1924, but in 1927 was still slightly below the pre-war level. Something similar happened in Guatemala, which was still struggling to import as much machinery in 1926–27 as in the years immediately prior to the war. After a fast recuperation of machinery imports in Honduras in the immediate post-war years till 1922, in the remaining early 1920s, this country showed negative growth rates. In 1927 and 1928 it performed worse than in 1913. The exception, once again, was Nicaragua, whose machinery imports in 1926 more than doubled those of 1913, achieving the highest growth rates in the whole region between 1913 and 1929.

Imports of Energy

Although apparent energy consumption[10] is less directly linked with producing or adding value to an economy, it is a good indicator of modernization, because the more modern energy is imported, the higher national productivity becomes. In current historiography it is generally accepted that economic growth correlates positively with apparent consumption of modern energy, with the proviso that these kinds of energies tend to be used in an economy's most modern sectors, exaggerating the relative differences between countries, giving more weight to industry, mining and countries with a high level of urbanization.[11]

In this paragraph we will analyse the apparent consumption of modern energies, consisting of coal, petroleum and hydroelectricity, in kilos of oil equivalents (koe). The first two types of energy, both fossil energies, were entirely imported, because the region did not have or use national coal or petroleum resources.[12] Hydroelectricity was especially important in Costa Rica, accounting for more than 10 per cent of the total modern energy consumption during the 1920s.[13] The rest of the region also generated hydroelectricity but at a smaller scale.[14] The Central American countries used other types of energy as well, mainly vegetal fuels, but these remained fairly constant in time: economic growth was more likely achieved with the use of fossil energies with higher energy density per weight.[15]

Although the First World War had a negative impact on the modern energy consumption in Costa Rica, there was also an increase in modern energy consumption in Nicaragua, El Salvador and Honduras *during* the war, while the level of energy consumption in Guatemala only decreased slightly towards the end of the conflict. After the war, Costa Rica did not achieve total recovery of its prewar energy consumption levels of almost 100 koe per capita, except for 1925. Measured between 1913 and 1929, Costa Rica was the only country in the region whose apparent consumption of modern energy *decreased*. Nicaragua's energy consumption increased steadily during the twenties, reaching 38 koe per capita in 1926, while that of El Salvador converged with the levels achieved by the rest of the region, from the beginning of the war towards the end of the decade, topping 32 koe per capita in 1929. The extremely low modern energy consumption of this country reveals its backwardness before the war, when it depended totally on the consumption of domestic organic energy sources and imported less than 1 koe per capita of modern energy between 1911 and 1913. The most remarkable growth was achieved by Honduras, which by the end of the period consumed more modern energy (mainly oil) than any other country in the region, reaching 175 koe per capita in 1929, coming from 8 koe per capita in 1912.

Not only Honduras was a large consumer of oil in the 1920s, the rest of the region also made the transition from coal to oil during the First World War, earlier than any of the European industrialized economies or the United States.[16] Due to its higher energy density per kilo, the consumption of oil is more associated with economic modernization than coal. Therefore, it is interesting to investigate how it could be possible that the Central American countries made this step so early and quickly.

In the Costa Rican trade statistics of 1927 it is stated that the oil consumption of the two foreign-owned railway companies accounted for the majority of the total oil imports of that year,[17] indicating that the sudden change from massive coal to massive oil imports was mainly caused by a change of fuel of these companies' locomotives. Although a lot of investigation into this sudden energy transition still needs to be done, a case study of the Costa Rican energy transition shows that already before the war, coal was getting more expensive and its imports were of diminishing quality. Costa Rican railroad companies, which before the war depended on coal imports, were preparing a smooth transition to oil-burning locomotives. When the war started, the transition had to be made faster because of exploding coal prices combined with relatively low-priced Mexican oil. Foreign-owned railroad companies (those owned by the UFCo) could make the transition from coal to oil burners in less than two years during the war, while the government-owned railway to the Pacific did not have the infrastructure, money nor contacts to do the same and, because of the lack of coal, had to use inferior national firewood during and even after the war.[18]

In other words, the First World War functioned like a modernization accelerator for Costa Rican foreign-owned railways, as well as an obstacle for the government-owned Railway to the Pacific. It is possible that other Central American countries, whose railways were mostly foreign-owned at the outbreak of the war,[19] could make an easier transition to oil burning locomotives, which explains their smaller drop in total modern energy consumption during and after the First World War.

Imports of Cement

Now that we have seen the tight link between modern energy consumption and the development of the railway sector, it is desirable to contrast these cycles against the apparent consumption of cement, the best simple indicator of activity in the construction sector which is one of the basic indicators for total investment in capital.[20] What this indicator has in common with modern energy consumption is that the analysis of the consumption of cement reflects and enlarges the relative differences between GDP levels of different countries. Only the richest sectors of relatively prosperous societies could afford to replace traditional building materials with imported cement.[21] The main difference between energy and cement as indicators for GDP differences among countries is that both indicators are based on the performance of entirely different economic sectors, namely railroads and construction. Analysing both indicators eliminates the risk of falsely identifying the growth of only one sector with that of the whole national economy.

In this paragraph, we will analyse the apparent cement consumption of all five countries in the region. The only Central American country that produced part of its own consumption of cement is Guatemala, which had a cement factory since 1901. This nationally produced cement of Guatemala is included in the figures. The leading cement consumer in absolute terms was again Costa Rica, with 17.9 kilos of cement per capita in 1913. The other countries followed at a distance, reaching 4.2 kilos in El Salvador, 3.7 in Guatemala, 3.0 in Honduras and 2.3 kilos of cement per capita in Nicaragua.

Studying cement consumption confirms partly what we have seen before, through analysing the energy consumption of the region: the impact of the war on cement consumption was extremely severe in Costa Rica, but not so dramatic in the rest of Central America. Where Costa Rican cement consumption was almost completely paralysed in 1918 (0.6 kilos of cement per capita), the other countries of the region showed, for the available years, only modest decreases of their cement consumption levels (between 1913 and 1918). After the war, Costa Rican levels of cement consumption recovered quickly, but because of the huge fall during the conflict, only surpassed its pre-war levels in 1925. The other Central American countries that did not suffer that much during the war kept on growing during the 1920s. Especially towards the end of this decade those countries expanded their cement consumption, reaching figures between 7.4 kilos per capita in Nicaragua and 15.6 kilos per capita in Guatemala. However, Costa Rica remained the leading cement consumer during the whole period and consumed over 52 kilos per capita in 1929.

The biggest differences with the energy consumption cycles occurred between 1923 and 1928, when Honduras performed a lot worse importing cement than importing energy and when Costa Rican cement imports tripled their pre-war level, while in the same period, its energy consumption struggled to reach its pre-war level. These differences between energy and cement consumption are probably rooted in the strict identification of energy consumption with the growth rate of the banana export sector in both countries. As we have seen, the majority of the imported oil in Costa Rica was used as fuel for locomotives. When banana exports expanded (like in Honduras in the 1920s), the locomotives that transported these fruits to the harbour needed more fuel. On the contrary, when banana exports declined, like in Costa Rica towards the end of the period, oil consumption of locomotives declined as well. In a country without banana exports, like El Salvador, modern energy consumption was extremely low, while the level of cement consumption ranked second in the region.

The fact that the apparent consumption of cement in these cases shows an entirely different cycle than the consumption of energy proves that an expanding (or contracting) export cycle did not mean that other sectors of the economy followed the same tendency.[22] In other words, we have to be very cautious identifying modern energy consumption with economic growth in small countries where the export sector had (at best) a limited spill over effect on the rest of the economy.

Imports of Foodstuffs

A substantial part of the total imports to Central America was importations of foodstuffs. At the beginning of the twentieth century, usually over 5 per cent of the import budget was used to finance the purchase of foreign wheat flower and maize.[23] More importantly, an analysis of the imports of these non-durable consumption products can tell us up to what point the Central American economies depended on the income of their agro-exports and suffered from global market fluctuations of imported as well as exported products. The more production factors were used for agro-exportation, the fewer possibilities remained for national cultivation of foodstuffs, which therefore had to be imported. According to Bulmer-Thomas, during the 1920s this resulted in a huge increase in the import of foodstuffs in Central America.[24]

However, commercial statistics on the imports of maize and wheat flour into Central America do not show such an increase. Moreover, foodstuff imports formed a very minor part of the Central American daily diet. Only Costa Rican habitants consumed imported wheat flour on a daily basis. Wheat flower was hardly produced in the region, except for Guatemala, which before and after the war produced part of its consumption domestically.[25] The rest of the Central Americans consumed far more nationally cultivated maize than imported foodstuffs.

The influence of the war on the already small imports of these two basic cereals was significant. Wheat flower imports decreased dramatically in all five countries, although Costa Rica and Guatemala resisted till 1917 cutting these kinds of luxury imports, whose prices exploded during the war. Initially, the cheaper home-made substitute, maize, could not replace the sudden drop in wheat flower imports, and as a result, maize imports rose in 1915. During the rest of the war, however, maize imports plummeted, probably because farmers adapted to the new situation and started to cultivate maize on a bigger scale, replacing foreign maize as well as imported wheat flower. The growth rates of maize and wheat flower together show a sharp decline in importations for Costa Rica and El Salvador between 1913 and 1918, and a moderate fall for Nicaragua and Guatemala.

Explaining the National Differences

Now that we have seen that the impact of the war was different in every Central American country and economic sector, the question remains as to why this war did not have the same impact on the whole region. In order to understand the differences between the five Central American countries, we have to dig into their economic history.

Costa Rica

Costa Rica depended, more than any of its neighbours, heavily on the exports of bananas and coffee. Because of a lack of labour caused by a relatively small population, and the big profits generated by coffee and banana cultivation, it was not very attractive to cultivate crops for national consumption. As a result, a relatively large proportion of food had to be imported. Till the outbreak of the war, the Costa Rican government taxed these imports with high duties, and an important part of its income was generated by taxes on imports, which explains why this government did not actively promote domestic food production.[26] This extreme model of export-led growth put Costa Rica on top of the region according to most social-economic indicators.[27]

However, when terms of trade worsened because of the war and imports collapsed, the government – in a desperate attempt to secure its revenues – rushed to introduce a new, import-independent indirect progressive taxing system, based on the amount of property owned. The coffee elites, that already suffered from the war because of the difficulties selling their coffee in Europe, revolted against the governmental plans to change the taxing system and, in 1917, a military regime took control under leadership of General Tinoco, who led the country into deeper crisis with his extravagant monetary policy, while not achieving recognition by the US government.

As we have seen analysing the apparent consumption of different products in Costa Rica, the war had a big impact on several sectors of this country's economy. Total modern energy consumption went down during the war and recovered slowly (and only partially) after it because of the failure of the government-owned railway to make a quick transition from coal to oil-burning locomotives. Capital investment showed a similar picture, while a new product like cement showed quicker recovery after the war. This indicates that although Costa Rica lost a decade of economic growth because of the war, during its recovery in the 1920s it started to modernize the structure of its economy, constructing stronger buildings (cement) and gradually burning fuels with higher energy density levels (oil).

Guatemala

Although of all Central American countries, Guatemala showed the most similarities with Costa Rica, the impact of the war was smaller in Guatemala and its recovery quicker. The causes of the differences in impact of the war on both countries lay mainly in the large population of Guatemala and the considerable contingent of Indians living in the higher and colder mountains. These Indian communities served the whole country with their harvests of foodstuffs.[28]

Although Guatemala did not develop any significant urban centres,[29] the big rural Guatemalan population not only served as cheap labour for the cultivation of coffee and food crops, it probably also served as a market for domestically produced goods. As a result, Guatemala was the only country in the region that not only possessed a big textile-producing factory (founded in 1885), and a cement factory that provided around three quarters of all cement consumed in the country, but also produced a considerable part of domestically consumed wheat flower.[30]

Although the economies of Costa Rica and Guatemala shared some similarities, like a strong coffee elite, a strong monopoly of the United Fruit Company and a high dependence on their coffee exports to Europe, the above-mentioned differences were what caused the relatively low impact of the war on the Guatemalan economy compared with the huge impact on the Costa Rican economy.

In particular, the fact that Guatemala, because of its sizeable internal market and foodstuff-producing Indians, depended less on imports of non-durable goods meant it had a greater ability to withstand the restrictions on trade during the war.

El Salvador

Although historiography stresses that El Salvador specialized extremely in coffee exports,[31] commercial statistics show that, in the period 1900–29, El Salvador was in fact the only Central American republic that imported virtually no maize or rice.[32] This means that this country must have cultivated a significant amount of basic cereals within its own borders, making it less dependent on imports of foreign foodstuffs, which helped the country to maintain its economic growth level during the First World War.

Another difference with the rest of the region was that El Salvador did not develop an agro-industrial banana export sector, because it lacked direct access to the Atlantic. Where other Central American countries attracted US capital to develop banana exportations and railways, El Salvador missed out on these investments and changed from the best commercially connected Central American country during its indigo exports in the nineteenth century,[33] to the most isolated economy in the region just before the outbreak of the war. At the beginning of the twentieth century, El Salvador imported less modern energy and capital goods than the other republics of the isthmus.

This relative backwardness and isolation from the world economy resulted in greater national sovereignty than in the rest of the region. El Salvador was the only country in Central America that did not have to cut commercial activities with the Germans during the war,[34] neither did it suffer from internal uprisings and almost all of its export earnings stayed in the country. At the beginning of the twentieth century, these coffee exports went mainly to France and Italy, but in the decade before the First World War, the United States began to gain interest in El Salvador and started to import its coffee, substituting the above-mentioned European countries. When the war broke out and the European coffee markets became difficult to reach, Salvadorian merchants benefited from these commercial contacts and sold a large proportion of their coffee in the United States. At the same time as the United States dominated Salvadorian trade, it also started to invest in railways, communication media and electricity in this country.[35]

After the end of the war, El Salvador started to modernize its economy and in some sectors this was already visible during the conflict, as we have seen in the beginning of this article. The war seems to have pulled El Salvador out of its economic isolation, introducing it to modern goods with high productivity imported from the United States, its new main trading partner.

Honduras

In contrast to the three above analysed coffee republics, Honduras did not know a coffee-based economical or political elite, because its fertile volcanic lands, where coffee was grown, were too difficult to access from the national harbours, resulting in very small-scale coffee exports.[36] Where in other countries in the region the big banana enterprises had to struggle against national political (coffee) elites, in Honduras, these fruit companies encountered hardly any serious opposition to their imperialistic goals. The quarrels between two giant banana companies, United Fruit and Cuyamel Fruit, resulted frequently in national political conflicts and even complete revolutions. The result of all this was a politically unstable country with high debts and a railway system that only served the banana companies on the Atlantic coast: at the time, it was faster to travel from the coast in Honduras to New Orleans than to Tegucigalpa.[37]

Already before the war, the foreign trade of Honduras was very straightforward: it exported bananas mainly to the United States and in turn it imported all it needed from the same country. Despite all the setbacks of this dependency on the United States, it also resulted in a lesser impact of the First World War on the Honduran economy: where the coffee republics had to find new buyers for their coffee, Honduras was assured of a big familiar market for their bananas in the United States. Of course, during the war, Honduras suffered from rising import prices, resulting in a temporary fall of capital investment in machinery, but because banana (FOB) prices at the Honduran harbour remained stable, as soon as the war was over and import prices normalized, the country was capable of quickly recovering its import levels.

It was especially the Atlantic region of the country that participated in the post-war bonanza. Oil imports exploded, but as we know, these were mainly burned by locomotives that were exclusively used to transport bananas to the Atlantic harbour and had a very limited spill-over effect on the rest of the country. The lack of growth of the national economy is confirmed by the poor performance of the Honduran import cycles of cement and machinery in the 1920s. While the banana export sector of Honduras was the biggest of the world,[38] in the same decade, the rest of the country kept on suffering from political instability[39] and economic backwardness.

Nicaragua

Although often neglected in the economic historiography of the region,[40] Nicaragua developed a coffee export sector that reached the same dimensions as in Costa Rica during the period under investigation, and was well connected (by railway) to the ports on the Pacific.[41] The difference with the Costa Rican situation was that in Nicaragua these coffee exports were accompanied by a great diversity of other export products like bananas, metals, several subsistence crops and cattle, destined to neighbouring markets.[42]

Although banana export opportunities were limited and no railway to the Atlantic was constructed, American interest in the country was high because of its ideal strategic location for the building of a canal that would link both oceans. The result was that Nicaragua became an American protectorate between 1912 and 1925 and lost the rights to build its own canal after signing the Bryan-Chamarro Treaty in 1916.[43]

According to the analysed figures at the beginning of this article, Nicaragua, together with El Salvador, suffered less of the First World War than other countries of the region: its capital investments (in machinery) remained more stable and also its levels of apparent consumption of energy and cement performed significantly better than in the neighbouring countries. This relatively positive wartime performance has several causes: Nicaragua did not rely that much on its coffee exports to Europe and, being a protectorate, already before the outbreak of the war depended extremely on the United States. This made the shock of the closing and difficult accessible European markets a less important issue for the country. Also, the diversity of its export products and its reduced dependency on imports of foodstuffs (that were produced inside the country) helped to maintain the stability of the Nicaraguan economy during the conflict.

Conclusion

In this article, I wanted to show and explain the impact of the war on the Central American economies. During the war, all five republics suffered from decreasing terms of trade, mainly because of more expensive import prices, but also, especially in the coffee republics, because their exports were less in demand and did not sell for the usual high European prices. From the nineteenth century, all five republics were, to a certain point, integrated in the global economy by either coffee exports or banana exports, so the decreasing terms of trade affected the whole region. However, as we have seen in the analysis of the apparent consumption of several products, the war had a different impact on all five countries and, within these countries, especially where banana companies worked in enclaves, on different economic sectors. The imports of machinery, indicative of investment in capital, decreased dramatically in the whole region, but the most in El Salvador, Guatemala and Costa Rica. These three coffee republics still imported the same amount of machinery in 1927 as they did before the war. The imports of products often linked with modernization, like energy and cement, showed better performances in all countries. Costa Rica seems to have suffered most during the war.

The main reasons why the war hit harder in Costa Rica than in the other countries of the region were that Costa Rica was extremely well integrated in the global economy, depended the most of all the countries on imported non-durable goods, exported the largest proportion of its coffee harvests to Great Britain and suffered from great political instability during the war. Other countries in the region depended less on imports of foodstuffs because they could count on greater domestic cultivation, often organized by Indian communities. Moreover, countries like Guatemala and, to a lesser extent, El Salvador, possessed factories of some scale (of cement and textile) for domestic consumption, which resulted in lesser decline in apparent consumption when these kinds of imports became more expensive. So, although these countries depended almost as much on their coffee exports to Europe as did Costa Rica, and consequently suffered from lower export income, their domestic production made a difference during the war. Nicaragua and Honduras could not rely on domestic production of textiles or cement, but cultivated (among other crops) almost enough rice and maize to feed its population. Moreover, both countries sold their exports to surrounding countries and the United States and therefore were not as affected by the war in Europe as was Costa Rica. El Salvador even seemed to have benefited from the war because of its increased commercial ties with the United States, bringing its modern energy and cement consumption to a significant higher level even before the end of the conflict.

7 ECONOMIC MODERNIZATION IN ADVERSE INSTITUTIONAL ENVIRONMENTS: THE CASES OF CUBA AND CHILE

César Yáñez

Introduction

Unlike what occurred in the central zones of the Spanish Empire in America, the Cuban and Chilean economies grew and modernized from the end of the eighteenth century. The expansion rate of production oriented to export markets appears to have been a stimulus for the modernization of productive structures and institutions. From early on, fossil fuel consumption, mainly coal used in steam engines, adapted to the economic activities of Cuba and Chile. In the early nineteenth century, this was a powerful sign of the adaptation of modern technologies in peripheral economies. Cuba and Chile's lead position in the consumption of modern energies (coal, oil and hydroelectricity) throughout the nineteenth century was also related to the existence of an elite which was capable of generating a stable political order that favoured business and promoted institutional modernization, though without losing its oligarchic character. It was probably the oligarchic character of the political order which proved to be an obstacle to the conversion of economic growth into long term economic development.

Economic Modernization on the Periphery

In recent years, the explanation for the economic backwardness of Latin America has been based on three ideas which, despite their solidity, can be revised and enriched in the light of a study of the Cuban and Chilean experience. The first of these ideas suggests that adverse institutional situations, represented by the political chaos inherited from the wars of independence, would have been an insurmountable obstacle to social, political and economic modernization. Local elites were not able to agree on a political order favourable to modern growth. The second is the affirmation that the Latin American economy stagnated between the mid-eighteenth century and the mid-nineteenth century. The region would only have awoken, triggered by opportunities brought by the first globalization from the end of the nineteenth century onwards. The third is that the economic stagnation of this period was caused by the absence of economic modernization. Heavy dependence on primary exports would have been an obstacle to the incorporation of technical innovations of the Industrial Revolution.

The comparison between Latin America and North America is the approach favoured by North, Summerhill and Weingast.[1] Their argument revolves around the consequences of the independence of the United States versus that of Latin America, where the latter would not have managed to build a stable political order and consensus among the elite to establish the rule of law. On the contrary, the political instability of the period of 'anarchy' and 'caudillismo' would have conspired against the establishment of ground rules favourable to the smooth running of the markets. For these authors, the root cause for the lack of consensus lies in the manner in which Spain governed its colonies. An excessive exercise of power, centralized in the hands of the colonial authorities had left the local elites with less political protagonism through which they might have accumulated experience and a tradition of agreements based on solid and stable consensus. The peripheral capitalism of the Hispanic tradition, defined by Haber as 'crony capitalism' would have failed to promote economic, political and social modernity.[2]

The chronology of Latin American economic backwardness, constructed with data from Coatsworth[3] and Maddison,[4] see Table 7.1, would confirm the assertions of the second affirmation. According to Coatsworth, Latin America's position had fallen relative to the United States between 1750 and 1913, while the per capita GDP documented by Maddison showed a decline of −0.3 per cent (accumulated annual rate) between 1820 and 1870, recovering later. If we were to use these figures to look for the historical moment in which Latin America fell behind, it would be reasonable to think as Coatsworth does: that backwardness started in the mid-eighteenth century in the context of a region under Spanish and Portuguese colonial control, that the wars of independence were extremely costly for the American economies and that the early decades of the republican era were harmful to regional economic growth. This opinion is shared by authors such as Haber[5] and Prados de la Escosura,[6] who rely on Maddison's figures. In any event, the weakness of this affirmation is that it is based on a limited number of observations which depend almost exclusively on measurements taken for Mexico and Brazil.

Table 7.1: Coatsworth's and Maddison's estimation of per capita GDP of Latin America

Coatsworth's estimation of per capita GDP for Latin America, as a percentage of per capita GDP of the United States		Maddison's estimation of per capital GDP at PPP for Latin America in $US of 1990	
1750	128 %		
1800	66 %	1820	692
1850	51 %	1870	681
1913	27 %	1913	1,481

Source: Coatsworth (1998) and Maddison (2001).

With regards the causes of backwardness, ideas point to the Iberian colonial institutions in America. Under neo-institutionalist theories the idea has taken root that archaic Hispanic institutions represent a dead weight for present-day Latin American prosperity. Colonial path dependence exercised a retarding force from which Latin America has not been able to free itself for the past 200 years.

Coatsworth himself is perhaps one of the authors who most vehemently point out colonialism's guilt for Latin American backwardness. Inefficiency in the use of productive factors can be explained by the predominance of cronyism and rent-seeking mechanisms characteristic of Iberian colonialism, as well as the absence of incentives to implement a regime with improved productivity.[7] Engerman and Sokoloff,[8] for their part assert that the 'bad quality' of the Hispanic colonial institutions is explained by the perverse incentive of the abundance of factors (land and labour), which would have given rise to extremely non-egalitarian societies which often resorted to slavery and where large landed properties predominated. The generous endowment of natural resources present in Latin America's exports basket would have reduced the economic growth alternatives to the fortuitous effect of the commodity lottery. By contrast, in some of the English colonies of North America, small and medium properties worked by European immigrant farmers, would have favoured a type of society where the mechanisms of capitalism would have adapted better.

In the following pages I will discuss these ideas in the light of what the Cuban and Chilean cases reveal. Historiography has been able to determine that both territories did not stagnate economically from the end of the eighteenth century, while our information on modern energy consumption (mainly coal, but also petroleum and hydroelectricity at the end of the period studied) speaks of a process of modernization in the productive structures. We would go as far as to suggest that this modernization relied on elites who founded a political order favouring their economic entrepreneurship. The long-lasting oligarchic order probably permitted the growth and modernization of the nineteenth century, but its exclusive dynamic could have led to the exhaustion and failure of this model of development.[9]

The Practice of Power and the Forging of Elites in Adverse Times

Early on, Cuba and Chile adapted their institutions to the economic and political changes of the end of the eighteenth century and start of the nineteenth century. Their trajectories differed according to their specific historical characteristics, but we must highlight that in both cases elites led processes of change, adapting to the opportunities offered by economic buoyancy and to the new political scenario. Two elements mark the difference between the Cuban and Chilean cases. One is of a marked political character, given that while the Cuban elite opted to remain within the frame of Spanish colonialism until 1898, the Chilean elite chose the path of emancipation, which was consolidated in 1818.[10]

The other element is clearly economic and social, and is linked to Cuba's slave economy,[11] compared with the Chilean experience which combined forms of free labour with mechanisms for tying the labour force to the land as tenant farmers.[12] In any event, the two experiences require a coalition of dominant groups to set up a political 'order' which would guarantee social 'order' as the base for the prosperity of their businesses.

Arango y Pareño united Cuban interests after the promotion of the sugar economy.[13] For them, the opportunity costs of getting involved in a war of independence or of rebuilding a 'colonial pact' with Spain inclined them towards the latter. Fraile and Salvucci[14] follow in the wake of Moreno Fraginals's thesis,[15] highlighting the Cuban elite's initiative to redirect the 'colonial pact' in favour of the expansion of sugar exportations dependent on slave labour. The social order of slave labour was guaranteed by the continuity of the Hispanic colonial regime, but it risked coming under threat if Cuba got involved in an anti-colonial liberation war, which would have required the mobilization of the slave labour force. The experience of Haitian Independence set a dangerous precedent for the Cuban elite and Spain showed greater willingness to reach pacts than it had with of its continental colonies.[16]

The colonial elite of Cuba and Spain would have started identifying common interests during the period of the English occupation of Havana (1762–3). The Cubans learned for once and for all that the metropolis needed them to sustain colonial control. Spain was not omnipotent before its enemies or its American subjects. Hence, Spain learned that, on occasions, its colonial system need to rely on the complicity of its local allies. From this moment onwards, the interference of Cubans in the governance of their affairs grew, while at the same time the new Bourbon Dynasty on the Spanish throne realized the urgent need to reform its colonial regime.[17]

The 1790s were brimming with initiatives on the part of the Cuban elite. The 'Speech on agriculture in Havana and ways to promote it' by Arango y Parreño in 1792 marked a milestone in the intention of Cubans to orient the colony's economic policy. From the Economic Society of Friends of the Country (Sociedad Económica de Amigos del País) and later from the Royal Consulate, the 'hacendados' and traders of Havana forged a solid coalition of interests which the Governors of the Island and the Madrid authorities could not afford to ignore. In the beginning, it was not a homogeneous group, since Cuban 'hacendados' in the mid-eighteenth century identified with different groups according to their region of origin or the type of crop cultivated on their lands; and traders, for their part, had different interests according to whether they were Spaniards or Cubans. At the same time, the colonial authorities, pressured by the different local lobby groups, revealed their weakness every time they had to confront one of their frequent conflicts within Europe.[18] Our hypothesis does not intend to demonstrate that the Spanish Crown was by nature disposed towards being flexible and negotiating with its governors in America, but in reality its capacity to govern its colonies effectively was questioned whenever conflicts in Europe distracted it from its responsibilities in America. The Cuban elite took advantage of this to gain concessions, to progressively forge a strengthening alliance around sugar production for exportation with slave labour, while at the same time weaving a dense network of complicity with the colonial authorities. The Cubans' renunciation of having their own state at the beginning of the nineteenth century did not imply renouncing participation in central decisions affecting their strategic interests. The group gained cohesion between the end of the eighteenth century and beginning of the nineteenth and represented an interlocutor for the colonial authorities in the reform of the colonial system within an extremely adverse context. A new colonial 'order' was emerging which would persist in Cuba unlike what occurred in the continental colonies.

In Cuba this convergence of interests was probably only feasible under the prosperity of the sugar industry, which broke all records at the turn of the century. In the forty years from 1790 to 1830 sugar production in Cuba grew at an annual rate of above 4.5 per cent, doubled between 1790 and 1800 and again between 1810 and 1820 (7.7 per cent and 5.9 per cent respectively).[19] For an activity still tethered to traditional extensive agriculture (supported only by organic energies), this growth is very difficult to match. In the case of Chile, well-documented by Carmagnani, no activity showed such buoyancy.[20] The exceptional nature of Cuba could thus be explained if we follow Acemouglu and Robinson[21] (2006), who propose the hypothesis that coalitions favourable to change are more probable in periods of economic growth, when there is surplus to be distributed without endangering the interests of those traditionally privileged groups.[22]

The Chilean colonial elite were no less faithful to the Crown than their Cuban counterparts.[23] The Creoles had their chance to prove this on the occasion of the English attack on Buenos Aires in 1806.[24] However, Chile's position within the Spanish Empire was far less important than that of Cuba – it was far from the centres of political power, it was not an obligatory stopping point on trade routes with the vice-regal capitals and it had not been especially favoured with its commodity lottery. Precious metals were scarce in Chilean territory. The colonial elite were composed of a few interrelated families whose pecuniary wealth was modest, but who were united and capable of influencing decisions of the colonial authorities. Jaques Barbier[25] highlights the capacity of this group to use both formal and informal channels in order to participate in the political and economic decisions affecting them. These formal channels would include petitions before the King and his administrators in the Viceroyalty of Peru, and among the informal channels there was the option of union through marriage to newly-immigrated Spaniards and to the bureaucrats of the Empire. But these informal channels were also a way to take advantage of the weaknesses in the colonial bureaucracy in order to influence its decisions. In this sense, administrative corruption favoured by Chile's remote location compared to other centres of power, in addition to slow communications, provided the ideal channel for the informal exercise of power.

If the Chilean elite found ways to intervene in local politics and thus feel that they shared colonial power, while simultaneously gaining cohesion; they never had the wealth of the sugar elite to bring to the negotiating table. The boom of the final decades of the colony certainly brought a new prosperity, but this prosperity was neither abundant enough to continue sharing it, nor did it require military power to dissuade potential domestic political threats, as occurred with the slaves in Cuba. The dominant position of the Chilean elite within society was neither contested nor threatened by subordinate groups. Chilean society 'externalized' its social conflicts in the form of border wars with indigenous communities,[26] imposing a severe social order within the country's 'haciendas'.[27]

In the face of the power vacuum that developed with the imprisonment of Ferdinand VII in Bayona, the group most in favour of emancipation was able to impose itself upon those who still entertained the possibility of a new 'colonial pact'. Initially however, the option of a liberation war was neither unanimous nor was it probably a majority option. In many senses the war was a civil conflict among Chileans.[28] Faced with this conflict, the Spanish Crown saw no advantages to power-sharing in the future, as it had been inclined to do in the Cuban case. At the end of the day, Chile was not much more than a Captain General that depended on the Viceroyalty of Lima, without the political or economic importance that would merit the Crown treating it any differently from Lima or Buenos Aires.

Both Cuba and Chile occupied a secondary position in the colonial administration, but for Spain, Chile was less important than Cuba. There are economic reasons for this. Cuba was not indispensable for the functioning of the Mexican economy, a Viceroyalty on which it depended administratively. Additionally, since sugar could be exported to the United States, the Cuban customs houses collected enough to be able to do without the 'situado' with which Mexico financed the administration of Cuba. In contrast, Chile was more integrated into the markets of the Viceroyalty of Peru; its cereal exports were important at specific moments and the subordination of Chile, while not essential, was part of the Viceroyalty's economy.

The singularity of Chile is that despite the fact that the Independence War represented a fracture in the cohesion of the elite, this was repaired in a relatively short time. Chile, in the Latin American context, seems like the paradigm of a successful state from the beginning of its life as a republic. The merit of this achievement has frequently been attributed to the leadership of Diego Portales, to the point where the expression 'Portaliano state' was coined to define the oligarchic order which prevailed in Chile from 1830.[29] However, Julio Heise's thesis[30] is perfectly sustainable: the political trial-runs prior to the 1833 Constitution should not be interpreted as a period of 'anarchy' resolved by the 'Portaliana' solution, but rather as the forces of an elite trying eagerly to recover political stability based on juridical regularity and legitimated by consensus. That may be, but it was an eminently oligarchic and authoritarian consensus which gave continuity to a tradition established in colonial times. In this sense, the reforms brought about by the Chilean oligarchy in subsequent decades, tended towards an institutionality which favoured their property rights and their business opportunities in the frame of exporter capitalism that required neither a civil society nor a vigorous domestic market.

The late nineteenth century was convulsive for both Cuba and Chile. The elites in power once more had to confront adverse scenarios. The Cuban sugar economy, as well as Chilean agriculture and mining, had to overcome the cycles that characterized the international economy.[31] On the political front, Cuba finally had to face an eighteen year-long War of Independence between 1868 and 1898, with a lapse in the accumulation of forces between 1881 and 1895. The solution to the conflict, which included the erosion of the slave-labour system, involved the intervention of the United States against Spain to seal the definitive emancipation of Cuba and also implied the recomposition of the Cuban elite, now more pro-North American than pro-Spanish. In Chile, on the other hand, the elites resolved the mid-nineteenth century crises with the War of the Pacific. The internal cohesion of the group and its hegemony over broader society was put at stake in a war which transferred the resources of the desert and the pampa from Bolivian and Peruvian hands to Chilean. The nitrate business took a central position in Chile's political conflicts and economic cycle from 1879.

At this point we could propose the hypothesis that the wars, against Spain in Cuba and against Peru and Bolivia in Chile, were the response of the elite when confronted with the declining prosperity of the previous period; and that the deepening of the oligarchic nature of the coalitions in power is also a response to this decline. If the Cuban and Chilean elites did not open up to power-sharing with new groups that emerged during the era of prosperity, it was because in adverse economic times it is less probable that those groups controlling the mechanisms of government are willing to share power with their adversaries. In times of crisis competition prevails over cooperation.[32]

In both Cuba and Chile, businesspeople interested in public affairs ran their countries throughout the nineteenth century. An oligarchic state represented the furthest point to be reached by the coalition of interests which took power.[33] They were successful in establishing their political project, and even in orienting economic modernization.[34] However, the aversion of the elites to sharing power and wealth beyond their tight social circles appears to have imposed a severe limitation on the opportunities to project modernization towards sustained growth leading to genuine economic development.

Economic Growth and Productive Modernization: A View from the Consumption of Modern Energies

Information available in historiography indicates that the Cuban and Chilean economies experienced significant growth from the mid-eighteenth century (see Table 7.2). There was expansion of the absolute product and per capita product in both countries, but from a certain moment, at the start of the nineteenth century, the pace tended to diminish. In Cuba this became evident after 1830 and in Chile subsequent to 1810. It is reasonable to think that in Chile the slowdown was the result of the War of Independence, but Cuba did not suffer such an episode. In any event, the growth rates of the Chilean economy before 1846 are clearly fluctuant.

Table 7.2: Economic growth of Cuba and Chile between 1750 and 1846

Estimation of Cuban production					Estimation of Chilean production				
Year	Total	Rate %	Product per capita	Rate %	Year	Agricultural	Rate %	GDP per capita	Rate %
1750	7.82		42.0		1750	62,830			
1775	7.86	0.03	45.9	0.37	1775	116,830	2.50		
1792	13.71	4.35	50.6	0.60	1800	154,704	1.13		
1831	48.60	6.88	68.8	0.97	1810	227,139	3.91	139,277	
1846	62.66	1.92	69.7	0.09	1820	213,480	−0.61	122,724	−1.25
					1830			124,363	0.13
					1840			146,104	1.62
					1846			159,897	0.90

Sources: For Cuba, Santamaria and García (2004) (total in millions of 1840 pesos and per capita total in 1840 pesos). For Chile, the agricultural product, Carmagnani (1969 and 2001) is the nominal value of the 'diezmo'; and the GDP/cap, Díaz, Lüders and Wagner (2000), in 1995 pesos.

The interpretation of the data in Table 7.2 goes beyond pure economic growth. There is reason to believe that in the 1840s Cuba, like Chile, approached the limit of expansion permitted by an organic economy, in the terms used by Wrigley.[35] The use of the factors of land and labour, conditioned only by the use of the vegetal biomass energy resources, would have allowed the economic growth of the eighteenth century. But, once in the nineteenth century, the oscillations in the growth rate and its downward trend would be a sign of exhaustion as it reached the limits of energy options.

If we look carefully at the Chilean GDP per capita, we will find reasons to support this assertion.[36] In 1820 Chile's per capita GDP at PPP (purchasing power parity) in US dollars of 1990, would be at US$694 according to Mad-dison's data.[37] This is a value between that of Mexico (US$759) and that of Brazil (US$646) and clearly below the United States (US$1,257) and the UK (US$1,706), which had started using fossil fuels, fundamentally coal some dec-ades earlier. Hypothetically, it could be maintained that GDP could not easily rise beyond US$1,000 at PPP of 1990 without the help of growing quantities of coal. Hence the question: How long might the Chilean economy have taken to start abandoning its dependence on vegetal biomass? If we trust that level of GDP per inhabitant at PPP will help us to clarify this question, we should find the answer between the decades of 1840 and 1850. It was at that moment when the Chilean economy began to show a steady dynamism which contrasts with the past. In 1845 it managed to rise to almost US$800 and in 1850 the figure rises above US$900, climbing to US$1,000 in 1857. The progression over these years speaks of an important change taking place in the Chilean economy. It was the arrival of coal and the steam engine which were breaking traditional moulds and inaugurating the cycle of the modern economy.

Only after 1840 does economic growth accelerate and becomes sustained in both cases studied. In Cuba, the product per inhabitant went from a growth rate of 0.63 per cent annually (1730–1830) to one of above 2.0 per cent (1850 and1913), 2.6 per cent (1850–95) and 2.1 per cent (1895–1913) according to Antonio Santamaría's estimations;[38] and in Chile, the GDP per inhabitant went from 0.69 per cent for the period of 1820–40 to 1.90 per cent for 1850–1913.[39] The cause of this acceleration is to be found in the modernizing effect of coal consumption: Cuba increased its consumption of modern energies to 4.38 per cent annually between 1850 and 1913 and Chile to 5.91 per cent annually between 1850 and 1913. The consumption of modern energies per inhabitant grew from 2 to 2.5 times more rapidly than the GDP.[40]

The leadership of Cuba and Chile in the region of Latin America and the Caribbean is evident around 1856. In that year 65 per cent of coal consumed in Latin America was consumed in Cuba and Chile. This hegemony in modern energies went on until the 1880s, when these countries still consumed more than 50 per cent of the regional total (see Table 7.3). At the beginning, as can be seen in Figure 7.1, modern energy consumption per inhabitant grew at an extremely rapid pace: above 20 per cent annually between 1844 and 1857 (27 per cent Cuba and 23 per cent Chile). One possible explanation is the low statistical start-ing point. But beyond this, the energy 'take-off' hides an intense transformation of the economy. In thirteen years modern energy consumption increases more than tenfold and the economy sheds the limitations of an organic economy and discovers the potential of the increase in productivity.

Table 7.3: Apparent consumption of modern energies of Cuba, Chile and Latin America (the Total in tonnes oil equivalent – TOE – and the per capita in thousands of TOE per inhabitant)

	CUBA				CHILE				Latin America and the Caribbean			
	Total		Per capita		Total		Per capita		Total		Per capita	
	Number	% over LA	Number	Annual rate %	Number	% over LA	Number	Annual rate %	Number	% over LA	Number	Annual rate %
	1	2	3	4	5	6	7	8	9	10	11	12
1845	4,294		4		9,416		7					
1850	31,728		28	47.1	24,588		17	19.4				
1855	52,441	30	43	9.0	39,419	26	26	8.9	225,657	100	8	
1860	77,805	21	61	7.0	114,398	31	69	21.6	368,416	100	11	7.8
1865	153,811	28	115	13.7	107,782	20	60	−2.8	551,772	100	15	7.0
1870	169,114	22	122	1.1	178,101	23	92	8.9	771,003	100	20	5.5
1875	188,820	16	131	1.4	397,527	34	189	15.5	1,155,282	100	28	7.0
1880	161,639	14	108	−3.8	471,577	41	208	1.9	1,136,780	100	26	−1.7
1885	172,450	12	111	0.5	473,384	32	194	−1.4	1,496,174	100	32	4.2
1890	220,352	11	136	4.2	564,569	27	216	2.2	2,090,196	100	41	5.4
1895	279,650	9	171	4.6	802,216	27	288	5.9	2,977,403	100	54	5.4
1900	264,954	8	160	−1.3	815,874	23	276	−0.8	3,509,036	100	58	1.6
1905	456,741	9	237	8.2	1,021,523	19	326	3.4	5,354,708	100	80	6.8
1910	652,020	8	294	4.4	1,481,087	17	446	6.5	8,489,450	100	117	7.7
1913	1,014,240	10	417	12.4	2,173,873	22	634	12.4	9,984,334	100	131	3.8

Sources: Cuban energy consumption was calculated based on coal and petroleum importations from Great Britain, the United States and Germany; for Chile see Yáñez and Jofré, '*Modernización económica y consumo energetico*'.

However, although the consumption of modern energies in Cuba and Chile was still higher than the Latin American average for the whole period of the first globalization, and both still led the region, the high growth rates tended to diminish in the long term. Once they had reached the mark of 75 tonnes of oil equivalent (TOE) per thousand inhabitants in 1957 (half a century before the region as a whole reached it in 1904), the pace moderated to 5 per cent annual accumulated, almost the same as the Latin American average over the entire period. Cuba and Chile's advantage was that they were the first to enter the steam and coal era.

With the initial period of rapid modernization over, the late nineteenth century until 1913 was tinged with short cycles of modernization, decades of long flat stretches of stagnation with rates of 2 per cent and stages where modern energy consumption dropped: in the case of Cuba during the two wars against the Spanish Empire and in the Chilean case at the time of the collapse of its international trade (−10.3 per cent between 1857 and 1863, −11.5 per cent between

1867 and 1871, and −0.8 per cent between 1895 and 1900). The true compensation for this irregular growth only came at the end of the period, in the decade just before the outbreak of the First World War. In those ten years the growth rates of modern energy consumption showed a renewed dynamism (above 8 per cent annually between 1903 and 1913) which was frustrated by the war.

Beyond Natural Resources

The apparent consumption of modern energies is an excellent indicator of economic modernization.[41] It is the activities that are intensive in modern energies which contribute most dynamism to the economy and which introduce the most technical innovation responsible for increases in productivity. In this sense, Cuba and Chile took the lead in Latin American economic modernization, incorporating fossil fuels into their economic activities. Cuba was the first to adopt steam in its maritime fleet, to build railways (1836) and to adapt sugar plants to the steam engine.[42] But all its modern fuel was 100 per cent imported. Chile, on the other hand, started to exploit coal deposits in the 1840s, thus covering 50 per cent of its consumption including steamships, railways, mining, agriculture and industrial activities.[43]

Foreign trade greatly boosted the Cuban and Chilean economies, and this was both a strong and a weak point for the two economies. Most new fuels were consumed in activities closely linked to the exportation of natural resources. The steam engine adapted to maritime transport was the means by which new technology was introduced to both Cuba and Chile. It was British and later the North American fleets visiting these ports which initially showed off these new technologies. The railways used in exportation activities completed the technological updating of the transport system. In Cuba the railroads were indispensable for transporting great volumes of sugar cane from the plantations to the plants and then the sugar to the export ports.[44] In Chile, the railways were first developed as a means of getting minerals from the mountain zones to the export ports.[45] However, it was in the mass-production industry where the steam engine showed its true worth. The strong increase in sugar production between 1830 and 1860 in Cuba was only possible with the aid of coal-generated steam.[46] Something similar occurred with metal foundry in Chile. The first Chilean copper cycle took advantage of both national coal as well as that imported from England to improve its output.[47]

What is striking in both cases is that export sectors based on natural resources had to adapt their production to technologies capable of augmenting output, so as to respond to market demands. In this sense, Cuba and Chile took a step beyond the strict exportation of unprocessed natural resources, also exporting primary commodities transformed through industrial processes that used modern energies. This lasting phenomenon was capable of generating positive externalities which benefited the entire economy.[48]

The Chilean and Cuban experience of economic modernization[49] may seem like that of a 'latecomer' from peripheral Europe. They were later than the leading countries in adopting steam and coal technology, but they did not remain on the sidelines. In this sense, in the mid-nineteenth century Cuba and Chile could have been on the verge of a jump in level of economic development which ended in frustration.[50]

This comparison is opportune (see Table 7.4), Cuba and Chile were ahead of Spain in the consumption of modern energies per inhabitant throughout the period, as well as ahead of Sweden until the 1880s, at least in the Chilean case, given that Cuba slowed down ten years earlier. The final decades of the nineteenth century give the worst results for these two Latin American economies. The recovery of the growth rate from the early twentieth century, although powerful is not enough to keep up with Sweden. The thrust of the Swedish economy in the twenty-five years preceding the First World War is no match for Cuba and only partly imitated by Chile. It makes sense here to highlight the trajectory of Chile in comparison with that of Great Britain and Holland. If in 1850 Chile consumed only 16 per cent of the modern energy that Holland did and 3 per cent that of Great Britain; in 1880 this proportion had grown to 40 per cent and 20 per cent respectively and later reached 50 per cent and 60 per cent in each case – which reflects well the British regression prior to the war of 1914. Cuban progress during these same years was less rapid, probably because Cuban modernization took off before the Chilean and tended to decelerate first.

The evidence emanating from the series on energy consumption attests to the idea that Cuba and Chile performed better economically than Latin America, which should permit a reconsideration of the chronology which until now has been used to describe the causes of the region's economic backwardness. It should also permit a revision related to the degree of economic modernization achieved by both Latin American countries throughout the nineteenth century.

Table 7.4: Comparison of apparent consumption of modern energies of Cuba, Chile, Spain, Sweden, Holland and England and Wales, 1850–1913 (in GJ per inhabitant)

	Cuba	Chile	Spain	Sweden	Holland	England and Wales
1850	1.12	0.73	0.32	0.71	4.63	22.64
1860	2.54	2.89	1.06	1.22	8.09	28.17
1870	5.12	3.84	2.03	3.19	15.01	32.75
1880	4.53	8.74	3.04	6.44	21.88	39.15
1890	5.72	9.02	5.25	10.53	25.42	43.76
1900	6.71	11.58	8.32	19.53	31.23	47.64
1913	17.52	26.61	11.73	31.44	52.94	40.73

Sources: For Cuba and Chile the same as Table 7.3. For Spain, Sweden and Holland, Gales, Kander, Malanima and Rubio, 'North versus South: Energy Transition', and for England and Wales, Warde, 'Energy Consumption in England & Wales'.

Corollary: The Virtuous Circle of Modernization and Its Limits

Ever since we have had information about the energy consumption of all the Latin American and Caribbean countries,[51] the position of Cuba and Chile in the region's economic history has appeared revaluated. Until 1880, both countries together represented more than half of all modern energy (basically coal) consumed in the region. In terms relative to population, the two always retained lead positions, accompanied by Uruguay initially and by Argentina after 1880.[52]

This Cuban and Chilean leadership which had gone unnoticed has historical fundaments. From the end of the eighteenth century, economic growth appears to have been faster on the periphery of the Spanish colonial system than in the vice-regal centres. There are signs suggesting that agricultural production oriented towards exportation demanded maximum output possible within the margins of an organic economy. The early incorporation of coal into the Cuban and Chilean economies could be explained by the need to advance from an organic economy to an inorganic one, to use Wrigley's terms. One could advance the hypothesis that the economic modernization implied by the use of the steam engine in transport and exportable production (sugar in Cuba and mining in Chile) would also have favoured the modernization of the main economic institutions which affected property rights and the organization of the state.

Unlike what occurred in most of the Spanish empire in America, in Cuba and Chile the crisis of independence was resolved by eluding political disorder and avoiding a serious economic crisis. In both cases the elite were capable of hegemonizing the process of creation of a new political order of oligarchic nature. The Cuban elite opted for the redefinition of the 'colonial pact' with Spain, while the Chilean tended to favour emancipation like the rest of America. There is reason to assert that both groups had gained cohesion and experience in government at the close of the eighteenth century and they projected into the future as an oligarchy conscious of its social and political hegemony. This distinguishing feature in the history of Cuba and Chile (strong united oligarchies capable of agreeing a new political order) coincided with a period of booming business and modernizing economic growth. Thus a virtuous circle was established of political and economic change, of institutional modernization and productive modernization led by coal and the steam engine, which favoured economic growth. This economic growth in turn favoured pacts which led to the establishment of a new order which dominated the Cuban and Chilean nineteenth century.

The oligarchic order that emanated from these groups would have given way to a form of state that was efficient for the government of public affairs to the benefit of the coalition in power. However, it failed to promote general interests, in the form of non-exclusive economic development and a political system that represented more than the hegemonic social group.[53]

8 CAPITAL GOODS IMPORTS, MACHINERY INVESTMENT AND ECONOMIC DEVELOPMENT IN THE LONG RUN: THE CASE OF CHILE

André A. Hofman and Cristián Ducoing

Introduction

Studies about machinery equipment investment have a long tradition in economics and economic history. Since the analysis of the Industrial Revolution and the growth studies of the twentieth century, there are indications that economic growth of countries has a strong nexus with investment in capital formation and specifically, with the machinery equipment investment. However, in the case of developing countries there is a lack of quantitative studies in the long run about the relationship between growth and machinery equipment investment.

This study about machinery investment and growth addresses three critical elements. First, most studies are for a short period of time, twenty-five years or less. Second, the majority of papers present correlations with a great number of countries without a comparison of the kind of investment. A growth process based on capital formation in construction (dwellings and non-residential structures) differs from growth based on machinery investment. More specific, there is another relevant disaggregation: non electrical machinery, electrical machinery and transport equipment that should be take into consideration.

Third, a developing country, Chile was elected to study its relationship with machinery imports in the long run, in an attempt to give to the debate about capital formation and growth another vision.

The article is organized as follows: in section 2, theory and empirics of growth and capital (machinery equipment) investment is presented; section 3 shows the methodology of the data base of machinery imports in Chile; section 4 presents the econometric model to fit the data with the theoretical approach; section 5 the results of causality tests and section 6 concludes.

The Relation between Investment and Economic Growth, Theory and Empirics

The controversy about the importance of fixed capital investment as a substantive element in economic growth remains an important discussion in modern economics. New developments in economic research regarding multi-factor productivity or advances in human capital do not dismiss the importance of investment and its determinants. Empirically, the growth performance of the Asian economies in the second half of the twentieth century was based upon high levels of fixed capital investment which enabled these countries to maintain rapid growth for more than three decades.[1] In this line of research a strong correlation was found between the levels of investment on machinery and equipment and economic growth for industrialized countries.[2]

However, development programmes[3] orientated to capital investment as realized in African countries after their independence in the 1950s and the 1960s, or indeed industrialization policies base on import substitution in Latin America did not obtain the same results. Among the facts explaining these results the literature points to erroneous investment decisions in obsolete capital goods or overinvestment, meaning the application of the Harrod Domar[4] model in countries that do not contain the minimal conditions for industrial developments.[5] Consequently, with this appreciation, studies using the augmented Solow Model[6] maintain that fixed capital is important as long as accompanied with a proportional investment in human capital. In the same line are the studies about economic growth in the Soviet Union which emphasize the enormous capital accumulation without increases in labour causing dismissing returns in capital investment.[7]

With respect to the USA, recently Field[8] concludes that there is an absence of evidence of a systematic positive relationship between rates of equipment investment and multi-factor productivity growth. However, the author recognized the important of the equipment investment in the long run.[9]

Mention should be made of the criticism by Blomstrong, Lipsey and Zejan,[10] arguing that the strong association between equipment investment and growth over the long run does not prove causality. Using the Granger-Sims causality framework, causality may run from GDP growth to capital formation. However, among the four main sources for economic growth that they mentioned, education, inflows of direct investment, lower population growth and the efficient use of investment, two of them are directly related to investment.

On the theoretical level, an important model to understand the relation between investment and growth has been the Solow[11] model. It expresses the importance of capital and its accumulation,[12] but also emphasizes that it is a finite factor (diminishing returns to capital) and does not explain the great differences of GDP per capita around the world. Further advances in economic models have emphasized factors like technology, research and education. In the framework of this discussion De Long[13] proposes two directions about the role of investment on growth. There is the historicism view (Rostow, Gershenkron), emphasizing the investment in machinery equipment and fixed capital like the engine of growth. Then there are the visions of development economists and new growth theorists:

> They have often concluded that the role of accumulation has been overstressed and that others factors – such as widespread formal education, the exploitation of economies of scale, appropriate terms of trade, the overcoming of structural rigidities, and the repairing of market failures – are more central to growth and development.[14]

For example, the classic Cobb Douglas production function:

$$Y = KA^{\alpha}L^{1-\alpha}$$

Where Y is the output, A is technical progress, K is capital and L is labour

The growth of capital stock increases output. This increases the growth rate of the economy depending of the time it takes for capital to reach its optimum and how much it takes for increases in capital to be effective on increases in output. Therefore the theory expresses higher rates of investment have subsequent effects on output, but decreasing effects of scale make constant increases necessary to have an effect on growth in the long run (Magendzo, 2002).[15] Another important input to theory is the development by Temple[16] and Temple-Voth[17] where capital is disaggregated in structures and equipment, changing the Cobb-Douglas production function as follows:

$$Y = E^{\alpha} S^{\gamma} H^{\beta} (LA)^{1-\alpha-\gamma-\beta}$$

Where E is equipment capital, S is structures capital, H is human capital and L is labour. The importance of this disaggregation is argued by Greenwood[18] indicating that the diminishing rates of equipment capital investment are related with the decrease of the growth rate of productivity in the United States in the decade of the 1970s.

The traditional theories of economic development after the Second World War and the new growth theory have a common element: the importance of productive linkages as fundamental sources of growth and inside this framework, the equipment as prerequisite of the human capital growth through learning by doing and productivity increases.[19]

In a consensus approach to the different positions, it is possible to claim the existence of a strong interdependence between investment in fixed capital and growth. In economic history, the growth process is accompanied by investment and vice versa because better economic expectations produce a rise of investment, and under normal conditions (*ceteris paribus*), this rise of investment brings a growth of output. The difficulty is to identify the causal relationship between the two variables. Tests are complicated because of circular arguments which are not conclusive. An agreement between the researchers about equipment investment and a growth nexus is the differences in the results for developing and development countries. The former obtain more benefits from investment than the latter, an argument that fits with the *gershenkronian* view of the 'advantage of backwardness'.[20]

The Database for the Study of Machinery Investment in Chile, Fluctuations and Stages

In studies about Latin American performance in the long run, there is a lack of quantitative studies mostly because of a lack of data. This work is in the area of quantitative economic history, not with the aim of undermine the traditional periodization of the Chilean economic history, but rather to substantiate this chronological classification with quantitative data. Moreover, it is demonstrated that the so-called *import substitution industrialization* was extremely productive when compared to the Great Depression Years, however it was less so in comparison to optimal growth potential.[21]

Three databases of machinery investment are used for Chile. The first, Hofman,[22] presents machinery investment data for Chile and another five countries from 1900 to 1997 (actually 2005). Between 1900 and 1940 this database is constructed using statistical yearbook from ECLAC 1949. The second is a new contribution of Tafunell[23] consisting of machinery investment data for ten countries of Latin America from 1890 until 1930, the historical period known as *first globalization*. The methodology of this work involves using exports of G-3 (the UK, the United States and Germany) representing nearly 85 per cent of the machinery imports of the above-mentioned region. The last database is part of the doctoral thesis of Ducoing,[24] and is built from the Chilean statistical yearbooks (1890–1960). We present the three series, for the years 1890–1930. The new data of Ducoing will be used, because it contains more information than the others mentioned.[25] From 1930, the differences between the series are less important; built with the data from ECLAC, INE and Central Bank of Chile.

Mention is made indistinctively of machinery investment and capital goods imports, because the principal input of machinery investment in Chile are capital goods imports. In the first years of this study (1890–1940) capital goods imports equal the machinery investment. From 1940 to 2005, national capital goods production is somewhat more important, but with shares that hardly rise above 15 or 20 per cent. This difficulty is avoided in the analysis taking into account a transition period between 1930 and 1940. Including in the analysis the national production of capital goods from 1940 to now does not change the principal results, and in concordance with others researchers[26] such as Gershenkron and Lee,[27] it is possible that the capital goods imports are an advantage for the developing countries, saving all the costs of research and development. However, for a complete analysis, we also include total machinery equipment investments in the regressions.

Maybe the long-run series, 1890–2005 should be subdivided to better understand the performance of the investment and its correlation with economic growth.[28] A simple method of peaks and valleys is used to divide the long base period of machinery investment (capital goods imports) and the GDP growth. As can be see, these sub-periods are in concordance with the classical chronology for Chilean economic history (and Latin America):

1890–1932: globalization and disruption of the global economy. During this period the growth rates of machinery investment have a high volatility, but a clear increasing tendency. The process of growth is sustained in the export of nitrates and the demand of the more productive sectors of the economy (mining and industry). The process of industrialization begins before this period, and forms part of the sustained growth period until the great depression years.

1933–75: inward-looking development. For a long time, this period has been considered the more productive in industrial development and machinery investment. The political economy of this period was centred on protectionism for national production, with tariffs and non-tariff barriers. The growth had a positive tendency, but at a low level.

1976–2005: sustained growth and financial crises. The abrupt final of the inward-looking development period started a new process with less state intervention in the economy and with an accelerated growth rate, but financial crises disrupted this process at two moments: 1982 and 1998. However, the share and the growth of the machinery investment increased in comparison with the previous period.

An Econometric Approach to the Contribution of Capital Goods Imports in Economic Growth in Chile 1890–2005: Is There Correlation and Causality?

Previous studies about capital goods and growth, or fixed investment in relationship with the output per capita, have two principal problems. First, multi-country models do not take into consideration in the analysis the obvious differences between these countries, especially the technological level of the investment. Second, the time series analysis is principally concentrated in relatively short periods. Only two authors use the equipment investment approach in the long run: De Long[29] and Kwan et al.[30] However, the first article is an analysis only for developed countries, and the second paper mentioned applied to China, using total fixed investment for a period of fifty years. However, the research objective of the present article is searching for the roots of economic development in the long run in a developing country using machinery equipment investment.

An initial problem to be addressed is related to the use of time series. Three possibilities to understand the cause and effect and the correlation between the variables GDP growth rate and machinery investment can be distinguished:

Using the share of the machinery investment in GDP, in an equation with the form:

$$DY_t c + Str_t + Mch_t + \varepsilon$$

Using the growth rate of machinery and the GDP growth rate in the following equation:

$$DY_t = c + \Delta Str_t + \Delta Mch_t + \varepsilon$$

Using a lag of one year:[31]

$$DY_t = c + \Delta Str_{t-1} + \Delta Mch_{t-1} + \varepsilon$$

The scatter graphs of Figure 8.1 show results as follows. The first graph shows the correlation between the share of machinery investment and GDP growth, the second between machinery growth in t and GDP growth, and finally, the third shows the correlation between machinery growth in $t-1$ and GDP growth.

The results of the scatter graph are similar between the growth rates of machinery (t and $t-1$) showing a positive correlation, but no correlation is found in the case of GDP growth rate in t with share of machinery in the GDP, contrary to the results of De Long and Summers (1991 and 1993). In order to validate the above correlation a co-integration test was applied using time series in a VAR framework, with the principal aim to measure the importance of the machinery investment without exogeneity. The following equations for machinery and GDP growth rates were used in a simple bivariate model:

$$y_t = \beta_{10} - \beta_{12} mch_t + \gamma_1 y_{t-1} + \gamma_{12} mch_{t-1} + \mu_{ty}$$
$$mch_t = \beta - \beta_{12} mch_t + \gamma_{12} y_{t-1} + \gamma_2 mch_{t-1} + {}^\mu mcht$$

Where y is the log of GDP, mch is the growth rate of machinery in t year and μ is white noise. Table 8.1 presents the principal results of this test.

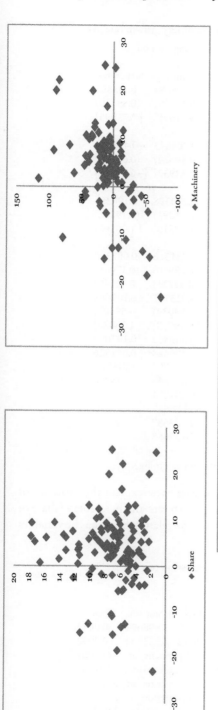

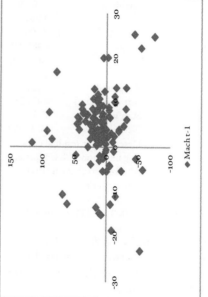

Figure 8.1: Scatter Graphs for *Mcb* Share, *Mcb* growth and *Mcb* growth in *t* −1

Source: Appendix

Table 8.1: Results of the VAR for machinery growth rate in *t*

Included observations: 104 after adjusting endpoints
Standard errors in ( ) and t-statistics in [ ]

	GDP	Machinery	Structures
GDP(−1)	0.030421	1.835084	1.608862
	(0.10963)	(0.34518)	(0.59150)
	[0.27750]	[5.31631]	[2.71995]
GDP(−2)	−0.213348	−0.204443	−0.493094
	(0.12266)	(0.38624)	(0.66186)
	[−1.73927]	[−0.52932]	[−0.74501]
Machinery(−1)	0.024043	0.220398	0.190254
	(0.03523)	(0.11091)	(0.19006)
	[0.68255]	[1.98710]	[1.00100]
Machinery(−2)	−0.000305	−0.051516	0.087300
	(0.03163)	(0.09960)	(0.17068)
	[−0.00964]	[−0.51721]	[0.51147]
	4.488015	4.013247	6.109683
C	(0.85125)	(2.68034)	(4.59307)
	[5.27226]	[1.49729]	[1.33020]
R-squared	0.512100	0.349862	0.107059
Adj. R-squared	0.471785	0.309648	0.051826
Sum sq. resids	4758.033	47172.89	138521.6
F-statistic	2.041088	8.699866	1.938306
Determinant residual covariance	22284271		
Log likelihood (d. f. adjusted)	−1322.517		
Akaike information criteria	25.83687		
Schwarz criteria	26.37083		

Source: Hofman (2000) and Ducoing and Hofman (forthcoming).

The results of the VAR model and the Johansen[32] test explain the existence of co-integration between the variables GDP growth rate and machinery (share of GDP, *t* and *t*−1).With these tests approved the correlation between the variables is validated as shown in Table 8.2.

Table 8.2: Results of the regression test in *t*

Dependent Variable: GDP
Included observations: 106

Variable	Coefficient	Std. Error	t-Statistic	Prob.
Structures	0.207305	0.020187	3.008694	0.0033
Machinery	0.446101	0.028942	2.923504	0.0042
R-squared	0.711077	Mean dependent var.		3.681061
Adjusted R-squared	0.602246	S. D. dependent var.		7.144050
S.E. of regression	6.918132	Akaike info criterion		6.724856
Sum squared resid	4977.498	Schwarz criterion		6.775110
Log likelihood	−354.4174	Durbin-Watson stat		2.082347

Source: Hofman (2000) and Ducoing and Hofman (forthcoming).

If using, instead of the machinery growth rate, the share of the machinery and structures in the GDP in the same year,[33] the results as seen in the scatter graph are different. In this case, as mentioned above, the correlation is not robust.

Table 8.3: Results of the regression of share of machinery in GDP

Dependent Variable: GDP
Included observations: 106

	Coefficient	Std. Error	t-Statistic	Prob.
Machinery	0.405238	0.093431	4.337319	0.0000
R-squared	−0.016955	Mean dependent var.		3.594623
Adjusted R-squared	−0.016955	S. D. dependent var.		8.093071
S. E. of regression	8.161390	Akaike info criterion		7.046095
Sum squared resid	6993.871	Schwarz criterion		7.071222
Log likelihood	−372.4431	Hannan-Quinn criter.		7.056279
Durbin-Watson stat	1.907158			

Source: Hofman (2000) and Ducoing and Hofman (forthcoming).

With the results shown above (machinery in *t*), a robust correlation was found, but with a great number of outliers, complicating the use of the Granger causality test. This problem was resolved using the Hodrick-Prescott filter eliminating the outliers that disrupt this model, using a smooth parameter.[34]

Results

It is possible to resume the results of the econometric approach in the results of the causality tests. The principal aim of this work is the search for the relationship between the variables machinery and GDP growth. The causality test is applied with the aim to discover what the dependent variable is, for example if investment in machinery causes the growth of GDP or instead, growth of GDP causes better expectations in the short and medium run and the agents decide to investment in machinery.

As the co-integration test was positive, it is possible to apply the Granger causality test. A problem of this test is the large number of years. This problem can be solved by dividing the whole period in the above indicated sub-periods. Better results are obtained with machinery in *t*, and this is the variable elected to test the direction of causality. First, the whole period will be examined. If Y_t is output *y*, mch_t is the growth rate of machinery in *t*, the VAR model is estimated as follows:

$$Y_t = a_1 + \sum_{i=1}^{n} \beta_i mch_{t-1} \sum_{j=1}^{n} \gamma_j \, y_{t-j} + e_{1t}$$

$$mch_t = a_2 + \sum_{i=1}^{n} \vartheta_i mch_{t-1} + \sum_{j=1}^{m} \delta_j Y_{t-j} + e_{2t}$$

It is not possible to find a robust Granger causality in the case of machinery in *t* for the whole period.[35] The same result appears when the causality test is applied for $t-1$. But different results are obtained if the whole period is separated in the sub-periods indicated above.

Table 8.4: Granger causality test for GDP and machinery in three sub-periods

Period	GDP causes machinery	F- statistic	Probability	Machinery causes GDP	F-statistic	Probability
First globalization	no	4.47589	0.01837	yes	1.90761	0.36314
Inward-looking development	no	2.39205	0.20583	no	1.08834	0.34760
Sustained Growth	yes	3.77841	0.43812	yes	0.58896	0.56305

Source: Ducoing and Hofman (forthcoming), Lüders (2007) and Hofman (2000).

The last result shows an important difference between the three sub-periods. The more surprising result is the lack of causality in the 'inward-looking development period', with a 'supposed' high rate of growth in the machinery investment and with the best performance in industrial output.[36] The result fits with the hypothesis that this period appears like a good growth period in comparison with the depression years, but is not the optimal in the long-run development of the country.

Conclusions

This article studied the relation between economic growth and investment and capital stock in the long run (1890–2006). It analyses the case of a developing country, Chile. As a result a long time database regarding investment and growth has been constructed. The principal conclusion is the confirmation of a positive relationship between these variables. However, the investment of machinery equipment is a much stronger predictor on economic growth than structure investment.

Further disaggregation of machinery equipment in electrical, non-electrical and transport equipment did not increase the explanatory level significantly. In the Granger test causality is found for sub-periods, but not for the whole period under consideration. This however is explained more by the weakness of this test in the long run than by the absence of a long-run relationship.[37]

Machinery investment is a fundamental element in long-run economic growth in a developing economy. Moreover, the present periodization and the results of the research about the inward-looking development period are in concordance with a new interpretation of Chilean economic development in the long run.

The interpretation presented in this article relates machinery investment and GDP growth and has two implications for the historical analysis of Chile's economic performance: First, the vision that the period of inward-looking development implicated an accelerated process of industrialization has come under scrutiny. Principally, industrialization needs machinery equipment investment and this period presents a low performance in machinery investment in comparison with the follower and predecessor period. Second, the growth analyses found correlation in the first and last period, but not in the second (inward-looking development). The Granger causality test refuted statistically the causality between machinery investment and growth. In a historical technology approach the type of investment used during the industrialization phase from 1933–76 was not on the frontier of technical progress and implicated lower levels of productivity and overall economic growth.

Appendices

Appendix A: GDP and Machinery Growth Rates

	GDP	Machinery		GDP	Machinery		GDP	Machinery
1890	10.2	6.3	1931	−18.69	−52.73	1974	0.97	−6.10
1891	7.23	−11.11	1932	−23.22	−74.53	1975	−12.91	1.61
1892	−1.12	43.75	1933	24.65	−1.86	1972	−1.21	−23.19
1893	5.17	−4.35	1934	19.92	89.57	1973	−5.57	11.57
1894	−4.27	−13.64	1935	7.49	93.00	1976	3.52	−12.15
1895	9.78	7.47	1936	3.4	19.56	1977	9.86	38.14
1896	5.09	−4.85	1937	12.84	8.34	1978	8.22	21.98
1897	−4.45	−15.07	1938	1.57	10.40	1979	8.28	14.43
1898	13.12	29.12	1939	2.53	−19.02	1980	7.94	21.02
1899	−0.15	24.63	1940	3.29	15.44	1981	6.21	16.29
1900	−4.09	20.67	1941	0.16	15.84	1982	−13.59	−45.69
1901	2.94	6.11	1942	3.29	−7.24	1983	−2.8	−31.41
1902	5.95	5.88	1943	2.86	4.88	1984	5.89	15.16
1903	−5.62	11.11	1944	1.89	−3.29	1985	1.97	15.50
1904	9.24	5.00	1945	8.63	12.57	1986	5.6	−3.40
1905	−2.03	42.86	1946	8.57	68.36	1987	6.58	36.76
1906	6.03	4.84	1947	−10.76	78.12	1988	7.29	20.69
1907	5.14	38.31	1948	16.6	10.64	1989	10.6	42.82
1908	9.27	16.09	1949	−2.16	46.17	1990	3.67	−3.74
1909	0.32	−30.69	1950	4.93	4.73	1991	7.97	3.32
1910	13.1	1.43	1951	4.35	45.16	1992	12.28	29.79
1911	0.54	9.86	1952	6.44	17.76	1993	7	16.81
1912	9.34	15.35	1953	7.54	11.16	1994	5.71	11.16
1913	1.37	11.15	1954	−3.24	21.94	1995	10.63	34.14
1914	−14.85	−56.58	1955	3.76	25.26	1996	7.4	7.01
1915	−5.3	−53.69	1956	1.68	16.81	1997	6.61	16.99
1916	22.08	85.10	1957	10.26	33.09	1998	3.23	0.86
1917	1.59	116.35	1958	5.49	0.27	1999	−0.76	−26.89
1918	0.79	8.15	1959	−5.66	−30.19	2000	4.49	23.16
1919	−15.26	13.79	1960	8.3	25.87	2001	3.38	4.05
1920	11.6	−14.26	1961	4.78	21.40	2002	2.18	0.58

	GDP	Machinery		GDP	Machinery		GDP	Machinery
1921	−11.17	−19.61	1962	4.74	−5.18	2003	3.73	5.34
1922	3.64	5.22	1963	6.33	−12.11	2004	6.06	21.17
1923	19.84	32.88	1964	2.23	9.30	2005	6.3	43.63
1924	7.25	21.15	1965	0.81	−12.74			
1925	4.02	5.23	1966	11.15	23.77			
1926	−2.77	47.84	1967	3.25	4.39			
1927	−1.98	−43.35	1968	3.58	14.34			
1928	25.18	14.33	1969	3.72	−1.70			
1929	2.76	61.15	1970	2.06	5.60			
1930	−12.84	−8.13	1971	8.96	−9.46			

Appendix B: Sources for Capital Goods Imports and Machinery Investment

1890–1940: Anuario Estadístico Chile: 1893, 1894, 1896, 1898, 1900, 1901, 1909, 1910–16, 1919–24, 1927, 1929, 1931–9 and Anuario de Comercio Internacional Chile: 1902–8, 1917, 1918, 1925–8.

1940–50: CORFO, Cuentas Nacionales de Chile, 1940–62, Table 5b, p.31, Santiago 1963.

1950–98: Official series collected by CEPAL.

1989–2005: Central Bank Chile, Statistical Yearbook of National Accounts.

Sources for GDP

1890–1900: Lüders

1901–50: Hofman

1951–60: ECLAC

1961–2005: Central Bank Chile.

9 THE SUGAR INDUSTRY, THE FORESTS AND THE CUBAN ENERGY TRANSITION, FROM THE EIGHTEENTH CENTURY TO THE MID-TWENTIETH CENTURY[1]

José Jofré González

Introduction

Cuba in the mid-eighteenth century was striking for having a higher level of economic activity than countries such as the United States and Argentina. However, at the beginning of the nineteenth century it started to lag behind the rest.

Authors such as Coatsworth,[2] Sokoloff and Engerman[3] point out that the success of countries like Cuba can be attributed to the combination of a relatively scarce workforce (free and slave) and access to abundant natural resources. Landes[4] adds that this led to the utilization of a large part of the territory for sugar-cane cultivation and the importation of all provisions – as tended to be the pattern in the plantation economies. Moreover, this type of societal organization led to enormous inequalities in income distribution and to the emergence of bad institutions[5] which became entrenched over time. These are the elements commonly used to explain how the rapid initial growth was later stunted and also to explain Cuba's present-day backwardness. However, this type of economic specialization also led to the near disappearance of Cuba's forests. This is a little-studied subject.

Generally, the process of Cuban economic growth has been associated with two factors: the availability of cheap energy obtained from the forests (where the land was the cheapest and most abundant productive factor on the island, in relative terms) and the availability of a slave workforce during the eighteenth and nineteenth centuries. These two elements defined Cuban economic growth potential along the lines of Boserup's bubble.

Cuban history demonstrates that as these factors started to become scarce, there was a change in the institutionality and new alternatives were sought in order for Cuba to continue participating in the international sugar market.

Cuba has been no exception in the energy transition, since once the primitive sugar-cane mills were transformed into large centralized factories at the beginning of the twentieth century a more efficient energy source was required to power the mills and boilers. This new energy source did not entirely replace plant biomass energy, instead they complemented each other.

This article is organized as follows: the second section presents the evolution of the Cuban sugar industry and its impact on the forests, the third focuses on the analysis of the energy transition and the fourth section deals with conclusions.

The Cuban Sugar Industry and the Use of the Forests[6]

The Advent of the Sugar Industry

Two events were key triggers for the development of the Cuban sugar industry. Firstly, in 1595 Phillip II granted the Portuguese Gómez Reynell licence to sell African slaves in the Indies. Secondly, on 30 December a Royal Charter was issued, giving Cuban producers the same privileges as those enjoyed by the sugar mill owners on Hispaniola. This Charter prevented the seizure for debt payment of sugar estate land, slaves, animals, machinery, etc.).[7]

The use of the forests was mainly associated with developments in the sugar industry. Initially, sugar mill owners tended to utilize the forests from which the navy had harvested timber for shipbuilding requirements and for the sale of valuable wood to Spain. The rest was burned two or three times and finally the remaining tree trunks were left as natural fertilizer and sugar cane was planted in this soil. Later, factory owners were granted authorization to make free use of the forests.

It is estimated that in the sixteenth century between 88 and 92 per cent of Cuba was made up of different types of forests, of which between 75 and 80 per cent were tropical forest and the rest, pine forest and low forest.[8] According to estimations, between 1492 and 1774 786,609 hectares were cleared – the equivalent of 7.87 per cent of the surface area of existing forests in 1492.[9]

In 1815 there was a new boost to the sugar industry with the liberalization of land use by way of a Royal Order of 30 August, allowing for all forests under the administration of the navy to be exploited.[10] This left only those forests which were Crown property as forest reserves. This measure (the end result of a long drawn-out conflict between the navy and sugar factory owners) permitted the change in land use, facilitating the demolition of haciendas and the emphyteutic leases of smaller estates (*cortes*), which led to an increase in the number of owners.[11]

At the beginning of the eighteenth century, favourable international conditions in the sugar market stimulated Cuba to intensely develop this productive activity.

Motivated by high sugar prices, the number of sugar factories in Cuba multiplied and *hacienda* owners put all their efforts and resources into reaping the benefits of the sugar business. This 'sugarocracy', seeking to maximize short and medium-term profits, launched themselves into sugar production destined for international markets. However, the 'sugarocracy' failed to take into account the fact that other producers in the world, operating under favourable natural conditions, could produce sugar – and most importantly, that while production grew prices tended to fall. This explains the systematic drop in the real sugar price until the 1930s and the growing rates of sugar production.

The sugar market was characterized by a pattern of fluctuations in the sugar price until the signing of international agreements in the 1930s in order to restrict supply and thereby to stabilize prices.

The Evolution of the Sugar Industry

Until the end of the eighteenth century sugar-cane farms were to be found close to Havana, but with the expansion of this activity in the nineteenth century, plantations moved towards the west and centre of the island, spurred by the introduction of railways. Finally, in the twentieth century sugar farming moved towards the eastern region of the country and once again, the railways played a central role in linking the plantations and the factories.

These changes in the utilization of the different regions bear witness to the depletion of adjacent and easily accessible energy sources, in addition to the exhaustion of the land due to intensive use, lack of fertilizer and lack of irrigation in the sugar plantations. The expansion of sugar farming displaced other smaller agricultural activities, such as the cultivation of tobacco, coffee,[12] subsistence farming and stock farming.

The bulk of sugar farming was concentrated initially in the region of Havana-Matanzas, later Las Villas, Camagüey, and finally in the eastern region. Certainly, if information was available about the degree of erosion of the territory over time, we would observe that the disappearance of the forests in Havana led the landowners to move to new lands.

The favourable natural conditions on the island allowed for transhumant sugar cultivation, which moved in search of new lands for planting cane and setting up factories; and in search of forests to exploit for fuel. In this way as sugar farming moved, the ecological damage spread to new places.[13]

From 1815, when the exploitation of the forests was permitted, we observe acceleration in the rate of deforestation with respect to the level in 1492.[14] This is hardly surprising, since from an economic perspective the sugar estate owners considered that within the process of sugar production the land (and by extension the forests and firewood) was the cheapest productive factor because virgin lands were abundant and therefore the intensive exploitation of forests would not have negative effects. They did not take into account all the externalities that arise with technology complexes.

A distinctive feature of the sugar business is that it began as an activity which the Creole sector of society engaged in, since the Spanish aristocracy was involved in the tobacco trade. This partly explains the behaviour of the sugar estate owners with regard the use of the forests. Hence we see how institutional elements conditioned the way natural resources were used. This is not to suggest that if other social classes had been involved in sugar farming, the results would have been any different. Rather, we should assume rent-seeking behaviour aimed at maximizing the short-term profits of this activity. As a consequence of such a mindset, the forest was exploited to the limit, damaging its capacity for renewal.

The evolution of the Cuban sugar industry, from the seventeenth century until the mid-twentieth, can be divided into five stages: 1) from 1602 to 1815, 2) from 1816 to 1868, 3) from 1869 to 1898, 4) from 1899 to 1926, and 5) from 1927 to 1955.

The following sections present a detailed analysis of the characteristic features of these periods and their impact on the forests.

1602–1815: The Beginning of Sugar Production

At the end of the seventeenth century there were sixty sugar mills and in 1759 this had risen to eighty-eight. In 1762 the mills in Havana occupied a surface area of over 61,000 hectares, with an average size of 134–61 hectares each. Generally, they were located in those areas where the best wood had been used to supply the Havana shipbuilding yard and the metropolitan state. In 1792 the average area per factory had increased to 295 hectares,[15] with double the land being used, which explains the rapid deforestation and the increase in sugar production during this period.

These new lands used for sugar production had previously been worked by small tobacco farmers (*vegueros*) because they were the most fertile, they had natural irrigation and had been cleared sufficiently yet retained enough forest, and there were roads linking them to the shipping ports.[16] Another activity affected was stock farming, in which case the established practice was to request the demolition of these haciendas once it had been demonstrated that they could not continue with this activity owing to the proximity of agriculture.[17] These elements explain the higher rates of exploitation of the forests and the achievement of higher rates of sugar production – not because of more efficient agro-industrial processes, but rather due to land rotation to new, more fertile lands.

Innovations such as mills with horizontal rollers and steel drums are characteristic of the beginning of the eighteenth century, as well as the use of steam as a motive force.[18] In the case of the boiler houses, there was a change in the positioning of the water pans and the type of fuel used.

Until the end of the eighteenth century the Spanish 'train' (a system of boilers)[19] was used, requiring an individual furnace for each water pan which meant a great quantity of fuel was needed. This was no problem as long as there were forests adjacent to the factories.[20] From 1796 the boiler system with a single furnace (the French 'train')[21] came into use, owing to the decreasing availability or firewood due to the destruction of the forests. This system worked using dry bagasse[22] as fuel. Therefore, the consumption of firewood was directly related to the system of boilers used.

The utilization of bagasse improved as Otaheite cane was planted.[23] The advantage of this type of cane was its greater yield – more sugar per area cultivated and on crushing the cane, more bagasse was obtained. This reduced consumption of firewood and the costs of maintaining vast forest areas close to the refinery for firewood, as well as chopping and transportation costs.[24] However, the use of bagasse was not without its problems and extra costs, since it had to be dried and later stored in a dry place until used, which meant using a significant number of slaves in the entire process, thus elevating sugar production costs. There was the additional problem related to the fact that the bagasse stores could be set on fire by the slaves, with consequent losses in production and installations.

From the last third of the eighteenth century until 1815 the fuel used in the sugar factories was firewood, which explains the high rates of disappearance of the forests. Also, until the mid-nineteenth century most factories used one furnace for each water pan in the process of sugar purging. Moreover, the labour force used in the cultivation and harvesting of the cane was slave labour, and therefore when this type of human exploitation was abolished, costs rose creating a new incentive to increase sugar-cane yields by clearing new territories.

In areas where there was no longer forest to exploit for firewood, sugar-cane mills were not established. Hence, the technological innovation of moving from the Spanish 'train' system to the Jamaican one in order to use less firewood and bagasse emerged in the deforested zones. In the other areas which did not suffer from a shortage of forest, firewood was the main energy source. Funes[25] points out that the criterion that determined the use of one system or the other was associated with the abundance and cost of firewood. When firewood did not pose a problem the Spanish system was used, and on the contrary mixed 'trains' were used.

The type of firewood burned depended on the type of forest close to the refinery, the type of soil and the climatic conditions. In terms of thickness, the thinnest wood was burned in the 'trains' and the thickest wood was used in the steam engines of the mills. Even when machinery was available, there was still dependence on firewood.

Generally, the sugar-cane mills which developed during the period of maximum pressure on the forests and which led to their depletion as a source of fuel

were semi-mechanized mills where the Jamaican 'train' was widely used in order
to rationalize the use of fire.

1816–68: Expansion and Transformation of the Industry

Sugar production in the period 1816–68 grew at an annual rate of 5.6 per cent,
exerting great pressure on other activities such as the cultivation and exportation of tobacco as well as stock farming. There was a surge in cash crops, as a
consequence of the comparative advantage they enjoyed, and a specialization
driven by profitability.[26] Thus, the 1840s saw a great expansion in the activity
of the sugar industry, supported by its technological and financial capacity to
face up to competition on the international markets and tax pressure from the
metropolitan state.[27]

From the mid-nineteenth century, the share of sugar in total Cuban exports
fluctuated at around 70 per cent. This evolution, however, depended on the
global behaviour of the sugar market. From Cuban independence onwards sugar
exports grew rapidly to over 80 per cent of total exports, which can be explained
by Cuba's absolute dependence on the United States once it gained independence from Spain.

The United States was the main market for sugar exports in 1841 representing 29 per cent of total sugar exported, Spain 15.3 per cent, Russia 9.9 per cent
and Germany 9.5 per cent. In 1860, the United States represented 58.5 per cent
of sugar exports, followed at distance by England at 16.7 per cent and Spain at
7.7 per cent. In 1880, 81.6 per cent of sugar exports were destined to the United
States. After Cuban independence all sugar was exported to the United States,
although without being fully processed. Instead, it was industrially processed
up to the raw sugar stage and finally the sugar was refined in the United States.

From this period until the beginning of the twentieth century Cuba began
the transition from an organic economy to a fossil fuel economy.[28]

Marrero[29] estimated that in 1827 90 per cent of Cuban territory was constituted by forest, woodlands and other landscapes, 4.2 per cent was cultivated and
5.8 per cent was used for pasture. In 1846 forests and arid lands made up 74.6 per
cent of the territory and in 1862, 57.4 per cent.[30] Between these dates the surface
area of the forests had dropped from 409.825 to 250.845 *caballerías*.[31]

Between 1828 and 1877 Funes[32] points out that 2,352,539 hectares of forest
disappeared, which represented 35.1 per cent of the area existing in 1828. The
forest was exploited in this way in order to obtain firewood, charcoal, wood for
use in the railways, by shipping companies, and in domestic and foreign timber
trade. Forest was cleared in other regions to gain territory for stock farming to
supply the plantations.[33]

The need to extend sugar-cane cultivation led to the construction of a railway system to provide access to new sugar plantations. Thus, in 1837 the stretch

of railway connecting Havana and Bejucal was inaugurated and in 1838 the line was completed to Güines.[34] In the 1850s the railway extended from the west to the centre of the island. As the rail system covered more and more territory, the cost of sugar transportation was reduced by approximately 70 per cent.[35]

The utilization of firewood can be divided into two periods:[36] a) 1815–40, which was the beginning of the steam era in the sugar refineries and b) 1840–60 when there was a biofuel crisis.

a) 1815–40: The Beginning of the Steam Era; Increased Use of Firewood and Need for Economy. The progress of the sugar industry in the early decades of the nineteenth century did not mean the substitution of the fuel used to drive the steam engines. The first steam engines were located in deforested areas and were used along with the Jamaican system of 'trains'. Sugar-cane factories operating in this manner were known as semi-mechanized and prevailed until the 1870s.

In the eighteenth century steam was used to a limited extent. Hence, for example in 1727 2.5 per cent of factories used steam mills with this percentage increasing rapidly to 19.8 per cent in 1846[37] and to 70.4 per cent in 1860.[38] Another important technological innovation was the adoption of the system of vacuum boilers,[39] which meant heat was used more efficiently and the sugar juice boiled at lower temperatures (in 1860 such boilers represented 5.1 per cent of boilers used in all refineries).[40]

The scarcity of forests for firewood to be used in the boilers and mills also affected the steam shipping companies. This gave rise to competition between these two activities and even greater deforestation driven by the exploitation of virgin territories.

b) 1840–60: The Fuel Crisis. Even though the use of bagasse partly reduced firewood consumption, this source of plant biomass energy was not very cost effective since it required more slave labour in the drying process and later for collecting and storage. Moreover, it required storage place in the refinery until it was used, however if it became damp it was useless. Furthermore, it meant an increase in the risk of fires on the sugar estates.

The problem of the use of biomass energy was significant as early as the 1840s, and was resolved with the use of coal – not only in the sugar industry but also in the railways[41] and the steam shipping companies. With this innovation Cuba joined the process of energy transition, which also allowed for the freeing up of labour power.

Moreover, coal was cheaper than charcoal and had a greater heat value. The relation between coal and firewood was: one ton of coal generated energy equivalent to four tons of bad firewood.[42]

From 1837 firewood was imported for the functioning of the railways, but in 1860 coal had already substituted firewood, with imports reaching 92,000 tons.[43] In the period between 1842 and 1843 an average of 65 tons of coal were imported.[44] The main coal suppliers were Great Britain and the United States, supplying 60,000 metric tons in 1855 which rose to 150,000 in 1864. In 1874 the port of Havana registered importations of 154,441 metric tons of coal.[45]

By the end of 1860 a significant number of mills were semi-mechanized (96.5 per cent used Jamaican 'trains' and 70 per cent used steam power) and just 9.4 per cent made use of the cutting edge technology of the time.[46]

1869–98: Consolidation of the Industry

The freeing of slaves exacerbated the rise in labour costs, leading to at the end of the nineteenth century a significant change in the organization of the industry and the vertical disintegration of the sugar production process. This saw the advent of centralized sugar factories that dealt with the industrial processing of its own cultivated sugar cane or cane bought from the tenant farmers and small farmers.

This change in organization was aimed once more at reducing production costs through the implementation of economies of scale. However, as was the trend in the evolution of the Cuban sugar industry, this did not impact positively on the forest, since now more land was required for the production of more cane for processing in factories with greater capacity.

The impossibility of storing cut cane during the harvest for more than twenty-four hours meant the factories developed their own railway systems guaranteeing ready transport from the plantations to the factories. Moreover, in order to avoid bottlenecks typical of greater volume cane production, relevant improvements were made in the crushing process and later in the system of evaporation to clarify the sugar-cane juice.[47]

The spread of centrifuges and their widespread use in the 1870s favoured the mechanization of evaporation, meaning a greater standardization of sugar was achieved. This led to production being centred on unrefined sugar with 96 per cent sucrose (so called raw sugar).

Other factors driving the modernization of the sector, which broke with the vertical integration of the factories, included the growth of international competition and difficulties in maintaining the slave trade and system of a servile workforce.[48]

Even though these innovations permitted the modernization of the sugar industry and the separation of the agricultural aspect from the industrial, pressure on the forests did not disappear given that more wood was needed to build bigger installations and more fuel for running the production process. Generally, the logic underlying large-scale mechanization was the advantage of the abundance of cane and the economizing on the labour factor, hence the boost in production. Unlike what had occurred up till then, this was due to an increase in productive capacities and not to a rise in the number of factories.

The Ten Years' War (1868–78) reduced the number of refineries in Cuba. The less efficient ones generally disappeared, especially those on the eastern half of the island, and sugar production was concentrated in the western region.[49]

Mechanization in the late 1870s and early 1880s meant an average of 8.0– 8.5 *arroba* of sugar was obtained per 100 *arroba* of cane, compared with yields of 5.5–6.5 *arroba* of sugar per 100 of cane achieved until the 1860s.[50]

In the second half of the nineteenth century and the first half of the twentieth century continuous production processes were introduced. This innovation boosted the productivity of the sugar industry, triggering a drop in international prices. All of this occurred within the framework of economic activity dependent on biomass energy. However, this improvement did not bring about the disappearance of slash and burn agriculture, causing greater pressure on the forests with the quest for new, unexploited lands – particularly in the new sugar-producing zones. On evaluating the phenomenon of centralization and concentration of the sugar industry, Funes[51] points out that:

> this had a bearing, in two opposite ways, on the progressive deforestation of the island. This centralization and concentration of the industry contributed to the abandonment of the old itinerant nature of the industry. However, the abundant forests in the central eastern half favored the continued practice of establishing new sugar estates on virgin territory, now with a far greater impact per unit. During this stage, the sugar industry was only at the start of its occupation of the eastern half of the island, which meant that there was less deforestation than in the period from 1815 to 1876 …

The reduction of the forests between 1878 and 1900 is estimated at 527,409 hectares. This represents 12 per cent of forests cleared in the period 1828–77. This implies that 50,419 hectares of forest were cleared annually in the earlier period, dropping to 26,208 hectares annually in the later period.[52]

Between 1890 and 1898, 92 per cent of Cuba's apparent consumption of fossil energy was coal.[53] The average price paid per ton of coal (in tons of oil equivalent) imported from the United States was US$3.99 and in the case of oil, US$20.4.[54] These values may appear high if we take into account that the average price received, during the same period, for each pound of sugar was 2.75 cents.

After gaining independence from Spain at the end of the century with the Independence War, Cuba found itself with a labour market undergoing a process of change and with 50 per cent of the forests it had in 1492.

1899–1926: The Sugar Industry and North American Capital

During the period 1899–1926 sugar production experienced growth rates of 10.7 per cent annually, which implies a rise from 332,000 metric tons to 5,386,000 metric tons. At the time sugar cane represented around 60 per cent of the world market, and Cuba occupied a relatively important position with approximately 20 per cent of the market. For its part, the real sugar price kept falling, excepting the years of the First World War when the price tended to rise – an exceptional period which lasted until the 1920s.

The start of the twentieth century was marked by more intensive exploitation of the forests, given that the factories built from 1898 onwards were larger,[55] controlling lands equivalent to one or more of the original haciendas. It was in this way that the sugar *latifundios* came into being. Land which was previously forest, grazing savannahs and cultivated areas or subdivisions of sugar factories was used exclusively for sugar plantations or pasturelands for oxen.[56] However, the expansion of the sugar industry continued to depend on the fertility of the forests cleared with slash and burn methods.

After the Cuban War of Independence, the island became a protectorate of the United States for three years, during which time lands were bought for the establishment of large centralized factories. These lands were surrounded by abundant forests and disposed of excellent conditions for the rapid commercialization of forest products.[57]

Evidence found by Santamaría García[58] shows that after the First World War the Cuban sugar industry began to intensify milling which cut the milling time (in Cuban historiography this process is known as *intensivismo*). The effects on industrial yield and on costs were felt in the second half of the 1920s.

From the perspective of apparent consumption of modern energies, oil constituted 6 per cent of total energy consumption (traditional and modern energies) and from 1917 this grew to over 20 per cent as oil gained importance within total energy consumed.

In the period 1900–27 Cuban forestlands shrank from 4,547,857 to 2,242,166 hectares – that is to say, they represented 41.3 per cent of the territory in the first year and 20.4 per cent in the final year. It is estimated that in the period 1900–13 102,544 hectares of forest were cleared – the incidence of greatest deforestation prior to 1921.[59] During the early twentieth century in the areas where the sugar industry had newly arrived, the existence of firewood meant this could be used as a supplementary fuel. Green bagasse-burning ovens also remained in use from 1860 until the early decades of the twentieth century.

After the period of utilization of green bagasse, oil helped resolve the insurmountable problem of deforestation, but the use of firewood was not completely abandoned. An analysis of information on the apparent consumption of fossil energies for Cuba between 1899 and 1926 indicates that coal represents on average 74 per cent of total fossil fuels, with the relative importance of oil starting to grow.

It is important to note that in Cuba the relative price of coal with respect to oil started to grow systematically from 1916. The necessary provisos and simplifications aside, we are able to indicate that as from the 1910s the Cuban economy began to use oil more intensely as an energy source due to a rise in the relative price of fossil fuels. We are also led to believe that, in the pursuit of greater economic profits the big sugar enterprises in Cuba favoured the use of a fuel with a higher heat value (as is oil) and for other less sophisticated processes bagasse was probably used.[60]

This period of analysis ends in 1926,[61] which is when legal regulations were adopted to curb the chopping down and burning of forests for use in the sugar industry – after more than a century of indiscriminate use of the forests. This can be understood as an attempt to halt the enormous expansion of this industry and its irreversible negative effects after more than a century of unbridled exploitation.

Finally, between 1926 and 1929 the government intervened to limit milling with a view to pushing up sugar prices, but evidence shows that Cuba was not powerful enough to trigger a price recovery.[62]

1927–55: The Sugar Industry under the Tree-Felling Proscription

The decree proscribing the clearing of forests did not instantly end the exploitation of the forest for the planting of sugar cane. But as Funes[63] points out we can state that the rise in sugar-cane yields – unlike in the past – depended on factors such as the use of a different variety of cane, agricultural mechanization, chemical fertilizers, irrigation and other elements characteristic of the green revolution.

This was a groundbreaking change, representing a modernization of agriculture associated with the sugar industry – something unheard of since the beginning of sugar-cane farming. We must remember that all the technological innovations adopted by the sugar industry were aimed at saving on the labour factor, whereas the availability of land for clearing removed the incentive for improvements in the area of the agricultural management of sugar production.

This final period of analysis is marked by a 0.06 per cent rate of decrease in annual sugar production.[64] This is among the lowest rates in the entire period analysed, however it can be explained by the drop in production in the mid-1920s[65] following a period of exceptionally high international sugar prices, the Great Depression of the 1930s, the agreements to stabilize the sugar price and then the impact of the Second World War. From the point of view of the relevance of sugar cane in the world market, this averaged 60 per cent and Cuba's presence in the world market tended to remain stable at around 10 per cent.

Through the evolution of the Cuban sugar industry the forest was the most important productive factor that sustained the economy for more than a century. As long as the land could provide rich soil (which had taken thousands of years to build up), the Cuban sugar industry was able to deal with international competition and achieve greater yields in sugar-cane production. Finally, with improvements to the industrial side of the process, sugar became an internationally competitive product. As we have observed, this model worked as long as forests were available, but in the long run it was not a sustainable situation.

The excessive pressure on the forests considerably reduced their size, to the point that in the 1950s there constituted only around 20 per cent of the previously existing forest of 1492. The most precise information from the 1943 census demonstrates that by that year 46 per cent of Cuban forests had been destroyed, and existing forests represented 18 per cent of the land, mangrove swamps and cays constituted 9 per cent and 23 per cent was savannahs, holm oak groves and open land.[66]

The Cuban Energy Transition

From the previous sections, it can be deduced that fossil fuels made a slow appearance in the Cuban energy basket since, as we have shown, forests provided firewood for the boiler houses and when the mills became mechanized, firewood was used in the steam engines.

With the mechanization of the factories, and in the face of the shortage of firewood from the forests, the sugar industry resorted first to the use of dry bagasse and later green bagasse as an energy source for the cooking process. But these innovations called for changes in the arrangement of the water pans and in the case of green bagasse, the ovens needed to be adapted. Once these changes were made, the use of bagasse began to spread. Simultaneously, coal was introduced for the generation of steam to drive the mechanized mills.

At the end of the nineteenth century when firewood was less available, oil was gradually introduced as long as it was cheaper in relative terms than coal. If we run through the technologies in use in the sugar industry at various points in time, we observe the coexistence of different factories that were at different stages in the energy transition. The most mechanized ones were most probably those which used fuels that yielded more energy per unit.

Following the logic of the intensive use of the lowest cost resource, at the times when relative prices of the different energies available changed, this should be reflected in the types of energies consumed. Evidence shows us that when slaves were more expensive, there was less incentive to use them in the gathering of firewood. During those periods coal was even more expensive, particularly if there were no adequate roads, and the incentive was to build an extensive railways system in order for coal to be used.

Finally, when the coal price rose oil began attract interest, especially between 1916 and 1948, to the extent that this energy source began to show higher participation in the energy basket. This led to the change in the consumption pattern of fossil fuels, as can be observed in Figure 9.1.

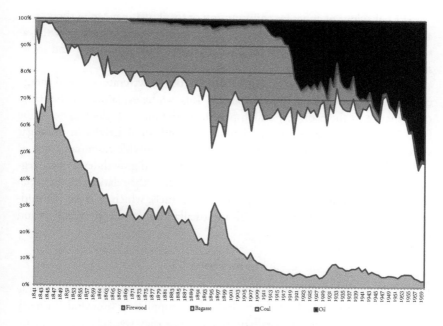

Figure 9.1: Energy basket composition: 1841–1960

Source: Own elaboration with information from the database of the research project *Importaciones y modernización económica en América Latina: 1890–1960* for modern energies and J. Jofré (2008) for the traditional energies. The negligible contributions of natural gas and hydroelectricity have been excluded.

The rise in prices of plant biomass energy on the island and the pressure to keep profits up on the world sugar market triggered the gradual move to coal and later oil.

The transition from coal to oil took place in the 1910s and early 1920s. This was a watershed period, since at the end of the nineteenth century Cuba was one of the countries with the highest growth in Latin America. Then from 1900 growth in apparent consumption of fossil fuels per capita in Cuba slowed down, but with the change from coal to oil Cuban energy consumption picked up. This behaviour is also influenced by the drop in production in the 1930s by 34.2 per cent compared with the previous decade. When compared with Uruguay, which has a pattern of weaker economic growth, what is evident is that Cuban apparent fossil energy consumption grew more rapidly until the 1920s and then the opposite occurred.

The Cuban energy transition is striking due to the use of mainly traditional energies until the first half of the twentieth century and the rapid introduction of oil in the early twentieth century.

The behaviour of apparent consumption of fossil fuels per capita shows that as from the decrease in sugar production in the mid-1920s economic growth was severely stunted. This probably triggered changes in the productive and social structure of the country.

Once Cuba began to use oil more intensely, the growth rates of fossil energy consumption per capita grew more slowly. This can be explained by the structural change in the economy which permitted the more efficient use of these fuels. This was rooted in the rationalization of industrial activity in the sugar sector, given that once the forests could no longer provide resources (such as firewood and fertile soil) to sustain the industry, record growth levels were registered. Other evidence that supports this statement is the relationship between the sugar price and the weighted price of fossil fuels, which as from the mid-1920s remained stable, with significant oscillations in the previous period (1880–1925).

Conclusion

It is hard to imagine Cuban sugar production and its later international trade without the forest, which played a vital role as supplier of firewood (primary energy source), timber for installations and, once they were cleared, freed up very fertile land.

From the eighteenth century firewood was the main source of energy in Cuba, which led to the destruction of the forests. Today, four centuries later, there is a new awareness of the impact of this situation in the face of growing desertification and drought. The shortage of firewood led initially to the use of dry bagasse for fuel, but pressure from the sugar industry for greater revenues meant the forest continued to be exploited as a source of biomass energy and new land was utilized with the growth in the number of factories and the enormous consumption of firewood in steam engines.[67] The shortage of firewood always favoured the use of other sources of energy as was the case with dry bagasse, but given that the process of obtaining the bagasse was more costly, at the end of the nineteenth century ovens were introduced that could burn green bagasse, which resolved problems of storage and risk of fires.

However, this technology complex was obliged to continue searching for the energy source that would substitute the already diminished forests. The adoption of steam engines powered by coal marked the start of a period of maturation of the technology. Although this curbed the chopping down of forests, vast tracts of cleared forest were still needed for the planting of cane in this extremely fertile soil.

The Cuban energy transition was not exceptional: once the sugar-cane mills grew into large centralized factories a more efficient energy source was needed to drive the mills and power the boilers. By no means did this new energy source completely substitute the use of plant biomass energy. On the contrary, findings demonstrate that this change was slower in Cuba than in countries with a similar level of industrial development, but where laws preventing the excessive exploitation of the forests and regulating the activity of the sugar industry (at both domestic and international levels) led to a change in energy uses.

Generally, the processes of economic growth in Cuba were associated with the availability of a cheap energy source obtained from the forests and a workforce that in the eighteenth and nineteenth century consisted of slaves. These two elements defined the growth potential, as per Boserup's bubble. The history of Cuba demonstrates that as these factors started to become scarce, there was a change in the institutionality and new alternatives were sought in order to continue exploiting the sugar resources.

10 EMPIRICAL DEBATE ON TERMS OF TRADE AND THE DOUBLE FACTORIAL TERMS OF TRADE OF COLOMBIA, 1975–2006[1]

Santiago Colmenares

Introduction

The causes and historical determinants of development and economic growth or, conversely, the causes of backwardness and poverty, constitute one of the main problems that deserve serious attention in the field of economics and economic history. Not in vain the book that for many is the cornerstone of modern economics was entitled *An Inquiry into the Nature and Causes of the Wealth of Nations*.[2] Through the centuries many ideas and schools of though have developed, some of whom can be defined according to the typology of explanations they formulate with respect to this particular problem.

This paper is about the Prebisch-Singer (P-S) hypothesis on international trade, which was formulated in the mid-twentieth century, and which we interpret as an attempt to create an analytical framework to explain the growing gap in welfare and develop levels among different regions in the world from its trade relations. In this sense we can say that the P-S hypothesis belongs to the fields of both economics and economic history. This hypothesis, besides being a significant challenge to the hegemony maintained by the neoclassical theory of trade, was the theoretical base for trade policies of many countries in the periphery during the middle decades of the twentieth century and, even though its influence in economic policy has been undermined in the last three decades, remains fervently debated in economics and economic history literature.

Given that there is a lot of remarkable analysis on this issue, and considering Love's reflection[3] when he said that a theory without empirical support is in danger of becoming mere ideology or doctrine, in this paper we choose to make an analytical assessment of the empirical literature around the P-S hypothesis.

However, as will be shown later on, we have found that there is a lack of correspondence between the original formulation of the P-S hypothesis and the direction taken by the empirical literature. The main problem is that the empirical analysis has focused almost entirely in the net barter terms of trade (NBTT), while in the original version of the P-S hypothesis labour productivity embodied in the economic sectors that compound the NBTT (i.e. the factorial terms of trade) has a central role. Therefore, a second objective of the present work is to elaborate a terms of trade series that, at least in what concerns the productivity factor, gets closer to the 'ideal' type or corroboration that the P-S hypothesis demands. In doing so we chose the case of the terms of trade between Colombia and the United States.

The paper is divided in three sections. Section one will consider the original P-S hypothesis and analyse some of its subsequent developments; section two will draw some of the main lines of the empirical debate on the subject and section three will study the terms of trade between Colombia and United States.

The Prebisch-Singer Hypothesis and Its Versions

The P-S hypothesis came out from and inductive type of reasoning. Both Prebisch and Singer observed that over time the periphery ('borrowing countries', as they were called by Singer in his original article), specialized in exporting primary products, suffer from a deterioration in its terms of trade, while at the same time its labour productivity grew less relative to the centre. This was against the neoclassical argument that states that productivity increments are reflected in lower prices. Therefore, in Prebisch and Singer's argument, besides the deterioration in the relative prices of exchange P_p/P_c[4] there was some differentiation in the labour productivity of their export sectors q_p/q_c.[5] Together, both phenomena determined the process of 'income differentiation' between the centre and the periphery or what is called the deterioration of the double factorial terms of trade (DFTT)[6] which can by expressed as $(P_p/P_c) \times (q_p/q_c)$.[7]

In other words, the P-S hypothesis means that over time not only a deterioration in the NBTT for the periphery could be noticed, but also that these occurred while productivity grew faster in the centre than in the periphery, and thus 'the income of entrepreneurs and productive factors have grown, in the centers, more than its productivity increments, and in the periphery, less than its according increment'. Therefore, 'while the centers have retained entirely the result of its industrial technical progress, the countries of the periphery have transferred a portion of the fruits of their own technical progress'.[8] In brief, the hypothesis argues that the periphery has suffered from a deterioration in its DFTT rather than its NBTT, and thus it is the DFTT that is the truly relevant measure in Prebisch and Singer's original conception to explain a widening in inequality and income level gap among different regions and countries in the world through time.[9] It is important to keep this in mind, because as will be seen later on, most of the empirical debate on the P-S hypothesis has been focused on the evolution of the NBTT and not the DFTT. In fact, in some recent contributions on this issue, when Prebisch's arguments are recalled, this important dimension of his hypothesis is not recognized.[10]

Regarding the *causes* of the deterioration of the terms of trade there exist at least two versions or models. In the first one, which Octavio Rodríguez called the 'cycles version', the prices of primary products have a wider price-cycle than the prices of manufactures.[11] Thus, during the upwards cycle, the relative prices of primary products vis-à-vis manufactures improve, while in the downwards cycle the relative prices of primary products decline. However, in the downswing, the prices of manufactures are characterized by strong rigidity, so at the end relative prices of primary products suffer a net fall.[12] This asymmetry in the determinants of price formation during the downward cycle between centre and periphery would by explained, in Prebisch's model, by asymmetries in the functioning of labour markets between the two regions. In fact, the net fall is produced in the factorial terms of trade, that in differences in labour remunerations, and through it in the NBTT.[13] While in the centre, productivity gains are absorbed by wages in an organized and almost fully employed workforce, the periphery is characterized by huge unemployment and weak organization of workforce.[14] However, taking into account that the demand of primary products depends somewhat in the demand for elaborated products, their prices are under enormous pressure to maintain certain levels that allow the processing sectors to reduce their costs and get some margin of profit. This version or model of the Prebisch hypothesis is a precursor of subsequent theoretical developments around 'unequal exchange'.[15]

The second model, first presented by Singer in 1950 and then reinforced by Prebisch in 1958, argues that the terms of trade of commodities versus manufactures tends to deteriorate due to different income-elasticity of demand of both types of products.[16] While the former has typically an income-elasticity of demand less than 1 (due to some causes related with Engel's law, or the fact that in the long run some commodities can be replaced by synthetic inputs in industrial processes), the later has normally an income-elasticity of demand larger than 1. Thus, they argue, during the process of economic growth, demand for manufactures became more dynamic than demand for commodities and this pushes down the NBTT of the latter. It is important to notice that while in the first model the deterioration happened in the factor markets, in this model it occurs directly in the product market.[17] Therefore, in this version the hypothesis could be directly corroborated in the NBTT without having to take into consideration labour productivity. Explaining this, Ocampo[18] developed a model in which changes in the NBTT of the centre depend on income-elasticity and price-elasticity as the following expression shows:

$$\Delta NBTT_c = (e_c g_p - e_p g_c) / (n_c + n_p - 1)$$

Where e is the income-elasticity of demand, g is the growth rate of the economy and n is the price-elasticity of demand (subscripts 'c' and 'p' corresponds to 'centre' and 'periphery'). From this expression it could be observed that there would be an improvement in the NBTT of the centre (and therefore deterioration in the NBTT of the periphery) if a) the income-elasticity of the products of the centre increases or the income-elasticity of the periphery decreases; and/ or b) the growth rate of the peripheral economy increases or the growth rate of the centre decreases. Hence, if we assume an equilibrated trade balance, the periphery is constrained to choose between deterioration in its NBTT or a lower growth rate relative to the centre, as illustrated in the expression:

$$g_p/g_c > e_p/e_c \rightarrow \downarrow P_p/P_c$$

For mid-twentieth century ECLA (the United Nations Economic Commission for Latin America and the Caribbean), this was an important point of concern in the view that the United States, the new 'main cyclical centre' and the main trade partner for most of Latin America was a much more closed economy (in relation with its economy size) than what the UK was in the past. Therefore, industrialization by import substitution was considered the only way to escape from the constraints placed above, because it was supposed to allow production and income to grow at a faster rate than global imports and exports.[19]

The Keynesian and neoclassical literature which get involved in the debate focused their attention in the above set of explanatory factors, something that could explain the little attention that the DFTT received in the empirical debate.[20] Nevertheless, the original contribution made by Singer was not limited to deriving conclusions about the fact that different countries trade products with uneven elasticities. The DFTT were central in his analysis, among other factors that contributed (in his view) to an uneven distribution of the gains of international trade between 'borrowing' countries and 'investor' countries.[21]

As is well known, at the beginning of the 1970s Singer radicalized his hypothesis, arguing that peripheral countries would suffer deterioration in its NBTT, no matter the type of products they exported, because the causes of the deterioration would not be related with the characteristics of products but with the country's distinctiveness.[22] In his argument, technology had a central role, specifically the fact that it was concentrated, developed and fabricated in developed countries, which gave them monopolistic power against 'borrowing countries'. Hence, in a situation of industrialization through the development of simple manufacturing sectors (who were the only sectors that arose from ISI policies), those products would have many of the characteristics that Singer had attributed before to primary products, and thus he predicted a deterioration of its prices vis-à-vis more technologically complex manufactures produced in the 'investor countries'. In neoclassical economics, technology and the capital–

labour relation is driven by factor endowments and the need to optimize costs. For Singer (in the 1970s), in the 'borrowing countries' this causation works the other way around: it is technology what imposes restrictions and determines the kind of goods to be produced, and the *effective* use of productive factors. In his view, typical phenomena of underdeveloped countries like chronic unemployment or overconcentration of capital in 'modern' sectors would be the consequence of misalignments between technologies (that were produced and designed in developed countries in accordance to their specific needs) and relative factor endowments. This 'new' hypothesis, formulated by Singer, triggered some studies about manufacturing NBTT and DFTT among developed and underdeveloped countries.

To sum up, there are two ways of testing the P-S hypothesis (NBTT and DFTT) and two explanation lines for the deteriorating terms of trade phenomena. One makes reference to labour market properties at each pole of the system, hence, to price formation mechanisms in export sectors. In this line, DFTT are the best measure to test the hypothesis. The second makes reference to income-elasticity of demand for products, and its testing could be made directly through NBTT. However, the hypothesis about income differentiation is closer to the first line. Finally, studies interested in the 'amplified' P-S hypothesis made by Singer in the 1970s, could broaden the scope of the typology of products to be analysed, going beyond the classical contraposition between primary products and manufactures to manufactures produced in *industrialized* countries vis-à-vis those produced in *industrializing* countries.

Great Twists in the Empirical Debate on Terms of Trade

The Old Debates

Theoretical concerns about terms of trade have existed since the times of classical economists. Authors such as John Stuart Mill and Adam Smith believed that prices of primary products relative to manufactures would improve in the long run, due to the law of diminishing returns in agriculture and the law of increasing returns in manufactures, as work division spread. At the beginning of the twentieth century, Keynes supported the same idea, and some empirical evidence built by D. H Robertson in 1915 and C. Clark in 1942 showed that terms of trade of Great Britain (the centre *par excellence*) had deteriorated through the nineteenth century.[23]

According to Lipsey, the first switch in the argument was done by Folke Hilgerdt in 1945, documenting a secular decline of NBTT for primary products in the League of Nations report 'Industrialisation and Foreign Trade',[24] notwithstanding the fact that two years before Kindleberger (1943) had argued: 'Inexorably the terms of trade move against agricultural and raw material countries as the world's standard of living increases ... and as Engel's law of consumption operates'.[25] But the study that made famous the hypothesis was the 1949 UN report 'Post-War Price Relations in Trade between Under-Developed and Industrialized Countries' which, as we now know, was made by Singer.[26]

On the other hand, terms of trade issues were very important in Latin America since the times of the oldest generations of professional economists. In the 1920s, Víctor Emilio Estrada, a former director of the Central Bank of Ecuador, explained the falling prices of cacao as a consequence of wage divergence between the United States and Ecuador. Besides, when ECLA was created, its first meeting (June 1948) ordered a study about Latin American terms of trade. Furthermore, its first director, Raul Prebisch, had been interested in the field since the mid-1940s when he wrote a pair of articles about the perils of permanent economic disequilibrium arising from import coefficient asymmetries between the United States – the new main 'centre' – and Latin America.[27] In 1949, Prebisch wrote his famous 'The Economic Development of Latin America and Its Principal Problems' where he reported an upward trend of the NBTT of Great Britain between 1876 and 1947, which he assumed to be correlated with a hypothetical deterioration of the NBTT of the periphery.[28]

During the 1950s authors such as A. Lewis, Kindleberger, Gundar Myrdal and many others sympathized with these kinds of ideas, developed economic models in those lines, and attempted to reinforce empirical evidences.[29] However, they were also heavily criticized by many scholars more aligned to orthodoxy. In the first place, the criticisms aimed at the use of NBTT of the UK as being representative of the whole group of industrialized countries and, therefore, attributing to this data the real evolution of NBTT of primary products versus manufactures. This was stated by Kindleberger, Meier and Baldwin, Haberler and Lipsey among others.[30] Second, some authors argued that primary products imported by the UK included several products acquired mainly from other industrialized countries.[31] Third, it was stated that while exports were valued in FOB prices, imports were CIF prices, thus, NBTT deterioration could respond to a sharp decline in transportation costs. Jacob Viner (in 1953) was among the scholars who stressed this point, and it is still possible to find studies that discuss and find empirical evidence on the issue, supporting or rejecting it.[32] Finally it was argued that the index of the UN report does not account for quality improvements in manufactures and, therefore, they overestimate the NBTT deterioration of commodities.

In 1976 ECLA dedicated a new series of publications entitled '*Cuadernos estadísticos de la CEPAL*' to the issue of the terms of trade, collecting NBTT indexes from several Latin American countries from 1928 onwards.[33] Even so, in academic circles the empirical debate remained focused in NBTT between types of products. In part, it is possible that this was because new NBTT indexes between manufactures and commodities were published by UNCTAD for 1900–70[34] and by the World Bank for post-Second World War years. In the first years of the 1980s, Spraos began a new wave of empirical investigations, in which his main conclusion was that the P-S hypothesis stands for the pre-Second World War years, but that it is less clear when the 1950–70 time span is included.[35]

Recent Discussions

During the 1980s the general tendency in the literature was to corroborate the P-S hypothesis, such as in quite favourable articles by Sapsford and Sarkar.[36] At this point, however, the main limitation faced by scholars interested in the subject was the lack of reliable data, since the United Nations and World Bank's price series were constructed and updated using different methodologies, product baskets and sets of countries over time. Thus, a project from the World Bank gave light to two studies containing new series of primary product prices since 1900: Diakosawas and Scandizzo, in 1987, and Grilli and Yang, in 1988.[37] The later reported a robust set of prices for twenty-four commodities between 1900 and 1986 which tended to corroborate the P-S hypothesis.

From that moment on, the availability of new data and the development of advanced econometrical tools for time series analysis enhanced the debate. Using the same data provided by Grilli and Yang (and sometimes other indexes too), new studies rejected the P-S hypothesis. For example, Cuddington and Urzúa[38] questioned the trend-stationarity of the Grilli and Yang index, while Powell[39] applied an Engle-Granger co-integration analysis that showed that Grilli and Yang series was trendless. Leon and Soto also rejected the P-S hypothesis based on an econometric analysis of the NBTT of sixteen Latin American countries.[40] All these studies were purely statistical, setting aside entirely the issues surrounding the causes of the phenomenon, or its consequences.

Nevertheless, there were also some studies that refuted those arguments from a statistical look.[41] Besides, the debt crisis in Latin America in the 1980s was joined by a sharp decline in commodity prices, and therefore, when Bleaney and Greenaway updated Grilli and Yang index to cover 1987–91, the deterioration of international commodity prices vis-à-vis manufactures seemed to be even greater.[42] One decade later, Ocampo and Parra updated again Grilli and Yang's indexes so that they covered the whole twentieth century.[43] Using econometric techniques they identified a breakdown in the series in 1920–1, and a downward tendency shift since the first years of the 1980s (the rest of the series i.e. 1900–19 and 1922–80, was found to be trendless). These scholars explained both events as been a lagged effect of the post-First World War depression and the oil shocks of the 1970s. The accumulated effect of NBTT deterioration for primary products is estimated to be around 50–60 per cent between 1920 and 2000. A similar statement was made by Zanias who, employing the Lumsdaine-Papell unitary root test, found that the NBTT of primary products did not follow a random path, nor a downward tendency, but remained constant except for two break-downs in 1920 and 1984.[44] The cumulative effect over the NBTT of primary products would have been 62 per cent throughout the twentieth century. How-ever, this complex debate about the identification of structural breaks or the best model to be used in time series analysis, although interesting, has set aside the original concern about the causes of the phenomena and its implications.

In recent years, an alternative literature that implicitly considers specialization in primary products for export as a bad thing for development has emerged, but its reasoning is different from that of Prebisch and Singer. In these studies it is considered that the main problem was the *volatility* of primary product prices. For example, Cashin and McDermott[45] – analysing the Index of Industrial Com-modity Prices made by *The Economist* between 1862 and 1999 – concluded that there has not been any structural break but a secular deteriorating trend of 1 per cent per annum in the relative prices of primary products, but they saw it as somewhat irrelevant in comparison with the volatility of prices, specially at the beginning of the twentieth century, when price cycles became wider, and in the first half of the 1970s, when the frequency of their ups and downs speeded up.

A similar statement was made by Blattman, Hwang and Williamson.[46] Sup-porting the idea that volatility in the export prices of the periphery constitutes its main problem, they show in an OLS regression a strong correlation between volatility in NBTT and GDP growth during 1870–1940 (the classical period in which Prebisch first tested his hypothesis). Their main conclusion is that secular changes in the NBTT were positively correlated with growth in the 'cen-tre', while in the periphery growth is inversely correlated with volatility. They also explore the hypothesis that the link between volatility and GDP growth was through the rates of investment, capital accumulation and foreign capital flows. However, the authors do not deal with the explanation of the positive correlation between (growing) NBTT and GDP growth in the centre, although Williamson and Hadass had argued that given the central role of the industrial sector for technological innovation and capital accumulation, a growing NBTT would have promoted greater specialization in these sectors, thus fostering the development of new industries and long-run economic growth.[47]

Moreover, Blattman, Hwang and Williamson took the argument further to suggest that the volatility of NBTT not only explains the difference in the economic performance between the centre and the periphery, but also the rela-tive economic success among the countries of the periphery.[48] Thus, 'commodity lottery' – a metaphor used by Carlos Díaz-Alejandro to make reference to the social, political and economical effects derived from the exploitation of certain natural resources – is interpreted in terms of the volatility of the international price experienced among different products.

It is worth noticing that in this type of argument, the explanatory variables of economic success in the centre are different from those that explain the relative failure in the periphery. Thus, while the periphery would have been negatively affected by volatility in their NBTT through diminishing capital flows, the centre would have been benefited from increasing NBTT through more specialization in manufactured products. Even more, in the mentioned article, Blattman, Hwang and Williamson suggest that the centre was not affected too much by volatility since the 'more sophisticated' institutions and 'better markets' of rich countries would have been more efficient to stop pressures derived from volatility. Therefore, 'our finding for the period up to 1940 agrees with a view of the post-war period that good economic performance was as much the result of good luck as it was of good policy'.[49]

Summing up, since the late 1980s the empirical debate on NBTT took the form of a statistical debate about time series in which the Grilli and Yang index has been frequently used. Subsequently, we notice the surge of debate over volatility, which could be seen as an attempt to raise an alternative to the P-S hypothesis, in the sense that its policy implications are similar (the message is that all countries should foster industrialization or, at least, avoid overspecialization in few primary products). None of these discussions, however, deals empirically or theoretically with the DFTT issue, the core of the P-S hypothesis, according to our view. However, while the discussion on relative prices of commodities and manufactures is worthwhile, in the end what really matters for countries is their specific relation of exchange. With the exception of Williamson's (and collaborators') contributions, this discussion has been given much less attention, although some studies deserve to be mentioned.

The Discussion on Countries

The studies on NBTT for underdeveloped countries have not reached any definitive conclusions regarding the P-S hypothesis. Due to the great diversity of experiences among different countries, the empirical evidence is more elusive in this matter. In some countries whose export sector relies heavily on a single commodity which has benefited from periodical upswings in its price, increasing NBTT has been normally the rule. By the other hand, it is obvious that no country exports only primary products and imports only manufactures, weakening the correlation between the debate on the relative price of goods and the actual experience of countries. In fact, manufactured exports from the resource abundant Periphery to the world have grown in the last half century.

Ocampo, for example, based on ECLA data between 1945–87 found that around half of Latin American countries did not have statistical significant trends in their NBTT, or some of them had increasing terms of trade, like Bolivia

(3.82 per cent annual), Colombia (0.4 per cent), Costa Rica (0.37 per cent), Peru (0.31 per cent) and Venezuela (2.18 per cent), although in the aggregate Latin American NBTT felt by 0.21 per cent annually.[50] A similar statement was made by Leon and Soto who analysed sixteen Latin American countries for a longer period (1928–93) concluding that five were characterized by random paths, while from the remaining three had declining NBTT and eight had stable or increasing NBTT.[51]

By the contrary, and as an example of the diversity of conclusions that these analyses could obtain, Ram stated from a sample of twenty-six underdeveloped countries around the world that twenty-one have had diminishing NBTT, with statistical significance in most of them.[52] Even more, its rate of deterioration is relatively high, since the simple average of the tendency among the countries analysed is −1 per cent annual for the period 1970–99. One important flaw in these studies is that their results are based on the trade of underdeveloped countries with *the world*, and therefore they are not able to establish the net effect in the bilateral trade between the periphery and the centre. Besides, as we already state, they do not take in account the DFTT.

A partial exception of the latter was a study by Sarkar and Singer, who analysed the manufacturing NBTT of developed and underdeveloped countries and considered the labour productivity in those sectors for each pole of the system.[53] These was supposed to shed some light on Singer's extended hypothesis (that is, the NBTT deterioration for the periphery in its manufacturing sectors), and gave some clues about the DFTT evolution. Based on data collected by the United Nations for the period between 1970 and 1987 plus some evidence on export unitary values for some individual countries, they found a 1 per cent annual deterioration of the manufacturing NBTT of underdeveloped countries. However, due to the increasing quantity of manufactured exports from those countries, they conclude that the absolute purchase power of these kind of exports have grown at almost 10 per cent per annum, and the relative purchase power of export 5 per cent per annum, explaining the commercial deficits of developed countries like the United States with South-East Asia, for example. Regarding the labour productivity issue, they found that it has increased more in developed countries than in underdeveloped nations, since for the first group it increased 4.1 per cent per year between 1960 and 1970 and 2.8 per cent per annum between 1970 and 1980, while the same figures for the periphery were 2.3 per cent and 0.4 per cent respectively. Hence, since manufacturing NBTT worsened for the underdeveloped countries, it could be expected that the DFTT would have worsened even more.

Those results were broadly confirmed by Maizels, who identified that while a group of developed countries increased its manufacturing NBTT with the United States at a rate of 1 per cent per annum over 1981–96, another group of underdeveloped countries went through a 0.9 per cent annual deterioration.[54] According to Maizels, the different kind of manufactures exported by developed and underdeveloped countries accounts for such an outcome. He noticed that the United States' manufactured imports from other developed countries were dominated by technologically complex products, like machinery and cars, whereas the underdeveloped countries' exports to the United States were mainly textiles, clothing and the like. Furthermore, exports of manufactured products of developed countries to the United States were based on qualified labour, oligopolistic markets, and patents, factors that push prices upward, while the opposite characteristics dominate in manufactured exports from underdeveloped countries.

In short, the analysis of the NBTT of specific countries reports more ambiguity regarding the corroboration of the P-S hypothesis, at least in comparison with the evidence that emerged in the discussion of the relative prices of primary products versus manufactures. However, the few works that studied the trade relation between the two poles, taking in account just manufactured products, concluded that the periphery lost, thus favouring the extended Singer hypothesis. Except for Sarkar and Singer's article of 1991, these studies have not explored DFTT and none of them deals with the problem we mentioned regarding the disaggregation of the 'intra-periphery' and 'intra-centre' trading when testing the P-S hypothesis. In what follows we will try to construct and index of the NBTT and DFTT of Colombia with the United States that overcomes theses limitations.

Colombian Terms of Trade

Although the P-S hypothesis was formulated to explain a dynamic of unequal development between the centre and the periphery in which international trade constitutes a key issue – and therefore there are severe limitations in making theoretical conclusions based on the experiences of individual countries – it is useful and interesting to analyse the foreign trade structure, that is, the NBTT, the DFTT and the simple factorial terms of trade (SFTT),[55] between countries with unequal degrees of development that have been commercially integrated. This is because such measures and concepts are useful to describe and explain specific phenomena related with the development and distribution of income between countries, and therefore are relevant to economic history.

Through the twentieth century, Colombian NBTT did not follow a clear upward or downward tendency.[56] A series elaborated by GRECO[57] starts with an index number of 88 in 1905 (were 1950 = 100) and ends with 44 in 2000, but in between it presents three peaks: 101 in 1911, 124 in 1954 and 141 in 1977. This evolution is clearly explained by the twentieth century booms in coffee prices. Other estimations made by IMF and ECLA follow very similar paths. The IMF reports an index number of 51 in 1905 (again, 1950 = 100), and 69 in

1997, with the mentioned peaks of 1911, 1954 and 1977 in between, estimated in this series by 73, 137 and 128 respectively.[58] This is shown by a simple visual inspection of different series reported by different sources (Figure 10.1).

The results reported by GRECO, IMF and ECLA are highly correlated. In the first part of the century, until the 1940s, there was a steady decline in the NBTT trend. This was followed by a sharp rise until 1954 and another fall until the late 1960s. During the 1970s the pattern changed again and the NBTT reached its highest point in 1977, as a consequence of a sharp rise in coffee prices. From that point until the end of the century the figure reports a steady decline again. The unitary value of exports used to elaborate these indexes are based almost entirely on international coffee prices, which had a declining tendency in the first half of the twentieth century, while in the second half it benefited from two booms: at the beginning of the 1950s and during the second half of the 1970s, as mentioned above. This procedure is justified, considering the historical significance of the coffee sector in the Colombian foreign trade structure.

Methodological Aspects

The NBTT measures how many units of an import product could be acquired in exchange of one unit of an export product. The DFTT is a measure that indicates how many workers (or hours-worked) are needed in a foreign country to produce an amount of value that is equal to the value produced with one worker (or in one hour of work) in the domestic country.[59] This is why this measure is close to unequal exchange theories. However, SFTT, by adjusting the NBTT only through the national productivity index, is a measure that describes the absolute welfare of a country derived from its foreign trade.

Three major issues influenced our decision to choose the manufacturing sectors to analyse the bilateral trade between Colombia and the United States. First, in the last decades manufacturing exports has increased its share in the total exports from Colombia to United States and the world. Manufacturing exports of Colombia to the world represented 29 per cent of the total in 1975, 31 per cent in 1981, 36 per cent in 1991, 42 per cent in 1995 and 45 per cent in 2005 (although there were some declines in some years in between).[60] Second, so far there is no study on the manufacturing terms of trade of Colombia. And third, there is no data on Colombian labour productivity in its primary products sectors, while the same information for the manufacturing sectors is fully available. In the same sense, the period under consideration (1975–2005) was chosen because of data availability.

On the other hand, we selected the United States for the analysis because in the theoretical context in which this exercise is framed this country could be considered the 'main centre', and also because it is Colombia's main trade partner. The share of the United States in the total exports of Colombia was above 30 per cent for almost every year along 1975–2005. In 2000 this climbed to 49.8 per cent, although it had fallen back to 40 per cent in 2005. In like manner, the share of the United States in the total imports made by Colombia was very high, even though it showed some decline during the last thirty years. Being 41 per cent in 1975 it kept around 33–5 per cent in 1980–2000 and finally dropped down to 28.6 per cent in 2005, still significant.

The elaboration of a NBTT series could be done through price indexes or through unitary value indexes. In the first case one should take into account a basket of specific products, while in the second case a set of SITC groups or categories is used, where the 'implicit price' results from dividing the value of the category (or group) exported/imported by the quantity (which is measured by its weight). Due to the large number of products that the manufacturing export and import sectors involve, it is very difficult to report NBTT employing price indexes; thus, we chose to elaborate unitary value indexes. It is worthwhile to mention that the share of the selected basket of manufacturing SITC groups in the total exports and imports of Colombia to (and from) the United States represents a good deal of the total bilateral trade. In the export sectors, it fluctuates between 44.5 per cent and 23 per cent of the total exports of Colombia to the United States, 32.8 per cent being the simple average. Regarding the import sectors, it fluctuates between 79 per cent and 95 per cent of the total imports of Colombia from the United States, being 86.5 per cent the simple average. The product categories that we used to elaborate our indexes are those of the industrial activities of the CIUU (rev. 2).

One of the main advantages of the estimations that we made here is that in elaborating the different versions of the terms of trade, we were able to work strictly with the bilateral trade data between Colombia and United States. This represents a considerable advantage compared with previous studies interested in centre–periphery relations which, as we noticed, could not 'fix' their results from the effect of the intra-underdeveloped and intra-developed countries' trade. This was possible because the source used here, the *Anuarios de Comercio Exterior del Departamento Administrativo Nacional de Estadística DANE*, presents Colombian international trade statistics disaggregated by foreign trading partners, that is, by countries of origin and destination.

Due to the large number of SITC categories used in our calculations, our sample seemed to be excessively responsive to the base year chosen when doing Laspeyres or Paasche indexes; for example, Paasche index changed considerably if we took 1990 instead of 1992 as base year. Thus, we decided to elaborate Colombia's export/import (to/from the United States) price index through the chained method, where we calculate for each year,

$$P_{EXP/IMP,tn} = \frac{\sum \left(P_{t1} \times q_{t0} \right)}{\sum \left(P_{t0} \times q_{t0} \right)} \times \frac{\sum \left(P_{t2} \times q_{t1} \right)}{\sum \left(P_{t1} \times q_{t1} \right)} \times ..... \frac{\sum \left(P_{tn} \times q_{tn-1} \right)}{\sum \left(P_{tn-1} \times q_{tn-1} \right)}$$

where P is the implicit price of exports/imports and q is the quantity exported/imported[61]. Finally, we made simple calculations to equalize, 1992 = 100, although, as we use a chain index, it cannot be said that 1992 is the base year.

In the elaboration of Colombian labour productivity index we used the *Encuesta Nacional Manufacturera* published by DANE, and the data of Atack and Bateman[62] in the case of the United States. Following the recommendations of Bonilla, Silva and Villamil[63] the procedure used was to divide the real aggregate value in the chosen manufacturing sectors by the number of workers in those sectors.[64] From this information we elaborate our productivity indexes taking 1992 as base year. As an alternative for the US labour productivity index, we also used the 'output per person' published by the Bureau of Labor Statistics.[65]

Finally, the procedure to obtain the DFTT series consisted in multiply the NBTT index by the relative labour productivity index between Colombia and the United States. In the same way, in the case of the Colombian SFTT we multiply its NBTT index by its national labour productivity index.

Results Analysis

Figure 10.1 reports the evolution of the NBTT and the DFTT of Colombia and the United States in their manufacturing sectors.[66] In the case of manufacturing NBTT, three phases could be identified. First, there was a clear upward trend for Colombia between 1975 and the mid-1980s, since its NBTT with the United States improved by almost fifty points (from 66 in 1975 to 111 in 1984). In the history of Colombian economic policies, this upward trend happened at the same time that policymakers were supporting non-traditional export sectors, by means of lowering or applying tariff exemptions to intermediate goods going to export sectors, enhancing credit for exporters, executing periodical devaluations, and so on. The mix of pro-export policies and growing prices in the manufacturing sectors resulted in increased income for Colombia, since the value of non-traditional exports rose from US$692 million in 1975 to US$1,487 million in 1981,[67] one year before the debt crisis in Latin America, and the highest point of Colombian NBTT with the United States during the whole period. However, the value of non-traditional exports move back to US$1,139 million in 1984, in the wake of international crises and a lowering in the *quantity* of non-traditional exports (the price index of Colombian exports of manufactures remained constant).

The second phase goes from the mid-1980s until the mid-1990s, during which the NBTT were fluctuating around 90 and 110, except for 1986 when it fell to 75 (see the line 3 in Figure 10.1). This period coincided with policy reform by Colombian authorities toward more liberal policies and free trade.

In the third phase, from the mid-1990s onwards, we see a sharp decline in manufacturing NBTT for Colombia, as a consequence of both a decline in (manufacturing) export prices for Colombia and an increase in the price of imports from the United States. While the former fell 42 per cent between 1997 and 2005, the later rose 81 per cent in the same years. At the end, in 2005, the NBTT reach the lowest point for the South American country in the whole period. Why did the prices of Colombian manufactures diverge so much from the US prices from 1997 onwards? Here we hypothesize that the sharp decline in the price of manufactures in the US market was due to an increase in supply as a result of increased imports of manufactured goods from East Asia and the countries involved in NAFTA. Nonetheless, this idea requires more research, as does the increase in the price of manufactured imports from the United States, for which we don't have any good explanation at the moment.

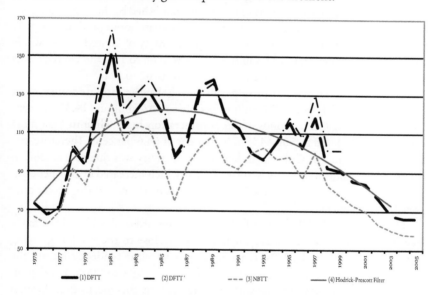

Figure 10.1: Manufacturing DFTT between Colombia and Unites States, 1992 = 100

Above all, we must say that during the last three decades we don't find any clear tendency, at least not a clear downward or upward tendency. This result does not match with the analysis made by Maizels (2000) and Sarkar and Singer (1991), who support the idea that the manufacturing NBTT of United States vis-à-vis underdeveloped countries had been growing.[68]

It is interesting, by the other hand, to compare the manufacturing NBTT with GRECO's index that depends on coffee prices. From the last years of the 1970s and through the 'lost decade' of the 1980s, where the NBTT of most Latin American countries fell in the context of debt crisis and the break-up of various cartel agreements, Colombia also suffered from deterioration in its 'coffee' NBTT. The index elaborated by GRECO falls from 223 in 1979 to 115 in 1990, being 1992 equal to 100.[69]. In contrast, manufacturing NBTT for Colombia improved in the last years of the 1970s and were almost trendless during the 1980s. In fact, it seems that from 1979 until 1989 both measures of terms of trade follow a scissors movement. This exemplifies how the primary product sectors were the most affected by the crises in Latin America through the 1980s.

Regarding labour productivity, in contradiction to what was expected and to what the extended Singer hypothesis states, Colombia's has had some incremental improvement in relation with that of the United States. In Appendix A we reported the labour productivity of each country, and the relative labour productivity between both (see columns 4 to 8 in Appendix A). These labour productivities indexes include only those CIIU groups that were chosen in the analysis of the bilateral trade (except for the 'output per person' published by the BLS). As can be seen, during the period under consideration Colombian labour productivity grew about 10 per cent in relation to the labour productivity of United States. While the Colombian index grew 127 points, passing from 68 to 196, the United States output per person grew 109 points, augmenting from 62 to 171.[70]

This result is even more surprising considering that the absolute employment of United States fell from 17.2 million people to 14.7 million (14.35 per cent reduction) in the CIIU groups under consideration here, while in Colombia it grew from 304,038 to 500,443, an increment of 64.6 per cent. Therefore, the better performance of Colombian labour productivity was due to a takeoff in the aggregate value of its manufacturing sector, which increased by 371 per cent. Instead, the aggregate value of the United States in its manufacturing sector only grew by 69.4 per cent.

However, the DFTT did not follow a clear upward or downward tendency (see Figure 10.1 above). Actually, it moved very close to the NBTT, growing from 1975 to the mid-1980s, remaining with no clear tendency during the next ten years, and following a sharp decline from 1997 to 2005. Relying on the intuitive interpretation that was presented before, this means that through 1975–84 fewer workers (or worker hours) were necessary in Colombia to produce an amount of value equal to the value produced by one US worker (or in one worker hour) in their manufacturing sectors (taking as 'value' the rate of prices between exports and imports in the bilateral trade). On the contrary, from 1997 onwards the opposite was the rule. At the end, the net effect on the index was a fall from 74 to 66, which speaks in favour of the idea that Colombia has suffered from 'unequal exchange' or the like in its manufacturing sectors, although this result is not significant since, as we already say, there was no clear downward trend along the period as a whole.

That said, it is important to stress two important flaws from our DFTT experiment. First, there is the problem that we gave the same weight to prices and labour productivity for the DFTT calculus, which is not strictly correct in a situation where not all of the production is being exported (or in which not all of the local basket of consumption is fulfilled by imports).[71] Due to the absence of appropriate data regarding this matter, we were unable to overcome this limitation. Thus, the implications of the DFTT in Figure 10.1 for the relative welfare between Colombia and the United States is somewhat distorted. Second, it is obvious that United States' income dependence on its trade with Colombia is negligible, and therefore the bilateral trade between the two countries cannot explain by itself the growing gap in the income per capita between both countries.

However, since for Colombian income its trade with the United States is much more relevant, it is interesting to analyse its SFTT with the North American economy. As shown in the last column in Appendix A, the manufacturing SFTT of Colombia with the United States improved through most of the period. The series reports an upward trend between 1975 and 1997, where the index number passes from 45 to 147, and a slightly downward trend thereafter, the index falling to 113 in 2005. The positive behaviour of the SFTT of Colombia basically responds to improving labour productivity in Colombia during the whole period. This meant that over the first twenty-three years Colombia produced in absolute terms a growing amount of value per worker-hour (again, taking 'value' as the price of exports relative to the price of imports) but, as a consequence of sharp decline in its NBTT from the mid-1990s onwards, the contrary was the rule: in the last eight years the income per worker-hour experienced a deterioration in its purchase power in terms of manufacturing bilateral trade (where productivity advances were included in the account).

Conclusion

In this paper we traced the history of a hypothesis that already has more than half a century of existence but which, nevertheless, still today is the object of a lot of discussion and controversy in academic circles. In the mid-twentieth century, the P-S hypothesis emerged at the same time that the neoclassical theory on international trade was refined by Paul Samuelson. Since that time, these two ideas have been used to justify free trade or interventionist policies, and also they were brought into play as explanations for the lack of convergence observed between developed countries and *most* of the Third World in the last 150 years.

In recent decades many studies have been written, and there have been also a lot of debates around the P-S hypothesis and its further developments made by neo-Marxist schools of thought, like the 'Dependency School'. However, in this paper we chose to pay closer attention to the empirical literature surrounding this subject. In his famous book, Octavio Rodríguez complained of the difficulty of this task, because

> the ECLA argument is linked to price movements in the very long term; it does not refer to trade in primary products and manufacture in general, but to the exchange of industrial goods produced in the central economies for commodities produced in the peripheral economies; [besides] the fundamental thesis on income differentiation requires to consider not only the relative prices of exchange but also to calculate productivity indexes.[72]

Since those times the empirical studies that have been produced are counted by dozens, from which we mentioned here only the main ones. In general, most studies tended to corroborate the P-S hypothesis when they dealt with the price of primary products vis-à-vis manufactures, although they introduced important modifications that drove them to make quite different assessments compared with the original hypothesis, for example, that there has not been a clear downward tendency but rather some structural breakdowns. Conversely, some scholars argued that this result does not necessary refute the standard theory on convergence, while others said that in the link between international trade and development there are other explanatory factors of much more relevance than the terms of trade.

On many occasions, the empirical debate on terms of trade forgot that the fundamental indicator in the P-S hypothesis was the DFTT, and in this paper we stress this point. By the other hand, in the mid-1970s Singer expanded his version of the hypothesis, fostering an interesting discussion on the changing terms of trade in manufacturing sectors, among countries with different degrees of development. These two elements drive this paper to elaborate the manufacturing DFTT between a peripheral country – Colombia – and the United States.

The results reported in this paper must be taken with precaution due to the lack of an accurate statistical analysis. Above all, we found that neither the NBTT nor the DFTT followed a clear upward or downward tendency in the case we studied here. But beyond the results obtained, some advantages of the present contribution deserves some attention: first, the original and essential concept of the P-S hypothesis, that is, the DFTT, was stressed; second, we were able to analyse exclusively the bilateral trade between a peripheral country and the main centre, which eliminates the effects of intra-periphery and intra-centre trade; third, empirical evidence on the relative productivity of labour was elaborated and forth, we presented a new series of Colombian terms of trade, based on its manufacturing sectors, whose share in total exports has been growing in recent decades.

Although we didn't identify any clear tendency in the evolution of the terms of trade, in strict sense the P-S hypothesis could only be corroborated if we take the whole periphery (or at least a considerable number of its countries) as our scope of analysis instead of a single country. That is why, in any case, in this attempt it would not have been possible to corroborate or refute the P-S hypothesis as such. However, we hope this work to be a starting point for further work on the matter.

Appendix A

Year	Colombian exports. Unitary value index	US exports. Unitary value index	NBTT	Colombia labour productivity index	US labour productivity index (Atack and Bateman)	US 'output per person', LBS	Relative productivity of labour COL-US	DFTT	Colombian SFTT
	1	2	(½)	3	4	5	(⅗)	(½) × (⅗)	(½) × 3
1975	21.91	32.94	66.52	68.46	61.78	62.1	110.23	73.32	45.53
1976	22.83	36.49	62.57	70.87	66.29	65.4	108.36	67.80	44.34
1977	25.93	37.29	69.55	70.45	68.42	68.4	102.99	71.63	48.99
1978	36.43	39.79	91.57	76.24	67.24	69	110.50	101.18	69.82
1979	38.06	45.75	83.19	76.19	67.01	68.1	111.89	93.08	63.39
1980	54.63	53.59	101.94	83.14	62.42	67.5	123.17	125.56	84.76
1981	75.22	60.24	124.86	83.20	63.46	68.1	122.17	152.54	103.88
1982	69.03	65.09	106.06	74.68	64.93	70.2	106.38	112.83	79.20
1983	74.95	65.54	114.36	79.69	69.70	74.6	106.83	122.17	91.14
1984	73.40	65.72	111.69	91.94	74.57	78.4	117.27	130.98	102.69
1985	72.37	75.96	95.27	102.58	77.42	81.2	126.33	120.36	97.73
1986	61.14	81.24	75.26	110.89	85.83	84.7	130.92	98.53	83.45
1987	79.95	85.35	93.67	101.04	89.96	87.5	115.47	108.16	94.64
1988	86.84	84.21	103.13	117.89	92.42	90.2	130.70	134.79	121.58
1989	95.70	88.03	108.71	114.67	91.59	90.3	126.99	138.05	124.66
1990	96.63	102.05	94.70	114.80	90.75	92.3	124.38	117.78	108.72
1991	95.98	104.46	91.88	114.95	94.17	93.7	122.68	112.72	105.62
1992	100.00	100.00	100.00	100.00	100	100	100	100.00	100.00
1993	105.52	102.65	102.80	97.30	102.57	103.8	93.74	96.36	100.02
1994	145.19	149.98	96.80	118.20	108.56	108.6	108.85	105.37	114.42
1995	157.70	160.85	98.04	133.09	110.24	112.7	118.09	115.78	130.48
1996	154.72	177.70	87.07	137.48	110.90	116.7	117.83	102.59	119.70
1997	188.01	187.39	100.33	146.73	112.87	124.2	118.16	118.55	147.22
1998	162.13	194.47	83.37	143.69	118.22	129.5	110.96	92.50	119.79
1999	159.19	204.05	78.01	158.82	122.21	136.5	116.35	90.77	123.90
2000	155.91	213.23	73.12	164.62		140.6	117.09	85.61	120.37
2001	159.12	226.79	70.16	167.67		140.0	119.79	84.05	117.64
2002	141.36	222.85	63.43	180.32		149.9	120.33	76.33	114.38
2003	135.62	225.43	60.16	179.56		158.8	113.09	68.04	108.03
2004	141.07	243.75	57.88	187.90		163.8	114.71	66.39	108.75
2005	155.42	268.63	57.86	195.91		170.7	114.78	66.41	113.35

11 PUBLIC REVENUES IN BOLIVIA, 1900–31[1]

José Alejandro Peres Cajías

Introduction

Latin American economic history is not always able to take regional economic diversity into account. The main reason is the lack of quantitative data which is particularly severe in the case of Bolivia. The present study goes one step towards remedying this with a presentation of two long-term series. Revising primary data brings a) the central state's fiscal income between 1900 and 1931; b) the mining fiscal burden between 1900 and 1929. However, this study goes beyond a mere descriptive strategy and proposes some interpretative clues to understand income evolution. The point is to study the Bolivian public finances taking into account its own restrictions. Undoubtedly, the central state fiscal income was strongly determined by the trade taxes. But looking at the profitability and – paradoxically – the stability of all the revenue sources, there was not a real option in the short or medium term. This research also shows that the mining fiscal burden grew considerably in the 1920s.

Economic history cannot always encompass the great economic diversity of Latin America. It is not unusual to find works understanding and defining the region basically from the study of the more developed countries in relative terms. This option can constitute a methodological approach. Nevertheless, it is usually no more than a resignation due to the lack of data, especially quantitative data.

Significant efforts taking into account every Latin American state are being made to fill the blanks.[2] This paper has the same approach and provides long-term series in the case of Bolivian economy, which is one of the cases with less quantitative evidence. Two fiscal series are brought forward. These series are reconstructed using a wide primary data compilation. In the first place, the real fiscal revenues of the Bolivian central government between 1900 and 1931, reconstructed in accordance with international parameters and also a significant level of disaggregation. The second series is the reconstruction of all real tax contributions made by the mining industry to the central government between 1900 and 1929.

Furthermore, apart from the quantitative evidence, some interpretative clues are given in order to understand the role of public finances during the first third of the twentieth century. Much as its Latin American counterparts, the Bolivian central government depended very much on the taxes levied onto foreign trade. This paper confirms a statement that has been frequently emphasized: dependence generates instability problems. Still, if we understand this dependence in terms of the actual limitations of the Bolivian state, then is clear that there were no alternative tax sources in terms of profitability. The partial evidence also shows that – paradoxically – there were no alternatives in terms of predictability.

Then, one of the classic dilemmas of the Bolivian political economy is discussed, namely the tax profiting of the revenues derived from the exploitation of natural resources. Given the limitations of the government to modify the tax structure, its second best is collecting at least enough[3] in order to have an effect on the economy through efficient public spending.[4] Considering the existing economic and political restrictions, it is stated that, in terms of tax pressure, perhaps the government performed better than what is commonly accepted. In the 1920s, total collection from the mining industry nearly doubled in terms of percentage over the value of mining exports. This fact cannot be underrated.

Central Government Revenues, 1900–31

The first quantitative reconstruction presented here, includes the revenues of the central government between 1900 and 1931. The estimate is based on a considerable collection of primary data that has been adapted to the classification proposed by the Government Finance Statistics Manual.[5] One of the initial considerations when elaborating the classification was the need to differentiate between tax revenues and non-tax revenues. The division is justified by the dissimilar implications in terms of legitimacy creation and fiscal capacities.[6] Later, in order to enable a higher level of analysis taxes are separated in three widely accepted large categories: direct tax, indirect internal tax and indirect external tax.[7]

Before showing the data reconstruction and describing the evolution of taxes, it is necessary to point out some methodological limitations. The lack of data on GDP for the years before 1950 hinders the assessment of tax collection in terms of economic significance. Furthermore, we must note that there is no reliable population data of the first half of the twentieth century. The only data available for this period is the information obtained in both the 1900 and 1950 censuses. Nearly every estimate of the Bolivian population for that period is based on lineal estimates using one of these information sources.[8]

The lack of data on the evolution of prices also poses a limitation for this work. The data is presented in current terms – current bolivianos (Bs) – because there is not a price index before 1931. Several historiography sources indicate, however, that throughout the period there were no sudden leaps at the price level, except in very specific periods. When analysing the market exchange value of the boliviano compared to pound sterling and controlling the information on the evolution of British prices, we observe a relative stability between 1900 and 1914, where year-to-year changes are more modest.[9] The most complicated period to analyse is the period between the beginning of the First World War and 1923, where the exchange value and British prices show lower stability. After 1923, both series recovered stability.

As exchange value leaps are never too sudden, it is possible to present an overall analysis of the Bolivian central government revenues both in pressure and tax structure terms. The first element that draws our attention is the high effective growth of the income of the Bolivian central government (Figure 11.1). This growth is explained basically by the ever-present preponderance of external indirect taxes. The evolution of Bolivian fiscal revenues depended basically on the exploitation of natural resources and the taxes derived from this activity.

Taking into consideration both the increase and the weight of external taxes, we can differentiate three sub-periods: 1900–13, 1914–22 and 1923–31. From the second half of the 1900s, the constant increase of the tax pressure is very clear. It is noticeable that until the beginning of the First World War, the external taxes constituted at least two-thirds of total revenues.[10] Afterwards, the First World War and its long-term impact on the stability of international markets had a clear effect on Bolivian tax evolution. From 1914 and until 1917 there was a constant decline of financial resources. Later, and until the end of the 1920–1 crisis, the volatility of external markets determined an unpredictable evolution of total tax collection. Furthermore, the volatility on external markets caused some reduction of the relative significance of external indirect taxes.

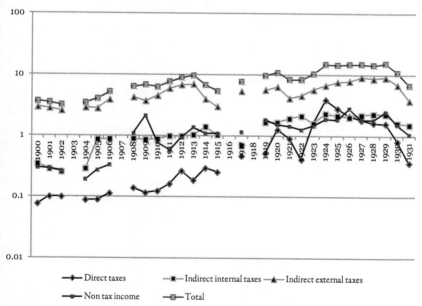

Figure 11.1: Bolivian government fiscal revenues per capita (log current Bs), 1900–31

Source: Own elaboration from data by Cuentas Generales. (see Methodological Annex).

Fiscal revenues did not resume a clear upward trend until 1923, once important fiscal reforms were undertaken. The crisis provoked a significant decrease of the central government revenues. Given the impossibility of reducing public spending, the Bolivian government had no other option but to resort to international capital markets. Gradually, the state continued to get into debt due to a) its inability to fill the financing gap; b) the need of refinancing the payment of previous international loans; and c) the demands of different lobbies. The necessity of making these payments, and the lobbying of international loaners boosted fiscal reform.[11] Through several policies, the government tried to increase the tax burden on the main tax sources and create certain tax diversification. Nonetheless, at the end of the decade the tax structure showed, in general terms, similar characteristics with those identified in previous periods. The reform did not entail a substantial reduction in the dependence of external indirect taxes. This constant centrality demands analysis of its causes and effects on the rest of the economy.

Dependence on Foreign Trade: Looking at the State Restrictions

One of the most important traits of the dependence on external tax resources is the fragility of the public finances compared to the evolution of international markets. This dependence shows a procyclicality on expenditures and fiscal revenues, which creates a problematic volatility.[12] In this respect, an analysis of the behaviour of the financial policies of different economies of the region after the recent boom of the price of raw materials would be illustrative.[13] It is graphically and econometrically confirmed, that in the period between 1980 and 2005, Latin American finances were procyclical. Later on, it is proved that between 1990 and 2004, both revenues and primary expenses were extremely volatile. Therefore, the volatility of revenues was higher mostly for economies which exported raw materials, particularly those with a stronger financial dependence on one particular natural resource. This was precisely the scenario of Bolivia's tax system at the beginning of the twentieth century.

The exports sector in Bolivia at the beginning of the century was characterized by a progressive trend to a high concentration.[14] During the rubber exports boom (1895–1915), mining exports constituted, on average, 70 per cent of total exports. After the First World War, this relative weight jumped to 90 per cent. Furthermore, during the 1920s, tin exports represented 70 per cent of Bolivian total exports. Given this concentration, the evolution of external markets determined the evolution of fiscal revenues of the central government. If the global economy suffered a backlash and the global demand of raw materials was reduced, the immediate effect was the reduction of exports and thus the duties derived from these exports. The reduction also entailed a decrease of the available amount of currencies used to import and therefore, the number of imports declined. As a result, fiscal revenues coming from the collection of customs duties also suffered.

Therefore, it came as no surprise that problems of instability arose. The ratio measuring the effective national revenues, compared to budget revenues, shows that effective revenues – as a part of budget revenues – had their lowest values in the years where the relevant international markets experienced difficulties. The impact of the crisis in the United States during the second half of the 1900s, together with the trade tensions caused by the First World War, explain to a great extent a 25 per cent difference between real revenues and budget revenues. During the 1920s, the higher instability of international markets is reflected also on this ratio. During the 1920–1 global crisis, or the Great Depression, the gap between effective income and budget income accounted for 30 per cent.

In this context, fiscal dependence limited the performance of the government itself. Policymakers were unable to anticipate external volatility. This generated an overvaluation of the future revenues of several years. The problem was that these estimated revenues were allotted to expenses that were not particularly flexible. Therefore, the government could not honour commitments. This generated social and political trouble, or debts that worsened its already weak fiscal position.

This dependence does not come as a surprise, and it is not exclusive to the Bolivian case. At a regional level, there was an awareness of the limitations imposed by the dependence but it went on.[15] In Bolivia, despite the fact that politicians and contemporaneous scholars stressed the potential dangers of external vulnerability,[16] it was not possible to end the tax dependence. So, the problem lies in understanding why this dependence endured.

A crucial motive was profitability.[17] In the Bolivian case, import duties and export duties were systematically the main fiscal resources throughout the first third of the twentieth century. As time went by, the relative importance of both categories diminished. All this indicates the accomplishment of certain tax diversification. Nevertheless, the Bolivian tax system diversification grew under an extremely fragile strategy of 'extensive' growth. The government opted for reaching agreements with very specific economic agents on very specific economic activities.[18] New tax items were charged over a very narrow tax base. Therefore, most of the new categories made a relatively small contribution. For instance, at the beginning of the century, the budget stated that, of every legally established tax, seventeen should make a relative contribution of less than 1 per cent of the total collection. At the end of the century, the number of items with a predicted relative contribution of less than 1 per cent increased to seventy-seven.[19] Then, it is clear that there was not a real alternative to external taxes in terms of collecting capacity.

The persistence of the dependence is understood also looking at the relative volatility of each tax source. By analysing the variation coefficient of the four big tax categories during the whole period, it is surprising to find that external taxes are less volatile in relative terms.[20] An analysis of shorter periods of time, however, shows that relative variability of external indirect taxes was not the lowest necessarily, and that it was not very different from the other categories. Nevertheless, if we analyse every category, the fact that import duties tend to be consistently presented as one of the less volatile tax sources is undeniable. Saying that import duties were less volatile does not imply that they were not volatile at all. The smaller relative volatility of customs duties could be the result of just an excessive volatility in the other contributions.

The inquiry of profitability and relative volatility in different tax burdens allows the drafting of two possible explanations. Dependence can be understood at an economic level: profitability and relative volatility were restricted by the size and stability of tax bases. But also from a political point of view: fiscal dependence was the result of government weakness. The government was unable to impose universal taxes in order to consolidate new tax sources that would be able to perform as a collection alternative. Sustainable agreements to allow the fiscal profiting of other tax bases permanently could not be reached with other economic agents. This limitation was particularly evident in the case of direct taxes and its subcategories. In contrast, it is true that the state consolidated some internal indirect taxes with a relative variability similar to that of import duties. Nevertheless, its tax profitability was extremely inferior.

Undoubtedly, the topic deserves more research. In any case, the previous review proves that in order to understand the main role and the dependence of taxes on external trade, it is necessary to understand the economically attractive options that the government enjoyed. In the short and medium term, there were no real alternatives to external trade taxes, in particular for imports, in terms of profitability and paradoxically, stability. So, in terms of collection, the state did not necessarily do it badly. This reassessment is clearer when mining taxes area analysed.

Rethinking the Mining Taxable Income

In this section we analyse the evolution of total mining taxes. This is possible thanks to another quantitative reconstruction: a series which shows all the taxes – direct and indirect – collected exclusively from the mining sector. There is a precedent to this.[21] Nevertheless, the information given by that work show aggregated amounts without an explanation of the considered taxes. By contrast, here is an estimate of the mining industry's fiscal contribution which includes all the contributions paid by the mining sector to the central government. They are identified and clearly differentiated.[22] Thus, it is possible: a) to learn which taxes are included in the estimate, b) to achieve a detailed understanding of the differentiated tensions provoked by the different levies.

In order to comprehend the growth of the mining royalty, it is necessary to understand the concentration of Bolivian exports. This process may be proved through the analysis of export taxes.[23] The relative importance of rubber becomes negligible at the mid-1910s. Later on, there was a quick concentration of mining exports, together with the almost exclusive main role of the tin sector. At the beginning of the century, a change took place in the mining export sector. The fiscal data show the speed of the process. The relative contribution of silver turned out to account for a 45 per cent of the export duties in 1900 and it just accounted for a symbolic 4 per cent four years later. In contrast, the fiscal relative contribution of the tin exports continued to increase steadily until it ended up contributing almost the whole sum of export duties (95 per cent).

The consolidation of the tin exports sector and the impediments to find another profitable resource, at least in the short term, gave the sector an undeniable fiscal appeal. It is probably difficult to deny that the mining sector was far from becoming an efficient 'driving force' to the development of the entire economy. However, the new series stresses that this inability was not necessarily a result of low tax pressure. The new empirical evidence proved that the tax pressure on the mining industry grew considerably in the 1920s, as some authors have pointed out.[24] Two indicators confirm this idea. On the one hand, the weight of mining taxes on total amount collected jumped – on average – from 20 to 27 per cent. On the other hand, the share of mining taxes on the value of mining exports also increased: from an average around 4 per cent (1900–22) to 10 per cent (1922–9).

It is possible to identify the establishment of several legal measures on the mining sector during the 1920s. Taxes on tin export taxes were increased. These exports played the leading role in the Bolivian mining sector. Furthermore, copper, silver and antimony export taxes were increased and there was a new levy on lead. The tax reconfiguration tried to make the most of the favourable junctures of ore in international markets, establishing rates that changed depending of the prices of ore. In 1923, the payment of the Impuesto a las Utilidades Mineras was at last imposed.[25] These changes in the policy explain to a great extent the doubling of the value of the mining taxable income as a percentage of the mining exports.

It could be argued that the Bolivian experience was not necessarily an atypical case in the region. It has constantly been stressed that the fiscal experience in Chile at the end of the nineteenth century depicts a government who was able to tax the mining sector considerably and also extend productive expenses.[26] Nevertheless, it should be stressed that tin market structure – both at a world and at a national level – created specific restrictions. Chilean exports could withstand higher tax loads, since they accounted for almost half of the world market of nitrate. The increase of the public revenues could be financed by the foreign consumer. In the case of Bolivia, the relative weight of the country in the world tin market kept increasing, but never surpassed 25 per cent. It was a high percentage, but it did not secure the profitability of a monopoly position in the market.[27] In regards to the national production structure, the concentration in the sector granted an additional power of negotiation to specific producers.[28]

If the government was unable to negotiate with them, any tax initiative was extremely fragile. The study of direct taxes makes clear this tension between the state and the mining sector. One of the outstanding elements is the persistent existence of increases and decreases in the collection of these taxes, which were basically taxes on the profit. In 1911 and 1919, the government passed several laws in order to impose a tax on mining profit. In each case, the year immediately after the enactment of the law, significant resources on this tax base were obtained. As time went by, however, the drive tended to disappear. Quickly, the direct mining contribution returned gradually to the previous level. The persistence of this process is an indicator of the state's incapacity to achieve a sustainable institutionalized commitment by the main economic industry of the country.

The former path did not end in 1923, when the Impuesto de las Utilidades Mineras was passed. One year after the law was imposed, for the first and only time direct mining taxes gave a higher amount of resources than mining export duties.[29] Due to the new pressure from the state, the mining industry adopted several strategies to resist the new taxation. In 1925, a lobby was created: the Asociación de Industriales Mineros.[30] Also, the big mining producers tried to negotiate directly with the government. For instance, Patiño offered a considerable loan in exchange for the government's commitment to freeze the tax tariffs for five years.[31] Tensions carried on throughout the second half of the 1920s. A decision by the Corte Suprema de Justicia enabled the state to take amounts owed by the big mining companies for the Impuesto a las Utilidades Mineras. Immediately after this, thanks to dextrous lobbying, the sector made the Kemmerer Mission (1927) to promote a reduction of tax rates on mining. The demand finally was approved by the Bolivian government.[32] However, the level reached after this measure was still higher than in 1922.

Therefore, it is noted that in specific periods of time, the government was able to increase its participation in mining income considerably. The increase of the fiscal pressure on the mining industry on the first half of the 1920s must not be belittled. The participation of the government in the total mining exports value doubled. So, despite some reversal on mining tax collection, the state achievements are evident when the study considers its own limitations.

Conclusions

The previous analysis of the Bolivian public revenues during the first third of the twentieth century makes two different contributions. On the one hand, it provides with quantitative information necessary to understand the Bolivian experience and put it into the regional debate. The reconstruction of economic series is very outdated in the Bolivian case. The work takes a step forward in overcoming this limitation. It provides two new fiscal series: a) the revenues of central state (1900–31); b) the total contribution of the mining industry to the public treasury (1900–29).

On the other hand, the work provides interpretative clues to understand the evolution of the revenues. The main feature of the Bolivian taxation system was its dependence on taxes derived from external trade. The increase of revenues derived from imports or exports was without a doubt the driving force of the growth of Bolivian fiscal revenues. The great limitation lay in the fact that dependence generated problems in terms of economic policies, basically in terms of instability.

However, the work goes beyond a mere descriptive strategy. It endeavours to understand the Bolivian taxation system within its own limitations. It is necessary to comprehend the dependence in a context where the government could hardly find an alternative source, at least in the short or medium term. This is made clear in terms of profitability. Also, the partial evidence shows that external trade taxes, particularly those derived from imports, were – paradoxically – among the less volatile in relative terms. The new empirical evidence also proves that the state achieved significant advances in terms of mining tax collection during the 1920s. Advances cannot be belittled either in terms of their weight on total fiscal income or in terms of their share on total mining exports.

So, the paper suggests that the Bolivian state did not necessarily do too badly in terms of tax collection, as is usually assumed.

Annex: Applied Methodology for the Reconstruction of Data on Central Government Revenues

There are previous reconstructions of data on the Bolivian central government fiscal revenues during the first third of the twentieth century. However, these reconstructions show several limitations. Therefore, it has been necessary to use primary sources for this work. Prior to this work, we must mention our own analysis of the budget revenues of the central government in four specific years: 1903, 1913, 1923 and 1930.[33] This reconstruction is useful to understand the building of the state and the tensions generated between the state and the taxpayers. However, from a quantitative point of view, the limitations of the time scope is evident, as well as the bias of using budget data. The alternative source is the effective revenues compiled by Delgadillo.[34] But this source is not satisfactory either.

The revenues are presented in an aggregated form and this hinders the analysis of the tax structure. Another option is the compilation made by McQueen[35]. Here the effective fiscal revenues are presented with a higher level of disaggregation for the period between 1910 and 1918. It is considerably exhaustive for the period between 1919 and 1922. Once again, the time scope limitation is the main restriction of this source.

The best existing estimate today is by Palenque, who reconstructed the effective fiscal revenues of Bolivia's Central Government with a significant disaggregation level for the period between 1911 and 1931.[36] But several reasons justify a new reconstruction considering primary sources. First and foremost, the time limitations arise. There is no disaggregated data available on effective revenues for 1900–10. This lack does not justify the elimination of a possible joint strategy once the first decade is established. However, Palenque does not present data on all income sources and this is particularly critical for reconstructing the mining tax burden.

Hence, this new reconstruction is essentially based on primary data. For the period between 1900 and 1918, the information provided by the Cuentas Generales and the Memorias del Ministerio de Hacienda are taken into account. For 1914–18, as the quantitative information provided only included the increase or decrease on the collected amount, it was necessary to consider the aggregated data of the Presupuestos in order to estimate the effective revenues. Between the years 1919 and 1922 and due to the impossibility of consulting the actual Cuentas Generales, the disaggregated data by McQueen was introduced.[37] In fact, the author states that his basic source of information are the Cuentas Generales. For the period between 1924 and 1929, the data by the Memorias del Ministerio de Hacienda e Industria and the Memorias de la Comisión Fiscal Permanente are taken into consideration. Finally, for the years 1930 and 1931, due to the impossibility of accessing the primary data, the series is reconstructed based on Palenque.

Taking into consideration the adapted classification from IMF, the different revenues present on the primary data have been inserted within the several categories. This was done after an analysis of the nature of the tax. In some cases, the name itself made the assignation obvious. However, when this was not possible, different information sources were used. The first option was locating the law that created the tax and then analysing the legislation. This option was made easy by the fact that the Presupuesto for 1931 showed all the legal information that justified the recollection of several revenues. When in doubt, the Cuenta General of 1901 was also used. It gives information even about the contributions made by specific agents. Lastly, the descriptions provided by McQueen were also very useful.

Finally, it is important to acknowledge that, based on the basic guidelines from the IMF, we opt to *not* take into consideration in this estimate the financial revenues, nor the delayed revenues. Issues relating to financial revenues, such as currency and public debt, loans, advance payments or variations of pending obligations, are useful to understand the management of deficit, rather that understanding the fiscal capacity of the government, defined as the possibility of imposing obligations or making use of specific income. Regarding the delayed revenues, they have been removed from the analysis due to the impossibility of detecting the origin of debts effectively and because their significance is on accountancy terms rather than economic terms.

12 THE CONSUMPTION OF DURABLE GOODS IN LATIN AMERICA, 1890–1913: ANALYSIS AND ESTIMATION OF A DEMAND FUNCTION[1]

Carolina Román Ramos

Introduction

Consumption is related to economic growth, standards of living, income distribution, urbanization, demographic structure and the modernization of a society, among other factors. Aggregate consumption has become a main source of data about living standards as it may capture welfare levels, and it is an indicator of standards of living as it constitutes an important component in people's welfare.[2] The types of goods consumed in a society and their variations over time yield information about standards of living and income distribution in that society. The incorporation of new goods into the consumption basket may be a result of economic progress in the sense that it may contribute to improving people's welfare, if these goods improve life quality in its different aspects – food, housing, transport, recreation – or make it possible to maintain life quality at a lower cost.

The period from the closing decades of the nineteenth century until the Great Depression, is considered the 'golden age' for most of the Latin American countries. The region enjoyed rapid growth based on the export of natural resources, although it remained a net importer of manufactured goods. The first globalization was characterized by decreasing transport costs and increasing trade, and the internal prices of goods converged to international levels. This period of big exports and economic growth made it possible to import consumer goods.

I work with series of durable goods for the period from 1890 until the First World War for six countries: Argentina, Brazil, Chile, Cuba, Mexico and Uruguay. My aim is to discuss the evolution of consumption and the relation between consumption and income levels in Latin America. During this period, almost all durable goods were imported, so I rely on external trade statistics to build series of imports as a proxy for the dynamic of domestic consumption. In addition, based on this information about consumption and income levels, I estimate the demand function using panel data, and I obtain estimations of income and price elasticities. Durable goods tend to have higher income elasticity and it is interesting to analyse if they were luxury goods during the period. I made the estimation for the aggregate series of durable goods, again using four groups: transport, clocks and watches, musical instruments and sewing machines.

This chapter is organized in six sections. In the next section I describe the variables affecting consumption from a theoretical point of view. In section three I present the methodology used for constructing the consumption series for the six countries and discuss its performance. In the fourth section I describe the estimation of consumption demand by panel data and I discuss the results. In section five I present my conclusions.

What Are the Factors Affecting Consumption?

In this study I focus on the behaviour of consumption demand affected by income and price variations, and I discuss other factors that theoretically may affect changes in demand.

The demand for goods mostly depends on income, so changes in income will alter consumption. However, when income changes, not all goods react in the same way; that is to say they exhibit different income elasticities. In general, we can divide goods into normal goods, those for which demand increases when income increases, and inferior goods, which have negative income elasticity. In addition, for some normal goods the income elasticity of demand is over the unity – luxury goods – while for others – basic needs – the elasticity is still positive but less so. This classification is due to Engel's law, which states that as income increases, the proportion of income spent on basic goods, especially food, falls.[3] I also distinguish non-durable goods, those consumed in one use, and durable goods, those that yield utility over time. Durable goods are usually the more elastic type of goods, and they have a strong positive relation with budget expenditure and income.[4]

Demand is also affected by relative prices, which will change with shocks on the supply side, for example, or with changes in the tax duty on imported goods.[5] Prices may change because of technological changes that affect production and the diffusion of consumption. Technological progress and innovations are especially important factors in the demand for durable goods. Income is important in demand, but we should also include other factors to explain the evolution of the consumption of new goods; the replacement of old by new ones and the velocity of these changes. Deaton (1981) argues that the diffusion of goods follows a life cycle or product cycle. At the beginning there are few consumers that can acquire the new item, and these play the role of carriers. This type of behaviour shapes a dynamic in demand that is slow at the beginning and then accelerates as the number of consumers increases, until it stabilizes at a saturation level.[6]

In addition, if we consider aggregate demand, consumption also depends on income distribution. As the basket consumption structure of each household depends on its income, income distribution among households will also affect the demand for the different types of goods. The influence of Engel's law on preference settings may mean that income distribution in a country affects consumption demand.

Changes in tastes and in consumption habits may also affect demand. Lastly, it is worth considering that several authors have criticized the standard theory, arguing that people's decisions are not independent of other decisions. Therefore we need to allow for social and institutional factors to explain some behaviour, especially that of individuals driven by the 'demonstration effect', as explained by Duesenberry.[7]

Although all these factors and variables may explain the evolution of and changes in consumption, we will focus on the effect of income level and relative prices, and we will make deductions about the effect of income distribution.

Analysis of the Consumption of Durable Goods

Domestic Consumption Based on Trade Statistics

I select some durable goods: carriages, vehicles and parts, bicycles and motorcycles, musical instruments, watches and clocks, sewing machines, photographic equipment and fountain pens. Changes in each of these groups have effects in several spheres of socio-economic activity. The introduction of new goods such as the motor car, one of the more complex goods at the end of the nineteenth century, had large positive effects on the cost, speed, comfort and flexibility of transport services.[8] Moreover, new goods may generate complementarities in three dimensions: the supply side (for example, petrol), public or external (roads) and changes in habits.[9] In addition, articles such as watches and fountain pens may be associated with cultural changes and/or labour organization. An increase in the consumption of photographic equipment and musical instruments may be associated with an expansion of entertainment activities. Finally, the introduction of sewing machines for domestic use may be related to new processes in clothing manufacture.

In the period between 1890 and the First World War most of these goods were imported and their domestic production in almost all the countries in Latin America may be considered irrelevant. Although industrialization processes were coming into being in some of these countries, especially the large ones, in the first decades of the twentieth century, import-substitution industrialization

(ISI) or state-led industrialization came later; it is considered a consequence of the Great Depression and the Second World War.[10]

In the light of the above we assume that imports of durable goods are a good approximation to domestic consumption in Latin American economies, but we must discuss some limitations on this assumption.

In the first place, we lack information to quantify inventory changes. A second aspect is that some of these countries – in particular Argentina, Chile, Cuba and Uruguay – were centres of regional distribution. For example, some of the trade that went into Argentina may have subsequently been sent on to Bolivia. The fact that there was intra-regional trade may generate some difficulties when the time comes to interpreting the results for the total level of imports as we may be overestimating domestic consumption. Finally, there is a third limitation on our use of import figures to measure domestic consumption: the existence of smuggling. This problem occurs especially in the case of watches, as they are goods of high value and small size.

In spite of all these limitations, the strategy of using trade statistics to measure domestic consumption has been widely used by economic historians. One reference is Mokyr,[11] in his analysis of the standard of living in the United Kingdom during the Industrial Revolution. The other important reference is Shammas,[12] who studies the behaviour of consumption demand in Great Britain and its colonies between 1550 and 1800. In both of these studies domestic consumption figures are based on trade information.

During the first globalization, in Latin America there was high concentration of trade by origin and destination of imports and exports, respectively. In 1913 France, Germany, Great Britain and the United States were the main markets for the region. These four countries accounted for 70.8 per cent of total exports and 75.1 per cent of total imports.[13] In the period 1890–1910 the average share of France, Germany, Great Britain and the United States in the total imports of our six economies (Argentina, Brazil, Chile, Uruguay, Cuba and Mexico) was 74 per cent.[14] Mexico had the highest concentration of imports, with 90 per cent, next came Chile and Cuba with 78 per cent, Argentina with 71 per cent, and lastly Uruguay with the lowest concentration of imports from this origin with 61 per cent.

When we focus on imports of durable consumption goods there is a higher concentration of imports. I consider two benchmarks, one near 1900 (with the exception of Brazil, for which have 1910) and the other towards the end of our period of analysis, 1913; and we find that durable goods have a pattern of higher concentration than that described above for total imports. On average 85 per cent of the total imports of durable goods came from the four industrialized countries. During this period, the share of the four countries in durable consumption imports was 92 per cent for Cuba, 89 per cent for Chile, 88 per cent for Mexico, 84 per cent for Brazil, 81 per cent for Argentina and 79 per cent for Uruguay.

I estimate domestic consumption based on the official trade statistics of the four exporter countries. That is, I consider the figures for what France, Germany, Great Britain and the United States exported to the Latin American region. This methodological approach has big advantages in terms of the availability of annual information, homogeneity and temporal and geographical coverage.[15] However, the use of these statistics led to problems when I compared foreign sources with domestic ones, as the data differed. There may be various reasons for these discrepancies, such as variations in the valuation procedure used in different countries, the assignation criteria of origin and destination of trade, and transport costs (*CIF* and *FOB* values). However, the accuracy of trade statistics has been analysed by other authors, who argue that these differences are within acceptable error margins and may be explained by geographic assignation.[16]

I use trade statistics from France, Germany, Great Britain and the United States to study consumption of durable goods in six countries in Latin America between 1890 and 1913. I produce series for seven groups of goods: carriages, vehicles and parts;[17] bicycles and motorcycles, musical instruments, clocks and watches, sewing machines, photographic equipment and fountain pens. I have several reasons for choosing these particular items: I selected categories of goods that were present and stable for most of the period. The only category which varies widely as regards its structure is 'carriages, vehicles and parts'. At the beginning of the twentieth century a new good appeared, the automobile, and demand for it grew rapidly. Imports of cars emerged as a separate item in trade statistics around 1904, although the absence of this item before that year does not mean there were no imports. A second aspect is that I tried as far as possible to choose goods that were for domestic consumption. However, in some cases, the statistics sources are not clear as to the final use of the item. Some secondary information may allow us to conclude that most imported sewing machines and automobiles were for domestic use and there are two pieces of evidence that support this conclusion. First, in 1922, in the trade statistics of the United States, the final use of sewing machines exports is broken down into 'domestic' and 'industrial'; sewing machines for domestic use amounted to 86 per cent of the total exported to these Latin American countries. Second, it was not until 1913 that United States trade statistics started to distinguish between automobiles for private use and those for commercial use. In that year, 93 per cent of automobiles exported were for private use. In addition, from the figures reported by Mitchell[18] we can calculate the percentage of cars for private use. Between 1900 and 1913 in the United States some 98 per cent of total automobiles were for private use, in 1905–13 in Britain some 50 per cent were for private use and in Germany some 88 per cent were in this category. Even though it is possible that some of the cars for private use might also have been used for domestic production, there is no information available to enable us to make such a distinction.

Finally, for each of our six Latin American countries we have data about imports of durable goods based on the 1890 to 1913 trade statistics of the four industrialized countries. In order to calculate the real evolution of consumption I deflate these series by an export price index, with 1913 as the reference year. I draw up this index based on export prices for industrial products in the four countries and I weigh them by the share of each country in exports of durable goods to Latin America. In addition, I correct the evolution of this index by unit values of automobile exports from Great Britain and the United States to Latin America.[19] Cars were the only group of goods whose unit value fell considerably over the period.

Evolution and Comparison

Figure 12.1 shows the evolution of per capita consumption of durable goods for the six Latin American economies in the period 1890–1913 and average growth rates for the whole period and for two sub-periods, 1890–1900 and 1901–13. This group of countries, except for Mexico, had the highest levels of durable consumption in Latin America.[20] At the beginning of the period Cuba, Argentina and Uruguay had the highest levels of consumption, but Cuba's high level may be explained by its lower demographic growth. This country shows a sharp decrease as the result of its war of independence (1895–8). Brazil underwent a steady decline towards the end of the nineteenth century as a consequence of an economic depression. At the end of the period Argentina showed the highest levels of consumption, followed by Uruguay, while Mexico still had the lowest levels, especially after 1910, because of the negative effect of the Mexican Revolution.

We observe a rapid growth of consumption. On average, it increased at an annual accumulative rate of 7.7 per cent, which reflects the economic growth experienced by these six economies. We can see from the average growth rates shown in Figure 12.1 that Argentina is outstanding and has the highest rate, followed by Chile, Uruguay, Cuba and Brazil. Mexico is the country with the lowest average growth rate. These results are consistent with the behaviour discussed above: those countries with higher levels show higher growth rates.

When we compare annual growth rates between the period 1890–1900 and the period 1901–13 we find results that vary. In the first decade of the twentieth century Brazil, Mexico and Uruguay had higher growth rates than in the previous period, while Argentina and Cuba performed better between 1890 and 1900 than after the turn of the century. Chile had similar growth rates in both periods.

The evolution of durable goods may reflect the economic performance of these economies and the difference between them. This hypothesis is based on the relation between income and consumption. We may expect that those periods of faster growth in consumption were periods of rapid economic growth.

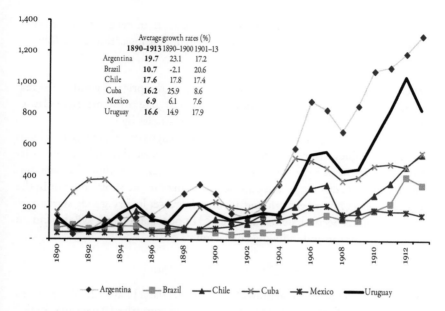

Figure 12.1: Real imports of per capita consumption of durable goods (in dollars per 1,000 inhabitants) and annual growth rates (percentages)

Source: Own elaboration based on sources reported in the annex. For details of its construction see Román, 'Importación de bienes de consume duradero y crecimiento económico en América Latina (1890–1913)'.

A second hypothesis is that differences in consumption levels between countries may be associated with income gaps. This may reflect a divergence pattern, as countries with higher levels have higher growth rates. However there are factors other than income that affect differences between consumption levels, such as income distribution, prices or changes in consumption behaviour. In addition, as regards the product cycle of Deaton,[21] differences in consumption levels and in growth rates may be explained by the fact that the countries were in different phases of the product cycle.

In the next section, we will study the relation between income and consumption by estimating consumption demand for the group of six countries.

An Empirical Analysis of Consumption Demand

In order to analyse consumption demand I used a specification of a double logarithmic function including real income and relative prices as explicative variables. In this way we can easily get the elasticity coefficients. This functional specification has been used in several empirical studies about consumption demand and the elasticity of different types of goods.[22]

In equation (1) the demand per capita for each item depends on per capita real income and relative price. The expression in double logarithmic is as follows:

$$\log q_i = \alpha_i + \beta \log \frac{Y}{\pi} + \lambda \log \frac{p_i}{\pi} \quad (1)$$

Where q_i is the quantity per capita of good i, p_i is the price of good i, Y is real income per capita, π is the price index, and α, β and λ are constants. Rent elasticity is represented by the coefficient β, and price elasticity by λ.

Equation (1) is a pragmatic approach to the analysis of demand as it includes the main variables we are interested in. Nevertheless, we should be aware of its limitations. In the first place, the elasticities are constant over time. This assumption has a lot of advantages and may be maintained in the short run, but in the long run, as economic growth and income increase, luxury goods start to be consumed more. Second, demand expressed in per capita terms will depend on income distribution and individual behaviour.[23]

Specification of the Model

I will estimate demand in equation (1) using panel data. I have 126 observations covering twenty-four years (1890–1913) and six countries (Argentina, Brazil, Chile, Cuba, Mexico and Uruguay).[24] The specification of the equation is as follows (equation 2):

$$\log M_{it} = \alpha_i + \beta \log(Y_{it}) + \gamma \log(PR_{it})(1 + t_{it}) + \mu_{it} \quad (2)$$

Where i = country i and $t = 1 \ldots 24$

M_{it} = Real imports of durable goods per capita from country i in year t

Y_{it} = GDP per capita of country i in Geary-Khamis dollars in year t

PR_{it} = Relative prices of country i in year t

t_{it} = Tariff rate on the imports of country i in year t

The coefficients to be estimated are: α_i individual effects that are characteristic of each country, β income elasticity and γ price elasticity. The relative prices for each country are the ratio between the international price index and the domestic price (this last one is the result of multiplying the consumer price index by the local exchange rate).[25]

Econometric Results

In this section I present a synthesis of the results of the estimation of the demand for imported durable goods using panel data. I estimate the equation using the model of fixed effect regressions to control for omitted variables that differ between countries but are constant over time.[26]

The fixed effects model assumes that the differences between countries may be captured by the differences in the constant coefficient, which means that the slopes are constant but not the intercept. Income elasticity and price elasticity will be the same for all the countries so we may interpret the estimations of the coefficients as an average. Therefore, equation (2) expresses the fact that the imports of durable goods of country i in year t depend on the fixed effects of each country, the income level (GDP per capita) and the relative prices adjusted by the tariff rate.[27]

Before presenting the results I must discuss two points. First, the fixed effects will represent not only the individual characteristics but all the missing variables that may affect each country's consumption but are not explicit in the model, such as income distribution, for example. Second, as we are using imports as a proxy for consumption there are some variables related to trade, such as transport costs, smuggling or intra-regional trade that may also be captured by the fixed effects and may affect the elasticities.

The coefficients of the estimations are statistically significant and with the correct effect: 2.2 for the income elasticity of demand and −2.5 for the price elasticity. The income elasticity of demand is positive and over the unity, which means that our durable goods are luxury goods. The price elasticity value is negative and over the unity (in absolute terms), which means that the demand is elastic. These results are consistent with the consumption theory and with other empirical evidence in estimations of demand for durable goods. Goldberger and Gamalestos compare the consumption pattern of thirteen countries from the OECD between 1950 and 1960 considering five categories of goods: food, clothing, housing, durable goods and others. They estimate a demand function and obtain a coefficient for the elasticity of income for durable goods over the unity, in a range between 1.16 and 3.58. A second paper, Clarida, presents an estimation of imports of durable goods from the United States in the period 1973–92, and obtains price elasticity over the unity (in absolute terms) and income elasticity over two.[28]

As regards individual effects, the coefficients reflect differences between countries, which can be explained by country characteristics such as income distribution and intra-regional trade that may explain the endogenous variable but are not explicit in the model. We order the countries according to their individual coefficients: Brazil (−8.9), Cuba (−10.1), México (−10.2), Uruguay (−10.6), Argentina (−10.6) and Chile (−11.2). Therefore, if we suppose the same level of income, Brazil and Cuba would have higher per capita consumption of durable goods than Argentina and Uruguay. This relation may reflect a worse income distribution in the first two countries, which is coherent with some of the historical context (such as the presence of slaves in Cuba and Brazil). Available estimations of income inequality show that during the period 1870–1920 income inequality in Brazil was greater and more persistent than in Argentina and Uruguay.[29]

I did the same estimation exercises using panel data but considering the demand for four categories or groups of goods: transport,[30] musical instrument, clocks and watches and sewing machines. The results for the income elasticity (first figure) and price elasticity (second figure) of demand for each group were all statistically significant and with the expected effects:[31] transport (1.71 and 5.0); musical instruments (1.31 and −1.7); watches and clocks (0.96 and −2.2) and sewing machines (1.01 and −1.75).[32] These results show that consumption includes goods with variations in their behaviour.

Transport and musical instruments have the highest income elasticity, which shows they are luxury goods. Automobiles started to be imported in the opening years of the twentieth century, and even though demand increased rapidly only wealthier population sectors could afford them.

We obtain lower income elasticity estimations for watches and sewing machines. Watches have a positive elasticity under the unity. Regarding the product cycle of Deaton,[33] we may think that these goods were in a phase of the product cycle in which more people could afford them. However, two other factors may also be affecting this result below the unity. First, the figures I use to estimate the consumption of watches do not consider imports from two big suppliers, Belgium and Switzerland.[34] Second, we cannot deny the existence of smuggling, as watches are small items with high value.[35] Both factors are limitations and may lead us to underestimate the consumption of watches. As regards sewing machines, the fact that their income elasticity is almost equal to one may mean that this good was not a luxury good. A possible hypothesis is that sewing machines were considered a production good and were used in the household to manufacture clothing for the market.

Conclusions

In this chapter I presented estimations of the evolution of consumption of durable goods in six countries in Latin America between 1890 and the 1913 in order to enhance our understanding of the performance of these economies and their improvements in standards of livings, except for some segments of their societies.

I found that the import pattern of durable goods was similar to total imports in terms of trade concentration, but was more concentrated. France, Germany, Great Britain and the United States accounted for 85 per cent of total imports of durable consumption. I based my estimations of consumption of durable goods series on the trade statistics of these industrialized countries. I analysed the evolution of consumption during the period and I related this behaviour to income by estimating a demand function using panel data.

The first globalization was a golden age for exports and most of the Latin American economies enjoyed rapid growth and material prosperity, especially for some groups and for the urban class that was emerging.[36] The increase in consumption during this period shows the positive economic performance of these regions, although the evolution within was heterogeneous. When we compare the performance of these six economies, those with higher levels show higher growth rates. Argentina is outstanding for its high growth rate, followed by Chile, Uruguay, Cuba and Brazil. Mexico is the country which shows the lowest average growth rate. A comparison of annual growth rates between the period 1890–1900 and 1901–13 yields varying results. In the first decade of the twentieth century Brazil, Mexico and Uruguay had higher growth rates than the previous period, while in contrast Argentina and Cuba performed better between 1890 and 1900 than after. Chile had similar growth rates in both periods.

The evolution of consumption, overall and between countries, may reflect the economic performance of these economies. At the end of the period, Argentina and Uruguay had the highest consumption levels, followed by Cuba, Chile. And at the bottom were Brazil and Mexico.

I also present some estimations of the demand function for durable goods. I first estimated an aggregate demand and then I worked with four categories of goods, looking for a variety of behaviour. The income elasticity of demand was positive and over the unity, which means that our durable goods were luxury goods. The negative value and over the unity (in absolute terms) of price elasticity means that demand was elastic. These results are consistent with the consumption theory and with other empirical evidence from estimations of the demand for durable goods. As to individual effects, the coefficients reflect the differences between country characteristics, such as income distribution differences. The results of the estimation for the four categories of goods enable us to identify different types of goods: those with higher income elasticity such as transport and musical instruments, and those with lower coefficients – watches and sewing machines.

Statistical Appendix

For Argentinian GDP I used the data from Cortés Conde (1890–1900) and Maddison (1900–1913); for external trade the *Anuario del comercio exterior*; and for exchange rate (ER) and Price Consumption Index (PCI), Bértola et al. and Flandreau and Zumer.[37] For Brazilian GDP, Maddison; and for external trade, *Commercio exterior do Brazil*; ER and PCI, Bértola at al. and Flandreau and Zumer.[38] For Chilean GDP, Lüders (1890–1900) and Maddison (1900–13); for external trade, the *Anuario Estadístico de la Reública de Chile, Comercio Exterior*; and for ER and PCI, Diaz, Lúders and Wagner.[39] For Cuban GDP see Santamaría García (1900–13); for external trade, *Comercio Exterior*; and for ER and PCI (1900–113), Oxford Latin American Data Base. For the PCI between 1900 and 1903, I calculate the PCI based on the variation of the PCI of the United States. Following Santamaría García and García Álvarez, the price index of Cuba and the United States between 1872 and 1914 were highly correlated. Actually, the correlation coefficient is 0.96 although they remark that the correlation was higher at the end of the nineteenth century than at the beginning of the twentieth.[40] For Mexican GDP, *Estadísticas Históricas de México* (1895–1900), and Maddison (1900–10 and 1910–13); for external trade *Anuario Estadístico: Comercio exterior y navegación*; and for ER *Estadísticas Históricas de México*, and for PCI Gomez Galvarriato and Musacchio.[41] The GDP of Uruguay in Maddison; external trade, *Anuario estadístico de la República Oriental del Uruguay*; and for ER and PCI, Bértola, Calicchio, Camou, and Porcile and *Anuario estadístico*.[42]

For French external trade, *Tableau générale du commerce et de la navigation*; and for exports prices of industrial products, Y. Breton.[43] The origin of German data is, for external trade, *Der Auswärtige Andel Deutschlands*; and for exports prices of industrial products, Hoffmann.[44] For Unites Sates, the external trade data from *The Foreign Commerce and Navigation of the US*; and for exports prices of industrial products, *Historical Statistics of the United States: Earliest Times to the Present*.[45] Finally, the United Kingdom external trade data, *Annual Statement of the United Kingdom with Foreign Countries and British Possessions*; and for exports prices of industrial, Mitchell.[46]

NOTES

Introduction

1. L. Bértola and J. A. Ocampo, *Desarrollo, vaivenes y desigualdad. Una historia económica de América Latina desde la Independencia* (Madrid: Secretaria General Iberoamericana, 2010).
2. http://www.ggdc.net/MADDISON/oriindex.htm (31 October 2011).
3. L. Prados de la Escosura, 'Lost Decades? Economic Performance in Post-Independence Latin America', *Journal of Latin American Studies*, 41:2 (2009), pp. 279–307.
4. Bértola and Ocampo, *Desarrollo, vaivenes*.
5. M. Rubio, C. Yáñez, M. Folchi and A. Carreras, 'Energy as an Indicator of Modernization in Latin America, 1890–1925', *The Economic History Review*, 63:3 (2010), pp. 769–804.
6. A. Dye, 'The Institutional Framework.', in V. Bulmer-Thomas, J. Coatsworth, and R. Cortés Conde (eds), *The Cambridge Economic History of Latin America*. (Cambridge: Cambridge University Press, 2006), vol. 2, pp. 169–207.
7. S. L. Engerman and K. L. Sokoloff, 'Factor Endowments,Institutions, and Differential Paths of Growth among New World Economies:A View from Economic Historians of the United States', in S. Haber (ed.), *How Latin America Fell Behind* (Palo Alto, CA: Stanford University Press, 1997), pp. 260–304.
8. D. C. North, W. Summerhill and B. R. Weingast, 'Order, Disorder and Economic Change: Latin America vs. North America', in B. Bueno de Mesquita and H. Root (eds), *Governing for Prosperity* (New Haven, CT: Yale University Press, 2000), pp. 17–58.
9. D. Acemoglu, S. Johnson and J. A. Robinson, 'The Colonial Origins of Comparative Development: An Empirical Investigation.', *American Economic Review*, 91:5 (2001), pp. 1369–401.
10. R. H. Bates, J. H. Coatsworth and J. G. Williamson (2007), 'Lost Decades: Postindependence Performance in Latin America and Africa' , *Journal of Economic History*, 67 (2007), pp. 917–43.
11. Haber, *How Latin America*.
12. C. Yáñez, 'Economic modernisation in adverse institutional environments: the cases of Cuba and Chile', paper presented at the Utretch Congress in 2008 and included this book (chapter 7).
13. See A. Carreras, Chapter 1 of this book.
14. R. Thorp, *Progreso, pobreza y exclusión. Una historia económica de América Latina en el siglo XX* (Washington, DC: BID, 1998).
15. Bertola and Ocampo, *Desarrollo, vaivenes*.

16. Thorp, *Progreso, pobreza y eclusión*.
17. Prados de la Escosura, 'Lost decades'.
18. Rubio, Yáñez, Folchi and Carreras, 'Energy as an indicator'.

1 Expectations, Instutions and Economic Performance

1. This research has been funded by Spanish Education and Science Ministry grants: SEC2003–00190 on 'Imports and Economic Modernization in Latin American and the Caribbean, 1870–1960', and SEJ2007–60445 on 'Energía y economía en América Latina y el Caribe desde mediados del siglo XIX a finales del siglo XX'. A first version was presented at the 'Tercer Congreso Internacional de la Asociación Mexicana de Historia Económica'. I thank Antonio Ibarra for the opportunity to present the paper to a wide audience and the comments provided by the discussants (Salomon Kalmanowitz and Luis Bértola) and by the public.
2. S. J. Stein and B. H. Stein, *The Colonial Heritage of Latin America: Essays on Economic Dependence in Perspective* (New York: Oxford University Press, 1970).
3. D. S. Landes, *The Wealth and Poverty of Nations: Why Some Are So Rich and Some So Poor* (New York: W.W. Norton & Company, 1998).
4. D. Acemoglu, S. Johnson and J. Robinson, 'The Colonial Origins of Comparative Development: An Empirical Investigation', *American Economic Review*, 91:5 (2001), pp. 1369–401; 'Reversal of Fortune: Geography and Institutions in the Making of Modern World Income Distribution', *Quarterly Journal of Economics*, 118 (2002), pp.1231–94.
5. R. Ransom, *The Confederate States of America: What Might Have Been* (New York: W.W.Norton and Company, 2005), on the Confederate States of America for a fully fledged and careful exploration of the counterfactual hypothesis of the US Civil War not finishing in the North victory but in an agreement providing the North with full territorial expansion rights and the South with political independence.
6. S. Engerman and K. Sokoloff, 'Factor Endowments, Institutions, and Differential Paths of Growth among New World Economies: A View from Economic Historians of the Unites States', in S. Haber (ed.), *How Latin American Fell Behind* (Palo Alto, CA: Stanford University Press, 1997), pp. 260–304; 'Institutions, Factor Endowments, and Paths of Development in the New World', *Journal of Economic Perspectives*, 14:3 (2000), pp. 217–32; 'The Evolution of Suffrage Institutions in the New World', *Journal of Economic History*, 65:4 (2005), pp. 891–921.
7. L. Prados de la Escosura, 'When Did Latin America Fall Behind?', in S. Edwards, G. Esquivel and G. Márquez (eds), *The Decline of Latin American Economies: Growth, Institutions and Crises* (Chicago, IL: The University of Chicago Press, 2007), pp. 15–57.
8. M. D. Bordo and R. Cortés-Conde (eds), *Transfering Wealth and Power from the Old to the New World* (New York: Cambridge University Press, 2001).
9. H. S. Klein, *The American Finances of the Spanish Empire: Royal Income and Expenditures in Colonial Mexico, Peru and Bolivia, 1680–1809* (Albuquerque, NM: University of New Mexico Press, 1998); R. Dobado and G. Marrero, 'Minería, crecimiento económico y costes de la Independencia en México', *Revista de Historia Económica*, 19:3 (2001), pp. 573–611; J. Coatsworth, 'Mexico', in J. Mokyr (ed.), *The Oxford Encyclopaedia of Economic History* (New York: Oxford University Press, 2003), vol. 3, pp. 501–7; 'Structure, Endowment, and Institucions in the Economic History of Latin America', *Latin American Research Review*, 40:3 (2005), pp. 126–44; 'Political Economy and Economic Organization', in V. Bulmer-Thomas, J. Coatsworth and R. Cortés Conde (eds), *The*

Cambridge Economic History of Latin America (New York: Cambridge University Press, 2007), vol. 1, pp. 237–73.

10. M. A. Irigoin, 'Macroeconomic Aspects of Spanish American Independence: The Effects of Fiscal and Currency Fragmentation, 1800s–1860s', Universidad Carlos III, *Economic History and Institutions Series*, Working paper 03–45 (2003); L. Prados de la Escosura, 'The Economic Consequences of Independence in Latin America', in V. Bulmer-Thomas, J. Coatsworth and R. Cortés Conde (eds), *The Cambridge Economic History of Latin America* (New York: Cambridge University Press, 2006), vol. 1, pp. 463–504; R. Grafe and M. A. Irigoin, 'The Spanish Empire and Its Legacy: Fiscal Redistribution an Political Conflict in Colonial and Post-Colonial Spanish America', *Journal of Global History*, 1 (2006), pp. 241–67.

11. But see the essays gathered in L. Prados de la Escosura and S. Amaral (eds), *La independencia americana: consecuencias económicas* (Madrid: Alianza, 1993).

12. J. Coatsworth, 'La independencia latinoamericana: hipótesis sobre sus costes y beneficios', in Prados de la Escosura and Amaral (eds), *La independencia Americana*, pp. 17–27; Prados de la Escosura, 'The Economic Consequence'.

13. D. C. North, W. Summerhill and B. Weingast, 'Order, Disorder and Economic Change: Latin America vs. North America', in B. Bueno de Mesquita and H. Root (eds), *Governing for Prosperity* (New Haven, CT: Yale University Press, 2000), pp. 17–58; J. H. Elliott, *Empires of the Atlantic World: Britain and Spain in America, 1492–1830* (New Haven, CT: Yale University Press, 2006).

14. J. Coatsworth and G. Tortella, 'Instituciones y desempeño económico a largo plazo en México y España (1800–2000)', in R. Dobado, A. Gómez Galvarriato and G. Márquez (eds), *México y España ¿Historias económicas paralelas?* (México: Fondo de Cultura Económica, 2007), pp. 47–74.

15. A. Dye, 'The Institutional Framework', in V. Bulmer-Thomas, J. Coatsworth and R. Cortés Conde (eds), *The Cambridge Economic History of Latin America* (New York: Cambridge University Press, 2007), vol. 2, pp. 169–207.

16. J. B. De Long, 'Productivity Growth, Convergence and Welfare: A Comment', *American Economic Review*, 8 (1988), pp. 1138–54.

17. W. J. Baumol, 'Productivity Growth, Convergence and Welfare: What the Long-Run Data Show', *American Economic Review*, 76:5 (1986), pp. 1072–85.

18. J. L. Gallup, J. D. Sachs and A. D. Mellinger, 'Geography and Economic Development', *International Regional Science Review*, 22:2 (1999), pp. 179–232.

19. C. Díaz-Alejandro, *Essays on the Economic History of the Argentina Republic* (New Haven, CT: Yale University Press, 1970).

20. T. Duncan and J. Fogarty, *Australia and Argentina: On Parallel Paths* (Carlton: Melbourne University Press, 1984); D. C. M. Platt and G. Di Tella (eds), *Argentina, Australia and Canada: Studies in comparative development, 1870–1965* (London: Macmillan & St Antony's College, 1985); I. Sanz-Villarroya, 'The Convergence Process of Argentina with Australia and Canada: 1875–2000', *Explorations in Economic History*, 42 (2005), pp. 439–58; L. Bertola, 'A los cincuenta años de la curva de Kuznets: crecimiento económico y distribución del ingreso en Uruguay y otros países de nuevo asentamiento desde 1870', Instituto Laureano Figuerola, dilf 0504, Universidad Carlos III (2005); P. Gerchunoff and P. Fajgelbaum, *¿Por qué Argentina no fue Australia? Una hipótesis sobre el cambio de rumbo* (Buenos Aires: Siglo XXI, 2006).

21. For instance, L. Prados de la Escosura and I. Sanz, Contract Enforcement and Long-Run's Argentina Decline, U. Carlos III, Economic History Working Paper 06–06, (2006).

22. Sanz-Villarroya 'The Convergence Process'.
23. A. Taylor, 'On the Costs of Inward-looking Development: Price Distortions, Growth and Divergence in Latin America', *Journal of Economic History*, 58:1 (1998), pp. 1–28.
24. Gerchunoff and Fajgelbaum, *¿Por qué Argentina no fue Australia?*.
25. Prados de la Escosura, 'When Did Latin America'.
26. L. Domínguez, *National Income Estimates of Latin America* (Washington, DC: Inter American Statistical Institute, 1945); 'National income estimates of Latin America', in *Studies in Income and Wealth* (New York: National Bureau for Economic Research, 1947), vol. 10, pp. 160–244.
27. The sixteen in A. Maddison, *Phases of Capitalist Development* (Oxford: Oxford University Press, 1982).
28. M. G. Mulhall, *Industries and Wealth of Nations* (London: Longmans, 1986).
29. Domínguez, *National Income* (1945).
30. Domínguez, 'National Income' (1947).
31. L. Prados de la Escosura, 'International Comparisons of Real Product, 1820–1990: An Alternative Data Set', *Explorations in Economic History*, 37 (2000), pp. 1–41.
32. Ibid., pp. 27–8.
33. A. Maddison, *Monitoring the World Economy 1820–1992* (Paris: OECD, 1985).
34. P. Astorga, A. Berges and V. Fitzgerald, 'The Standard of Living in Latin America during the Twentieth Century', *Economic History Review*, 58:4 (2005), pp. 765–96.
35. J. G. Williamson, 'Real Wages Inequality and Globalization in Latin America before 1940', *Revista de Historia Económica*, 17 (1999), pp. 101–42; B. Sánchez-Alonso, 'Labor and Immigration', in Bulmer-Thomas, Coatsworth and Cortés Conde (eds), *The Cambridge Economic History*, vol. 2, pp. 377–426.
36. Better known as CEPAL according to its Spanish name – 'Comisión Económica para América Latina'.
37. ECLAC, *Series históricas del crecimiento de América Latina*, Cuadernos estadísticos de la Cepal, 3 (Santiago de Chile: Cepal, 1978).
38. ECLAC, *Economic Survey of Latin America, 1949* (New York: United Nations, 1951) and a number of highly valuable detailed country monographs prepared during the 1950s under the general title 'Análisis y proyecciones del desarrollo económico': Guatemala, 1951; Ecuador, 1953; Brazil, 1956; Colombia, 1956; Argentina, 1959; El Salvador, 1959; Panama, 1959; Peru, 1959 and Honduras, 1960. A review of them is available in C. Yáñez y X. Tafunell, 'Informe sobre la recuperación del patrimonio documental estadístico histórico de la CEPAL. Las series de larga duración sobre las principales variables macroeconómicas de América Latina y el Caribe', CEPAL, Documento LC/R.2119, 17 de julio de 2004.
39. A. Maddison, *Dynamic Forces in Capitalist Development: A Long-Run Comparative View* (Oxford: Oxford University Press, 1991); 'Monitoring the World', *The World Economy: A Millennial Perspective* (Paris, OECD, 2001); *The World Economy Historical Statistics* (Paris, OECD, 2003); V. Bulmer-Thomas, *The Economic History of Latin America since Independence*, 2nd edn (Cambridge: Cambridge University Press, 2003); R. Thorp, *Progress, Poverty and Exclusion* (Baltimore, MD: The Johns Hopkins University Press, 1998); Astorga, Berges and Fitzgerald, 'The Standard of Living'.
40. Astorga, Berges and Fitzgerald, 'The Standard of Living'.
41. W. M. Scammell, *The International Economy since 1945* (New York: St Martin's Press, 1980).

42. C. Feinstein, P. Temin and G. Toniolo, *The European Economy between the Wars* (Oxford: Oxford University Press, 1997).

43. C. Wilcox, *A Charter for World Trade* (New York: Arno Press, 1972; reprint of Macmillan Company, 1949).

44. That is, time to prepare for switching into full currency convertibility.

45. Wilcox, *A Charter for World Trade*, and W. A. Brown, Jr., *The United States and the Restoration of World Trade: An Analysis and Appraisal of the ITO Charter and the General Agreement on Tariffs and Trade* (Washington, DC: The Brookings Institution, 1950), are extremely detailed in explaining the remote and immediate origins of the Havana Charter, as well as the major criticisms that appeared after its initial approval, in the road to national parliamentary ratifications.

46. H. Feis, 'The Confict over Trade Ideology', *Foreign Affairs*, 25:2 (1947), pp. 217–28; J. Viner, 'Conflicts of Principles in Drafting a Trade Charter', *Foreign Affairs*, 25:4 (1947), pp. 612–28.

47. Feis, 'The Conflict'.

48. Viner, 'Conflicts of Principles'.

49. Ibid., p. 638.

50. Wilcox, *A Charter for World Trade*; Brown Jr., *The United States*.

51. A. S. Milward, *The Reconstruction of Western Europe, 1945–1951* (London: Methuen, 1984); A. S. Milward, G. Brennan and F. Romero, *The European Rescue of the Nation-State* (London: Routledge, 1992); B. Eichengreen, 'Institutions and Economic Growth: Europe after World War II', in N. Crafts and G. Toniolo (eds), *Economic Growth in Europe since 1945* (Cambridge: Cambridge University Press, 1996) pp. 38–72; L. Neal and D. Barbezat, *The Economics of the European Union and the Economies of Europe* (New York and Oxford: Oxford University Press, 1998).

52. A good summary is available in Eichengreen, 'Institutions and Economic Growth'.

53. It is worth reminding that countries which by 2001 had quite similar per capita GDP such as Thailand, Malaysia, Argentina, Mexico and Uruguay (6383, 7756, 8137, 7089 and 7557 US international Geary-Khamis dollars, respectively), were much more diverse in 1950 (817, 1559, 4987, 2365 and 4659, respectively). Maddison, *The Economic History*.

54. That is, Europe was only for the Europeans.

55. Neal and Barbezat, *The Economics of the European Union*.

56. And also of Franco and Castro!

57. For the paragraph 'in totto', A. Carreras and X. Tafunell, *Historia económica de la España contemporánea* (Barcelona: Crítica, 2003).

58. F. Guirao, *Spain and the Reconstruction of Western Europe, 1945–1957: Challenge and Response* (London and New York: MacMillan/St Martin's Press, 1998).

59. Guirao, 'Spain and the Reconstruction'; O. Calvo-González, '¡Bienvenido, Míster Marshall! La ayuda económica americana y la economía española en la década de 1950', *Revista de Historia Económica*, 19 (2001), pp. 253–75; 'Neither a Carrot Nor a Stick: American Foreign Aid and Economic Policymaking in Spain during the 1950s', *Diplomatic History*, 30:3 (2006), pp. 409–30; 'American Military Interests and Economic Confidence in Spain Ander the Franco Dictatorship', *Journal of Economic History*, 67:3 (2007), pp. 740–67.

60. The argument was made both by scholars and by contemporary observers. An approach taking into full account the importance of expectations in the consolidation of Spanish transition to democracy can be found in B. Weingast, 'Constructing Self-Enforcing

Democracy in Spain', in J. Oppenheimer and I. Morris (eds), *From Anarchy to Democracy* (Palo Alto, CA: Stanford University Press, 2004) pp. 161–95.

61.   Ransom, *The Confederate States of America*, plays with the counterfactual that an independent Confederate States of America would have conquered or bought Cuba and made it a full member of the CSA.

62.   A. Dye, 'The Smoot-Hawley Tariff and Crisis in Cuba', paper prepared for the ISNIE conference, Barcelona (September 2005).

63.   E. F. Denison, *Why Growth Rates Differ* (Washington, DC: Brookings Institution, 1967); A. Maddison, 'Growth and Slowdown in Advanced Capitalist Economies: Techniques of Quantitative Assessment', *Journal of Economic Literature*, 25 (1987), pp. 649–98; N. Crafts and G. Toniolo, 'Postwar Growth: An Overview', in N. Crafts and G.Toniolo (eds) *Economic Growth in Europe since 1945* (Cambridge: Cambridge University Press, 1996), pp. 1–37.

64.   Crafts and Toniolo (eds), 'Economic Growth in Europe'; N. F. R. Crafts and B. van Ark (eds), *Quantitative Aspects of post-war European Economic Growth* (Cambridge: Cambridge University Press, 1996).

65.   Eichengreen, 'Institutions and Economic Growth'; B. Eichengreen, *The European Economy since 1945: Coordinated Capitalism and Beyond* (Princeton, NJ: Princeton University Press, 2006).

66.   G. Ofer, 'Soviet Economic Growth, 1928–1985', *Journal of Economic Literature*, 25:4 (1987), pp. 1767–833.

67.   A 'normal' approach is shared by Astorga, Berges and Fitzgerald, 'The Standard of Living'; A. Hofman, *The Economic Development of Latin America in the Twentieth Century* (Cheltenham-Northampton: Edward Elgar, 2000); J. Coatsworth, 'Structure, Endowment, and Institucions in the Economic History of Latin America', *Latin American Research Review*, 40:3 (2005), pp. 126–44. For contrary evidence, Prados de la Escosura, 'When Did Latin America'.

68.   Hofman, 'The Economic Development', obtains slightly more optimistic results on the role of TFP, but his various estimating procedures suggest that the range of uncertainty is still very high.

69.   Astorga, Berges and Fitzgerald, 'The Standard Of Living', p. 785.

70.   A. Carreras, and X. Tafunell, 'The European Union Economic Growth Experience, 1830–2000', in S. Heikkinen and J. L. Van Zanden (eds), *Explorations in Economic Growth* (Amsterdam: Aksant, 2004) pp. 63–87.

71.   Carreras and Tafunell, 'The European Union Economic Growth'.

72.   By 'recently' I mean 2005, 2006 and 2007.

73.   G. Oddone, *El crecimiento económico de Uruguay en el siglo XX* (PhD thesis, University of Barcelona, 2006).

74.   S. Haber, 'It Wasn't All Prebisch's Fault: The Political Economy of Latin American Industrialization' (unpublished manuscript, Stanford University, 2002).

75.   L. Bethell and I. Roxborough, 'Conclusion', in L. Bethell and I. Roxborough (eds), *Latin America between the Second World War and the Cold War, 1944–1948* (Cambridge: Cambridge University Press, 1992), pp. 327–34. The authors go into this direction when they suggest that Prebish's new paradigm was the unifying theme behind the changes in Latin America during the critical 1944–8 years. Prebish and CEPAL were still to come, and they were nothing more than a reaction. It is true that the new ideas can become the future vested interests, and they became so, indeed. Haber's title: 'It Wasn't All Prebisch's Fault' suggests a new look at Prebisch and his historical environment.

76. D. C. North, J. J. Wallis and B. Weingast, *Violence and Social Order: A Conceptual Framework for Interpreting Recorded Human History* (Cambridge: Cambridge University Press, 2009).

2 On the Accuracy of Latin American Trade Statistics

1. This chapter is the result of research at an early stage of a project entitled 'Imports and economic modernization in Latin America 1890–1960', which is financed by the Spanish Ministry of Education (Project No: BEC2003–00190 MCYT). We are obliged to the rest of the team members for their encouragement and help: A.Carreras, X.Tafunell, C.Yañez and A.Hofman. The authors gratefully acknowledge the research assistantship of F. Notten. The usual disclaimers apply.
2. G. Parniczky, 'On the Inconsistency of World Trade Statistics', *International Statistical Review*, 48 (1980), pp 43–48; J. Rozansky, and A. Yeats, 'On The (In)Accuracy of Economic Observations – An Assessment of Trends in the Reliability of International-Trade Statistics', *Journal of Development Economics*, 44 (1994), pp. 103–30; B. Makhoul and S. Otterstrom, 'Exploring the Accuracy of International Trade Statistics', *Applied Economics*, 30 (1998), pp. 1603–16.
3. G. Federico, and A. Tena, 'On the Accuracy of Foreign-Trade Statistics (1909–1935) – Morgenstern Revisited', *Explorations in Economic History*, 28 (1991), pp. 259–73.
4. A. Carreras, A. Hofman, X. Tafunell, and C. Yañez (2003): 'El desarrollo económico de América Latina en épocas de globalización- Una agenda de investigación', *Estudios Estadísticos y Prospectivos, Naciones Unidas: CEPAL: Centro de Proyecciones Económicas*, 24 (2003); A. Carreras, C. Yañez, A. Hofman, X. Tafunell, M. Folchi D, and M. D. M. Rubio (2004): 'Importaciones y modernización económica en América Latina durante la primera mitad del siglo XX. Las claves de un programa de investigación', II Congreso Nacional de Historia Económica. Asociación Mexicana de Historia Económica, Mesa Temática N° 6, Universidad Autónoma de México (2004).
5. O. Morgernstern, *On the Accuracy of Economic Observations* (Princeton, NJ: Princeton, 1963).
6. S. Naya, and T. Morgan, 'The Accuracy of International Trade Data: The Case of South Asian countries', *Journal of the American Statistical Association*, 64 (1969), pp. 452–67.
7. A. J. Yeats, 'On the Accuracy of Economic Observations: Do Sub-Saharan Trade Statistics Mean Anything', *The World Bank Economic Review*, 4 (1990), pp. 165–56.
8. Rozansky and Yeats, 'On The (In)Accuracy'.
9. Makhoul and Otterstrom, 'Exploring the Accuracy'.
10. Ibid.
11. Rozansky and Yeats, 'On The (In)Accuracy'.
12. Yeats, 'On the Accuracy'.
13. A. J. Yeats, 'Are Partner-Country Statistics Useful for Estimating "Missing Trade Data"?', *World Bank Policy Research Working Paper*, 1501 (1995), pp. 1–44.
14. R. G. D. Allen and E. J. Ely, *International Trade Statistics* (New York: Wiley, 1953).
15. Federico and Tena, 'On The Accuracy Of Foreign-Trade Statistics'.
16. Y. Don, 'Comparability of International Trade Statistics: Great Britain and Austria-Hungary before World War I', *Economic History Review*, 31 (1968), pp. 78–91.
17. D. C. N. Platt, 'Problems in the Interpretation of Foreign Trade Statistics before 1914', *Journal of Latin American Studies*, 3 (1971), pp. 119–30.

18. W. P. McGreevey, 'La investigación cuantitativa en la historia latinoamericana de los siglos XIX y XX', in Landes et al. (eds), *Las Dimensiones del pasado: estudios de historia cuantitativa* (Madrid: Alianza, 1975), pp. 325–54.

19. Federico and Tena, 'On The Accuracy Of Foreign-Trade Statistics'.

20. Argentina: Dirección General de Estadística, *Anuario del comercio exterior de la República Argentina* (Buenos Aires: various years); Belgium: Ministère des Finances, *Tableau annuel du commerce avec les pays étrangers* (Brussels: various years); Bolivia: Dirección General de Aduanas, *Comercio especial de Bolivia. Exportación-Importación* (La Paz: various years); Brazil: Directoria de Estatistica Commercial, *Commercio exterior do Brasil* (Rio de Janeiro: variours years); Chile: Oficina Central de Estadística, *Anuario Estadístico de la República de Chile: Comercio Exterior* (Valparaíso: various years); Colombia: Departamento de Contraloría, *Anuario Estadístico. Comercio Exterior* (Bogotá: various years); Costa Rica: Dirección General de Estadística, *Anuario Estadístico* (San José: various years); Cuba: Secretaría de Hacienda, *Comercio Exterior* (Havana, various years); Dominican Republic: Receptoría General de Aduanas, *Report of the … fiscal period: Together with Summary of Commerce* (Washington, DC: various years); Ecuador: Dirección General de Estadística, *Comercio Exterior del Ecuador en los año …* (Quito: various years); El Salvador: Dirección General de Estadística, *Estadística comercial* (San Salvador: various years); Germany, *Der Auswärtige Handel Deutschlands* (Berlin: various years); Guatemala: Ministerio de Hacienda y Crédito Público, *Memoria de las labores del Ejecutivo en el ramo de Hacienda y Crédito Público* (Guatemala: various years); Mexico: Departamento de Estadística Nacional, *Anuario Estadístico: Comercio exterior y navegación* (Mexico City: various years); Nicaragua: Administración de Aduanas, *Memoria del Recaudador General de Aduanas y las Estadísticas del Comercio de* (Managua: various years); Paraguay: Dirección General de Estadística, *El comercio exterior del Paraguay* (Asunción: varoius years); Peru: Superintendencia General de Aduanas, *Estadística especial del Perú* (Callao: various years); Unites States: US Department of Commerce, *The Foreign Commerce and Navigation of the United States* (Washington, DC: various years); United Kingdom: Statistical Office of the Customs and Excise Department, *Annual Statement of the Trade of the United Kingdom with Foreign Countries and Britain Possessions* (London: various years); Uruguay: Dirección General de Estadística, *Anuario estadístico de la República Oriental del Uruguay* (Montevideo: various years); Venezuela: Ministerio de Hacienda y Crédito Público, *Estadística mercantil y marítima* (Caracas: various years).

21. Ibid.

22. U. Ricci, 'Sulle Divergenze fra Statistiche del Movimento Commerciale', *Riforma Sociale*, 21 (1914), pp. 337–412.

23. A. Carreras-Marín and M. Badía-Miró, 'Geographical Deviations in Foreign Trade Statistics: A Study into European Trade with Latin American Countries 1925', *Economics Working Papers* (Barcelona: Universitat Pompeu Fabra, 2005).

24. C. Moneta, 'The Estimation of Transportation Costs in International Trade', *The Journal of Political Economy*, 67 (1959), pp. 41–58.

25. Ibid.

26. M. D. M. Rubio and M. Folchi, 'Energy as an Indicator of Modernisation in Latin America by 1925', Universitat Pompeu Fabra, *Economics Working Papers*, 868 (May, 2005), 1–37.

27. Sources are quoted in the references under the heading 'official publications'.

28. Société Des Nations, *Mémorandum sur le Commerce International et sur les Balances de Paiements, 1912–1926* (Geneva: Publications de la Société des Nations, 1928).
29. General trade accrued imports for home consumption plus the imports deposited in entrepôts, generally excluding trans-shipment trade and trade in transit. European countries tended to use the 'Continental system' and reported 'special trade' instead, which only includes the imports for domestic consumption. The few Latin American countries using the continental system were: Argentina, Bolivia, Chile, Paraguay and Peru. See Société des Nations, Ibid.
30. M. Folchi, and M. D. M. Rubio, 'El consumo aparente de energía fósil en los países latinoamericanos hacia 1925: una propuesta metodológica a partir de las estadísticas de comercio exterior', II Congreso Nacional de Historia Económica. Asociación Mexicana de Historia Económica, Universidad Nacional Autónoma de México (Mexico City, 2004).
31. US Department of Commerce, *Commerce Year Book* (Washington, DC: United States Government Printing Office, 1925 and 1926).
32. P. A. G. van Bergeijk, 'The Accuracy of International Economic Observations', *Bulletin of Economic Research*, 47 (1995), pp. 1–20.
33. Federico and Tena, 'On The Accuracy Of Foreign-Trade Statistics'.
34. Société Des Nations, *Mémorandum sur le Commerce*.
35. van Bergeijk, 'The Accuracy of International'.
36. Rubio and Folchi, 'Energy as an Indicator'.
37. Ibid.
38. J. M. Bland, *An Introduction to Medical Statistics* (Oxford: Oxford University Press, 1995).
39. H. Motulsky, *Intuitive Biostatistics* (Oxford: Oxford University Press, 1995).
40. R. Lowry, *Concepts and Applications of Inferential Statistics* (Poughkeepsie, NY: Vassar College,1999), available at <http://faculty.vassar.edu/lowry/webtext.html>.
41. Motulsky, 'Intuitive Biostatistics'.
42. F. Wilcoxon, 'Individual Comparisons by Ranking Methods', *Biometrics Bulletin*, 1 (1945), pp. 80–3.
43. Do not confuse the Wilcoxon Matched-Pairs Signed-Ranks test with the other main test by the same author, the Wilcoxon Rank-Sum test, which compares one group with a hypothetical median.
44. M. Friedman, 'The Use of Ranks to Avoid the Assumption of Normality Implicit in the Analysis of Variance', *Journal of the American Statistical Association*, 32 (1937), pp. 675–701.
45. Lowry, *Concepts and Applications*.
46. A. D. Quang, and B. T. Hong, *Statistical Data Analysis* (Hanoi: UNESCO Training Course, http://www.netnam.vn/unescocourse, 2000).
47. Friedman, 'The Use of Ranks'.
48. Bland, 'An Introduction to Medical'.
49. W. J. Conover, *Practical Nonparametric Statistics* (New York: John Wiley and Sons, 1998).
50. Federico and Tena, 'On The Accuracy Of Foreign-Trade Statistics'.
51. Yeats, 'Are Partner-Country Statistics Useful'.
52. S. Kuntz, 'Nuevas series del comercio exterior de México, 1870–1929', *Revista de Historia Económica*, XX (2002), pp. 213–70.

3 Latin America and Its Main Trade Partners, 1860–1930

1. V. Bulmer-Thomas, *La historia económica de América Latina desde la independencia* (Mexico City: Fondo de Cultura Económica, 1998); J. Coatsworth and J. Williamson, 'The Roots of Latin American Protectionism: Looking before the Great Depression', *NBER*, 8999 (2002); J. Coatsworth, and J. Williamson, 'Always Protectionist? Latin American Tariffs from Independence to Great Depresión', *Journal of Latin American Studies*, 36 (2004), pp. 205–32; R. Thorp, *Progress, Poverty and Exclusion: An Economic History of Latin America in the 20th Century* (Washington, DC: Inter-American Development Bank, 1998).
2. Bulmer-Thomas, *La historia económica de América Latina*.
3. M. Rubio, 'Protectionist but Globalised? Latin American Custom Duties and Trade during the Pre-1914 Belle Époque', *UPF Working Papers*, 967 (2006); X. Tafunell, 'On the Origins of ISI : The Latin American Cement Industry, 1900–30', *Journal of Latin American Studies*, 39 (2007), pp. 299–328; X. Tafunell and A. Carreras, 'América Latina y el Caribe en 1913 y 1925: Un enfoque desde el consumo de bienes de capital', *Trimestre Económico*, 75:3 (2008), pp. 715–73.
4. S. Kuntz, 'Las oleadas de americanización en el comercio exterior de México, 1870–1948', *Revista Secuencias*, 57 (2003), pp. 159–81.
5. A. Carreras-Marín and M. Badia-Miró, 'La fiabilidad de la asignación geográfica en las estadísticas de comercio exterior: América Latina y el Caribe (1908–1930)', *Revista de Historia Económica - Journal of Iberian and Latin American Economic History*, 26 (2008), pp. 355–73, justify the use of the foreign trade statistics of the UK and United States in those works which analyse the overall region because they offer homogenised and comparable data.
6. Carreras-Marín and Badia-Miró, 'La fiabilidad de la asignación geográfica'.
7. Bulmer-Thomas, *La historia económica de América Latina*.
8. Cluster analysis groups different objects with similar patterns related to some chosen variables. This allows us to find data structures without previous explanations or interpretations. M. S. Aldenderfer, *Cluster Analysis* (Newbury Park, CA, 1984) pp. 347–94.
9. A. Zeileis, C. Kleiber, W. Krämer and K. Hornik, 'Testing and Dating of Structural Changes in Practice', *Computational Statistics and Data Analysis*, 44 (2003), pp. 109–23.
10. J. Bai, 'Least Squares Estimation of a Shift in Linear Processes', *Journal of Time Series Analysis*, 15 (1994), pp. 453–72.
11. J. Bai, 'Estimating Multiple Breaks One at a Time', *Econometric Theory*, 13 (1997), pp. 315–52; J. Bai, 'Estimation of a Change Point in Multiple Regression Models', *Review of Economics and Statistics*, 79 (1997), pp. 551–63; J. Bai and P. Perron, 'Estimating and Testing Linear Models with Multiple Structural Changes', *Econometrica*, 66 (1998), pp. 47–78. The algorithm used in the estimation of the breakpoints is the one derived from J. Bai and P. Perron, 'Computation and Analysis of Multiple Structural Change Models', *Journal of Applied Econometrics*, 18 (2003), pp. 1–22, to obtain multiple breakpoints simultaneously. The distribution function used is the one used of Bai, 'Estimation of a Change Point in Multiple Regression Models' and the ideas which are behind of that implementation is the one obtained from A. Zeileis, C. Kleiber, W. Kraemer and K. Hornik, 'Testing and Dating of Structural Changes in Practice', *Computational Statistics and Data Analysis*, 44 (2003), pp. 109–23. The objective of the algorithm is to work out the triangular matrix RSS which show us the quadratic sum of the residues for a segment which starts with the observation j and ends in i' where $i' > i$.

12. In 1917, Denmark sold this territory to the United States. This explains the extreme dependence between this territory and the United States.
13. Kuntz, 'Las oleadas de americanización en el comercio'.
14. An interesting comparative analyis about the importance of the railways in Latin America can be seen in A. Herranz, 'The Contribution of Railways to Economic Growth in Latin America before 1914: The Cases of Mexico, Brazil and Argentina', *Documentos de trabajo de la AEHE*, 3 (2009).

4 The Structure of Latin American Investment in Equipment Goods during the Mature Period of the First Globalization

1. E. Cárdenas, J. A. Ocampo and R. Thorp (eds), *An Economic History of Twentieth-Century Latin America, Vol. 1, The Export Age: The Latin American Economies in the Late Nineteenth and Early Twentieth Centuries* (Houndmills: Palgrave/St Antony's College, 2000); V. Bulmer-Thomas, *The Economic History of Latin America since Independence*, 2nd edn (Cambridge: Cambridge University Press, 2003); V. Bulmer-Thomas, J. H. Coatsworth and R. Cortés Conde (eds), *The Cambridge Economic History of Latin America* (Cambridge: Cambridge University Press, 2006), vol. 2.
2. For GDP, A. Maddison, *The World Economy: Historical Statistic* (Paris: OECD, 2003), and L. Prados de la Escosura, 'When Did Latin America Fall Behind?', in S. Edwards, G. Esquivel and G. Márquez (eds), *The Decline of Latin American Economies: Growth, Institutions, and Crises* (Chicago, IL: The University of Chicago Press, 2007), pp. 15–57. A bibliographic compendium of GDP estimations made for the main economies of the region in L. Bértola and J. G. Williamson: 'Globalization in Latin America before 1940', in Bulmer-Thomas, Coatsworth and Cortés Conde (eds), *Cambridge Economic History*, pp. 648–50.
3. See the studies cited in note 1.
4. For transport equipment, X. Tafunell: 'La inversion en equipo de transporte de América Latina, 1890–1930: una estimación basada en la demanda de importaciones', *Investigaciones de Historia Económica*, 14 (2009), pp. 39–67; and for machinery, X.Tafunell, 'Capital Formation in Machinery in Latin America, 1890–1930', *The Journal of Economic History*, 69:4 (2009), pp. 928–50. In X. Tafunell, 'The Electric Revolution in Latin America', Working Paper 1236 (Barcelona: Department of Economics and Business of the Universitat Pompeu Fabra, 2010), the author provides a similar calculation to previous studies, but for electrical equipment. In X. Tafunell and A. Carreras: 'La América Latina y el Caribe en 1913 y 1925. Enfoque desde las importaciones de bienes de capital', *El Trimestre Económico*, 75:3 (2008), pp. 715–53, a quantitative estimation – non serial, but more comprehensive – includes investment in capital goods in general.
5. United Nations, *System of National Accounts 1993* (Washington, DC: International Monetary Fund/World Bank/Commission of European Communities, 1993). For Latin America from 1900 onwards, A. Hofman, *The Economic Development of Latin America in the Twentieth Century* (Cheltenham: Edward Elgar, 2000).
6. J. B. De Long and L. Summers, 'Equipment Investment and Economic Growth', *Quarterly Journal of Economics*, 106:2 (1991), pp. 445–502; X. Sala-i-Martin, 'I Just Ran Two Million Regressions', *American Economic Review*, 87:2 (1997), pp. 178–83; J. Temple and H. J. Voth, 'Human Capital, Equipment Investment, and Industrialization', *European Economic Review*, 42:7 (1998), pp. 1343–62; and L. Qui, 'The Relationship

between Growth, Total Investment and Inward FDI: Evidence from Time Series Data', *International Review of Applied Economics*, 21:1 (2007), pp. 119–33.

7. The assumption of the representative nature of the G3 in importations of equipment goods is weighed up in Tafunell and Carreras, 'Latin America and the Caribbean'. Several authors have insisted that domestic production of these types of goods was irrelevant, and that, therefore, it is valid to use importation data as an approximation for capital formation. See, for example, for Brazil, W. Suzigan, *Indústria brasileira: Origem e desenvolvimento* (Sao Paulo: Editora HUCITEC/DA UNICAMP, 2000) p. 384; and for Mexico, S. Haber, 'Mercado interno, industrialización y banca, 1890–1929', in S. Kuntz Ficker (ed.), *Historia económica general de México. De la Colonia a nuestros días* (Mexico City: El Colegio de México/Secretaría de Economía, 2010), p. 417.

8. See note 4, above.

9. The German and American statistics are far more detailed than those of the United Kingdom, which does not make it difficult to exclude equipment goods not destined for mining or for industry. We must bear in mind that the United States almost immediately came to lead the sales of modern devices used in the service sector.

10. American statistics clearly distinguish household appliances in the second half of the 1920s. Possibly, prior to this date sales were of little importance, particularly in Latin American markets. British and German trade statistics do not detail these types of goods, or they do not do so appropriately. The problem of household appliances aside, it must be remembered that there was electrical material which could have been both a consumer good and an investment good, such as lamps and light bulbs. We can assume that in aggregate terms, the magnitude of electrical investment goods was far superior to that of electrical consumer goods. In any case, it is worth pointing out that electrical machinery does not figure among the former, since industrial machinery includes electrical and non-electrical alike.

11. The compound annual growth rates of investment in machinery and other equipment goods for significant periods are as follows:

Years	AL-9	AL-20.
1890–1929	5.0	5.1.
1890–1913	5.2	5.2.
1913–1929	4.8	4.9.
1890–1900	−1.1	−0.7.
1901–1913	11.1	10.8.
1913–1920	0.0	0.4.
1921–1929	8.9	8.0.

12. For the Brazilian case, Suzigan, *Indústria brasileira*, pp. 87, 124 and 250–9.

13. A. Dye, *Cuban Sugar in the Age of Mass Production: Technology and the Economics of the Sugar Central, 1899–1929* (Palo Alto, CA: Stanford University Press, 1998); and A. Santamaría, *Sin azúcar no hay país. La industria azucarera y la economía cubana (1919–1939)* (Sevilla: CSIC, 2001).

14. The Argentinean situation appears highly exceptional. It became, along with Canada, the main foreign market for the United States' powerful agricultural machinery industry. The Argentinian investment structure was incomparable even with its small neighbour Uruguay, though they shared some strong likenesses. Although it is not possible to determine the quantity of agricultural and industrial machinery which Uruguay bought from Britain, American exports of these goods have been quantified. The calculation yields a

proportion that is not lower than for the AL-9, Argentina excluded, but instead, higher: the value of industrial machinery quadrupled that of agricultural machinery.

15. Two recent essays which defend this viewpoint can be found in R. Salvucci 'Export-Led Industrialization' and S. Haber 'The Political Economy of Industrialization', in Bulmer-Thomas, Coatsworth and Cortés Conde (eds), *Cambridge Economic History*. I myself have held the optimistic thesis in a study on the early development of the cement industry in X. Tafunell 'On the Origins of ISI: The Latin American Cement Industry, 1900–1930', *Journal of Latin American Studies*, 39:2 (2007), pp. 299–328.

16. Bulmer-Thomas, in his detailed and solid interpretative global study of the region, adds Peru and Uruguay to the aforementioned countries, pointing out that in Colombia and Venezuela only 'modest beginnings' were visible. Bulmer-Thomas, *The Economic History*, p. 180. Nevertheless, there are many nuances to his perspective: 'Despite the recent interest in early industrialization efforts in Latin America, it is difficult to escape the conclusion that the results were modest before the First World War', p. 136. Chile provides us with an example of conflicting viewpoints. Mamalakis sustains that the early development of the national industry was curbed by its poor efficiency, resulting in it being replaced by foreign industry. See M. J. Mamalakis, *The Growth and Structure of the Chilean Economy: From Independence to Allende* (New Haven, CT: Yale University Press, 1976) pp. 16 and 71–2. But other authors, like Palma, have argued that the process of industrial imports substitution started long before 1930. See G. Palma: 'From an Export-Led to an Import-Substituting Economy: Chile 1914–39', in R. Thorp (ed), *An Economic History of Twentieth-Century Latin America, Vol. 2, Latin America in the 1930s: The Role of the Periphery in World Crisis* (Houndmills: Palgrave/St Antony's College, 2000) pp. 43–4 and 51–5.

17. M. Rubio, 'The Role of Mexico in the First World Oil Shortage: 1918–1922: An International Perspective', *Revista de Historia Económica – A Journal of Iberian and Latin American Economic History*, 24:1 (2006) pp. 69–96, and its bibliography. For Colombia, see M. Wilkins, 'Multinational Oil Companies in South America in the 1920s: Argentina, Bolivia, Brazil, Chile, Colombia, Ecuador and Peru', *Business History Review*, 48:3 (1974) pp. 414–46; and D. Montaña, *La industria del petróleo en Colombia. Síntesis de su proceso historic* (Botorá: Tunja, 1975).

18. K. J. Mitchener and M. D. Weidenmier, 'The Baring Crisis and the Great Latin American Meltdown of the 1890s', *The Journal of Economic History*, 68:2 (2008), pp. 462–500.

19. Bulmer-Thomas, *The Economic History*, pp. 146–51.

20. This evolution tallies with the thesis defended by Haber, who in a recent study of the industrializing process in Mexico until 1929, maintains that this was the result of the growth of the export sector during the decades of the dictatorship of Porfirio Díaz, and that after the revolution and the civil war, it experienced a slowdown, which the author attributes to reduced growth opportunities once national industry substituted importations. See Haber, 'Mercado interno', pp. 412 and 431.

21. For the entire period, agricultural machinery acquired by Argentina made up 64 percent of the agricultural machinery exported by the G-3 to the AL-9.

22. What contributed to this, both in the case of Colombia and of Peru, was the 'dance of the millions' in the second half of the 1920s, that is, the massive influx of foreign capital to preferentially finance infrastructures. See R. Thorp and C. Londoño, 'The Effect of the Great Depression on the Economies of Peru and Colombia', in Thorp (ed.), *An Economic History of Twentieth-Century*, p. 72. With regards the parallelism in the construction of the railways see F. Polo, 'El ferrocarril en Colombia, Venezuela y Ecuador

(1855–1995): un análisis comparativo', in J. Sanz (ed), *Historia de los ferrocarriles de Iberoamérica (1837–1995)* (Madrid: Ministerio de Fomento, 1998), pp. 211–48. Very recently, Safford has insisted on the idea that the lack of development of transport in Colombia during the nineteenth century was possibly the most deciding factor in its economic backwardness. See F. Safford, 'El problema de los transportes en Colombia en el siglo XIX', in A. Meisel and M.T. Ramírez (eds), *Economía colombiana del siglo XIX* (Mexico City: Banco de la República/FCE, 2010), p. 523.

23. If we consider the length of the railway lines per inhabitant in 1913, Colombia was at the tail end, followed by Venezuela. Of the remaining countries making up the AL-9, Guatemala and Peru were in last place. See W. Summerhill, 'The Development of Infrastructure', in Bulmer-Thomas, Coatsworth and Cortés Conde (eds), *Cambridge Economic History*, p. 307.

24. The investment boom led to the appearance of innumerable unrealizable projects such as the 'railways to the moon' and unbridled speculation which ended with the Baring crisis of 1890. See A. Rodríguez, 'El ferrocarril en la Cuenca del Plata', in Sanz (ed.), *Historia de los ferrocarriles*, p. 136. The enormous investment cycle was possible thanks to a flow of foreign capital of extraordinary magnitude, possibly larger, relative to GDP, than any emerging economy has experienced. See A. Taylor, 'Capital accumulation', in G. Della Paolera and A. M. Taylor (eds), *A New Economic History of Argentina* (Cambridge: Cambridge University Press, 2003), p. 173.

25. Tafunell, 'The Electric Revolution'.

26. In keeping with this fact, the electric company which led the electrification of Argentina and Chile, like Uruguay (the group of the German firm German Transatlantic Electric Company) became the most important direct industrial investment outside of Germany. See W. Hausman, P. Hertner and M. Wilkins (eds), *Global Electrification: Multinational Enterprise and International Finance in the History of Light and Power, 1878–2007* (Cambridge: Cambridge University Press, 2008), p. 100.

27. Tafunell, 'La inversión en equipo' and 'Capital Formation'.

28. This empirical contribution would instead endorse Bulmer-Thomas's interpretation that in the case of Central American economies, once normality was restored after the World War, the elites of these countries prepared themselves to reestablish the traditional agro-export model. V. Bulmer-Thomas, *The Political Economy of Central America since 1920* (Cambridge: Cambridge University Press, 1987), and 'Central America in the Inter-War Period', in Thorp (ed.), *An Economic History of Twentieth-Century*, pp. 244–72.

29. We must bear in mind Cuba's early economic development before the beginning of electricity. For example, the Cuban railways were built out so early that already in 1860 80 per cent of sugar production (the economic base of the island) was transported by railway. O. Zanetti and A. García, *Caminos para el azúcar* (La Habana: Editorial de Ciencias Sociales,1987), p. 98. At that moment, half of the railway lines in Latin America were to be found in the small territory of Cuba. J. Sanz: 'Conclusiones generales', in Sanz (ed.), 'Historia de los ferrocarriles', p. 375.

5 Factorial Distribution of Income in Latin America, 1950–2000

1. F. Rodriguez, 'Factor Shares and Resource Booms: Accounting for the Evolution of Venezuelan Inequality', in G. A. Cornia (ed), *Inequality, Growth, and Poverty in an Era of Liberalization and Globalization* (Helsinki: UNU/WIDER, 2005); J. Graña, 'Distribución Factorial del Ingreso en la Argentina, 1935–2005', Working Paper 8 (Buenos

Aires: Instituto de Investigaciones Económicas, Universidad de Buenos Aires, December 2007); J. Lindenboim, 'Distribución funcional del ingreso, un tema olvidado que reclama atención', *Problemas del Desarrollo, Revista Latinoamericana de Economía*, 39:153 (2008), pp. 83–117.

2. F. Rodriguez, and D. Ortega, 'Are Capital Shares Higher in Poor Countries? Evidence from Industrial Surveys', *Wesleyan Economics Working Papers*, 23 (2006), pp. 1–41; E. Frankema, 'Reconstructing Labor Income Shares in Argentina, Brazil and Mexico, 1870–2000', *Revista de Historia Económica*, 28:2 (2010), pp. 343–74.

3. J. G. Williamson, 'Real Wages, Inequality and Globalization in Latin America before 1940', *Revista de Historia Económica*, 17 (1999), pp. 101–42; L. Bértola, L. C. Castelnovo, J. Rodriguez. and H. Willebald, 'Income Distribution in the Latin American Southern Cone during the First Globalization Boom, ca: 1870–1920', *Working Papers in Economic History*, WP 08–05 (Madrid: Universidad Carlos III de Madrid 2008).

4. J. Rodriguez, 'Los tiempos de la desigualdad. La distribución del Ingreso en Chile, entre la larga duración, la globalización y la expansión de la frontera, 1860–1930' (Master dissertation, Universidad de la República, Montevideo, 2009).

5. B. Kliksberg, 'Desigualdad y desarrollo en América Latina: El debate postergado', *Reforma y Democracia*, 14 (1999), pp. 1–48.

6. J. De Gregorio, 'Economic Growth in Latin America', *Journal of Development Economics*, 39:1 (1992), pp. 59–84; B. Bernanke and R. Gürkaynak, 'Is Growth Exogenous? Taking Mankiw, Romer, and Weil Seriously', *NBER Macroeconomics Annual*, 16 (2001), pp. 11–57.

7. I. Diwan, 'Labor Shares and Financial Crises', *The World Bank Working Paper*, Preliminary draft (November 1999).

8. See E. Bakir and A. Campbell, 'The Effect of Neoliberalism on the Fall in the Rate of Profit in Business Cycles', *Review of Radical Political Economics*, 38:3 (Summer 2006), pp. 365–73; L. Ellis and K. Smith, 'The Global Upward Trend in the Profit Share', *Bank for International Settlements Working Papers* 231, Monetary and Economic Department (2007), pp. 1–23; D. Ortega and F. Rodriguez, 'Openness and factor shares' (Caracas: Office of Economic and Financial Advisors (OAEF), National Assembly of Venezuela, October 2002); N. Berthold, R. Fehn and E. Thode, 'Falling Labor Share and Rising Unemployment: Long-Run Consequences of Institutional Shocks?', *German Economic Review*, 3:4 (2002), pp. 431–59; A. E. Harrison, *Has Globalization Eroded Labor's Share? Some Cross-Country Evidence* (University of California at Berkeley and NBER, 2002), pp. 1–43; F. Jaumotte and I. Tytell. 'How Has the Globalization of Labor Affected the Labor Income Share in Advanced Countries?', *International Monetary Fund Working Paper* WP/07/298 (2007), pp. 1–54.

9. Gollin, D., 'Getting Income Shares Right', *Journal of Political Economy*, 110:2 (2002), pp. 458–72.

10. A. Harberger, and D. Wisecarver, 'Private and Social Returns to Capital in Uruguay', *Economic Development and Cultural Change*, 25:3 (1977), pp. 411–45; De Gregorio, 'Economic Growth in Latin America'; A. Krueger, 'Measuring Labor's Share', *American Economic Review*, 89:2 (May, 1999).

11. De Gregorio, 'Economic Growth in Latin America'; V. J. Elias, *Sources of Growth: A Study of Seven Latin American Economies,* (International Center for Economic Growth, 1992); A. Young, 'The Tyranny of Numbers: Confronting the Statistical Realities of the East Asian Growth Experience', *Quarterly Journal of Economics*, 110 (1995), pp. 641–80.

12. Bernanke and Gürkaynak, 'Is Growth Exogenous?'.

13. Ortega and Rodriguez, 'Openness and factor shares'.
14. Harrison, *Has Globalization Eroded Labor's Share?*.
15. Rodriguez and Ortega, 'Are Capital Shares Higher in Poor Countries? Evidence from Industrial Surveys'; R. Agacino (ed.), 'Crecimiento y distribución funcional del ingreso en la industria chilena. Un análisis sectorial' (Santiago de Chile: Informe De Investigación FONDECYT, 1996).
16. Frankema, 'Reconstructing Labor Income Shares'.
17. Young, A., 'The Tyranny of Numbers'.
18. The 4th Revision of the System of National Accounts (1993 SNA) includes a 'Mixed Income' category where the income of the own-account workers is accounted for. Even if the 'shadow wage' and the operating surplus are still confounded, this provides some idea of the weight of the sector and a clear interval in which to apply the estimation of shadow wage.
19. As argued in D. Gollin, 'Getting Income Shares Right'.
20. And, in the gross measurement, the capital depreciation is also included. It is a broad measurement: pre-direct taxes, the benefits, rents and interest are confounded, etc. For a revision of the differences between benefits and gross operating surplus, see J. Chan-Lee and H. Sutch, 'Profits and Rates of Return', *OECD Economics Department Working Papers*, 5 (Autumn 1985), pp. 127–67; and F. Lequiller and D. Blades, *Understanding National Accounts* (Paris: OECD Publishing, 2006).
21. For further details, see V. Neira, 'Distribución factorial del ingreso en América Latina, 1950–2000: nuevas series a partir de las cuentas nacionales', paper presented at the Second Latin-American Congress of Economic History, Mexico City (2010), which provide in annex full details of the procedure and national series.
22. The general criteria are: a) temporal: as the data published subsequently could include corrections and revisions of the accounts we can expect a better reliability (besides, the last years of a published series are less reliable or are estimations even where not explicitly stated); b) contextual: coincidence of different sources, plausibility of strong jumps in the series, internal coherence of the primary distribution of income tables, etc. It is possible that this process, in some specific cases, has smoothed real cycles, but avoiding this risk demands a complete study of other macro variables. Such is beyond the scope of this paper.
23. When the change of the base year introduces a jump in series, we assume that the value of the first year of the new series is correct and the gap is due to the time-growing distortion of the previous indices. Thus, we have assumed that the first value of the previous series is correct too, and we weigh the intermediate values according to their time-proximity of each base year.
24. Neira, 'Distribución factorial del ingreso en América Latina'.
25. ECLAC, 'Estado de avance de la aplicación del SCN 1993 en América Latina y el Caribe', Documento de referencia DDR/1, Tercera reunión de la Conferencia Estadística de las Américas de la Comisión Económica para América Latina y el Caribe (Santiago de Chile: 2005).
26. Gollin, 'Getting Income Shares Right'.
27. For recent years, they can be complemented by labour force surveys (LFS), especially in some countries where such surveys were done more frequently. However, there exist important discrepancies between census and LFS, so it is more reliable to only use one of them. We use the censuses because they provide information for early years.
28. I estimated a *CLSh* for Chile, which includes sectorial-wage gaps, but the effects on the results are modest. I hope to improve and present this study soon.

29. Gollin, 'Getting Income Shares Right', for Bolivia and Ecuador; and Harrison, *Has Globalization Eroded Labor's Share?*, for a more extensive sample of countries.
30. Ibid., p. 17, raises the point that in Gollin's sample the underdeveloped countries are under-represented, and thus, the weight of the developed countries in the sample is the cause of the apparent stability of the FD concluded by the author.
31. For example, between 1987 and 2006, the auxiliary family workers represented 0.18% of the employed population. In 1991, the E.U's values fluctuate between 2% for Spain, and 0.7% for the UK.
32. P. Sáinz, and A. Calcagno, 'En busca de otro modelo de desarrollo', *CEPAL Review*, 48 (1992).
33. Gollin, 'Getting Income Shares Right'; Bernanke and Gürkaynak, 'Is Growth Exogenous?'.
34. For example Rodriguez, 'Factor shares and resource booms'.
35. Ibid.
36. A. Guscina, 'Effects of Globalization on Labor's Share in National Income', *International Monetary Fund Working Paper* WP/06/294 (Western Hemisphere Department. 2006), pp. 1–33; S. Bentolila and G. Saint-Paul, 'Explaining Movements in the Labour Share', *Contributions to Macroeconomics* 3:1 (2003), pp. 1–31.
37. P. Sáinz and A. Calcagno, 'En busca de otro modelo de desarrollo'; Cornia, G. A., *Liberalization, Globalization and Income Distribution* (Helsinki: World Institute for Development Economics Research, United Nations University, 1999); N. Giammarioli, J. Messina, T. Steinberger, y C. Strozzi. 'European Labor Share Dynamics: An Institutional Perspective', *European University Institute Economics Working Papers* N 2002/13 (2002), pp. 1–30.
38. F. Rodriguez, 'Inequality, redistribution, and rent-seeking', *Economics and Politics*, 16:3 (2004), pp. 287–320.

6 The Influence of the First World War on the Economies of Central America, 1900–29

1. Based on my PhD thesis: F. H. Notten, 'La influencia de la Primera Guerra Mundial sobre las economías de Centroamérica. Un enfoque desde el comercio exterior (1900–1929)' (PhD Thesis, University of Barcelona, 2009). This paper was presented at the World Economic History Congress (WEHC) in Utrecht, 2009. As a research assistant of the project Importaciones y modernización económica en América Latina, 1890–1960, I would like to acknowledge its members for all comments received during my investigation and Sandra Kuntz for her valuable input during the WEHC in Utrecht 2009. I would also like to thank Xavier Tafunell, tutor of my PhD thesis, for giving me ideas and criticisms during the investigation.
2. See for example: R. Thorp, *Progress, Poverty and Exclusion: An Economic History of Latin America in the Twentieth Century* (Baltimore, MD: Johns Hopkins University Press, 1998), pp. 97–100; V. Bulmer-Thomas, *La historia económica de América Latina desde la independencia* (Mexico City: Fondo de Cultura Económica, 1998), p. 188; M. Samper Kutchbach, 'Los productores directos en el siglo del café', *Revista de la Universidad de Costa Rica*, 4:7 (July–December 1978), p. 184–5; L. Hearst, 'Coffee Industry of Central America', *Economic Geography*, 8:1 (1932), p. 65–6; T. Schoonover, 'Imperialism in Middle America: United States, Britain, Germany and France Compete for Transit Rights

and Trade 1820s–1920s', in R. Jeffreys-Jones (ed.), *Eagle against Empire, American Opposition to European Imperialism* (Aix-en-Provence: Université de Provence, 1983), pp. 41–58, on p. 50; R. L. Woodward, *Central America, a Nation Divided* (New York: Oxford University Press, 1975) pp. 158 and 184.

3.	A. Carreras, M. Folchi, A. Hofman, M. Rubio, X. Tafunell and C. Yáñez, 'Importaciones y modernización económica en América Latina durante la primera mitad del siglo XX. Las claves de un programa de investigación', *Serie estudios estadísticos y prospectivos*, 44, CEPAL (2006).

4.	V. Bulmer-Thomas, *The Political Economy of Central America since 1920* (New York: Cambridge University Press, 1987), p. 42; A. C. Román Trigo, 'El comercio exterior de Costa Rica (1883–1930)' (thesis, Universidad de Costa Rica, 1978), pp. 320–23; Woodward, *Central America, a Nation Divided*, p. 163. In general, foreign direct investments and loans were too small to finance a structural balance of trade deficit. See Notten, 'La influencia de la Primera Guerra Mundial', chapters 5 and 6. M. Samper Kutchbach, 'Café, trabajo y sociedad en Centroamérica (1870–1930): una historia común y divergente', in V. H. Acuña Ortega (ed), *Historia general de Centroamérica. Las repúblicas agroexportadoras (1870–1945)* (Madrid: Ediciones Siruela S.A., 1993), vol. 4, p. 32.

5.	R. Thorp, *Progress, Poverty and Exclusion: An Economic History of Latin America in the 20th Century* (Washington, DC: Inter-American Development Bank, 1998), pp. 97–8.

6.	Costa Rica: Dirección General de Estadística, *Anuario Estadístico* (San José, Imprenta Nacional, 1927); El Salvador: Dirección General de Estadística, *Anuario Estadístico* (San Salvador, tipografía 'La Unión' de Dutriz Hnos, 1924 and 1925); Dirección General de Estadística, *Estadística Comercial* (San Salvador, tipografía 'La Unión' de Dutriz Hnos, several years); UK: Department of Overseas Trade, *Survey of Economic and Financial Conditions in the Republics of Honduras, Nicaragua, El Salvador and Guatemala, 1921–1922* (London: HMSO, 1923); Guatemala: Secretaria de Hacienda y Crédito Público, *Memoria* (Guatemala City: Tipografía Nacional, several years).

7.	Notten, 'La influencia de la Primera Guerra Mundial', see chapters 3 and 4 for a detailed analysis of the quality of the foreign trade statistics of the Central American republics. In the appendix on chapter 7 I explain why, in this particular case, it is better to work with Central American trade statistics instead of those of its main trading partners.

8.	A. Carreras and X. Tafunell, 'La América Latina y el Caribe en 1913 y 1925. Enfoque desde las importaciones de bienes de capital', *El Trimestre Económico*, 75:3 (2008), pp. 715–53.

9.	To obtain constant prices, I have used the methodology of X. Tafunell, 'Capital formation in machinery in Latin America, 1890–1930', *Journal of Economic History*, 69:4 (2009), pp. 928–50.

10.	Fossil energy: all kinds of oils (gasoline, benzene, kerosene, petrol, etc.) and coals. Modern energy includes fossil energy and hydroelectricity.

11.	M. Rubio, C. Yáñez, M. Folchi and A. Carreras, 'Energy as an Indicator of Modernization in Latin America, 1890–1925', *Economic History Review*, 63:3 (2010), pp. 769–804.

12.	M. Rubio, 'Economía, energía y CO2 en América Latina: los comienzos del siglo XX', paper presented during el Primer Congreso Latinoamericano de Historia Económica, Montevideo, Uruguay (2007), p. 9.

13.	Notten, 'La influencia de la Primera Guerra Mundial'.

14.	X. Tafunell, 'La reconstrucción del consumo hidroeléctrico en América Latina en el primer tercio del siglo XX', in M. del M. Rubio and R. Bertoni (eds), *Energía y desar-*

rollo en el largo siglo XX: Uruguay en el marco latinoamericano (Montevideo: Universitat Pompeu Fabra and Universidad de La República, 2008), pp. 73–80.

15. M. Folchi and M. Rubio, 'El consumo de energía fósil y la especifidad de la transición energética en América Latina, 1900–1930', paper presented for the International Economic History Congress, Helsinki, Finland (2006).

16. Ibid.

17. Dirección General de Estadística, *Anuario Estadístico* (San José: Imprenta Nacional 1927), pp. 510–17.

18. F. H. Notten, 'La transición energética en Costa Rica y sus consecuencias', *Revista de Historia*, 53–4 (2006).

19. Bulmer-Thomas, 'The Political Economy of Central America', pp. 5–7.

20. X. Tafunell, 'On the Origins of ISI: The Latin American Cement Industry, 1900–30', *Journal of Latin American Studies*, 39:2 (2007), p. 320.

21. Tafunell, 'On the Origins of ISI', p. 323.

22. According to Bulmer-Thomas, 'The political economy of Central America', appendix, during the 1920s, Central American agricultural exports share of GDP only surpassed 30 per cent in the case of Honduras towards the end of the decade.

23. Notten, 'La influencia de la Primera Guerra Mundial'.

24. Bulmer-Thomas, 'The Political Economy of Central America', p. 39; and 'Economic Development over the Long Run, Central America since 1920', *Journal of Latin American Studies*, 15:2 (1983), p. 286.

25. Notten, 'La influencia de la Primera Guerra Mundial', chapter 7.

26. R. Facio, *Estudio sobre economía costarricense* (San José: Editorial Costa Rica, 1990), p. 104.

27. Notten, 'La influencia de la Primera Guerra Mundial', chapter 1.

28. C. Hall, and H. Pérez Brignoli, *Historical atlas of Central América* (Norman, OK: University of Oklahoma Press, 2003), p. 197.

29. Bulmer-Thomas, 'The Political Economy of Central America', p. 20.

30. See for example, Guatemala: *Secretaria de Hacienda y Crédito Público, Memoria* (Guatemala City: Tipografía Nacional, several years), p. 5; UK: Department of Overseas Trade, *Survey of Economic and Financial Conditions in the Republics of Honduras, Nicaragua, El Salvador and Guatemala, 1921–1922* (London: HMSO, 1923), p. 60.

31. See for example, M. Samper Kutchbach, 'Café, trabajo y sociedad en Centroamérica', p. 28. Samper even writes about the 'mono-cultivation' of coffee in El Salvador. See also C. Cardoso, 'Historia económica del café en Centro América: siglo XIX, estudio comparativo', *Estudios Sociales Centroamericanos*, 4:10 (1975), p. 54.

32. Dirección General de Estadística, *Anuario Estadístico* (San Salvador: tipografía 'La Unión' de Dutriz Hnos, several years).

33. H. Pérez Brignoli, 'Las economías centroamericanas, 1860–1940', in E. Cárdenas, J. A. Ocampo and R. Thorp (eds), *La era de las exportaciones latinoamericanas de fines del siglo XIX a principios del XX* (México City: Fondo de Cultura Económica, 2003), p. 130.

34. D. A. Luna, *Manual de historia económica de El Salvador* (San Salvador: Editorial Universitaria de El Salvador, 1971), p. 227.

35. A. M. Frassinetti, 'Economía primaria exportadora y formación del proletariado. El caso centroamericano (1850–1920)', *Economía Política*, 19 (1981), p. 56.

36. Pérez Brignoli, 'Las economías centroamericanas', p. 131.

37. M. Posas, 'La plantación bananera en Centroamérica (1870–1929)', in Acuña Ortega (ed.), 'Historia general de Centroamérica', p. 112.

38. Posas, 'La plantación bananera en Centroamérica', p. 150.
39. J. Dunkerley, *Power in the Isthmus: A Political History of Modern Central America* (London: Verso, 1988), pp. 67–8.
40. Frassinetti, 'Economía primaria exportadora'; and Cardoso, 'Historia económica del café' ignore Nicaragua completely in their comparative economic histories of Central America, while Thorp, 'Progress, poverty and exclusion', p. 85, denies the liberal reforms of the country.
41. Hall and Pérez Brignoli, 'Historical Atlas of Central América', p. 203.
42. Samper Kutchbach, 'Café, trabajo y sociedad en Centroamérica', p. 22.
43. J. Weeks, *The Economies of Central America* (New York and London: Holmes and Meier, 1985), pp. 22–4; C. Cardoso, 'The liberal era, c. 1870–1930', in L. Bethell (ed.), *Central America since Independence* (New York: Cambridge University Press, 1991), p. 65; Dunkerley, 'Power in the Isthmus', pp. 68–9.

7 Economic Modernization in Adverse Institutional Environments

1. D. C. North, W. Summerhill and B. Weingast, 'Order, Disorder and Economic Change: Latin America vs. North America', in B. Bueno de Mesquita and H. Root (eds), *Governing for Prosperity* (New Haven, CT: Yale University Press, 2000), pp. 17–58.
2. S. Haber, *Crony Capitalism and Economic Growth in Latin America: Theory and Evidence* (Stanford: Hoover Institution Press, 2002).
3. J. Coatsworth, 'Economic and Institutional Trajectories in Nineteenth-Century Latin America', in J. Coatsworth and A. Taylor (eds), *Latin America and the World Economy Since 1800* (Cambridge: Harvard University Press, DRCLAS, 1998), pp. 23–54.
4. A. Maddison, *The World Economy: A Millennial Perspective* (Paris: OECD, 2001).
5. S. Haber, *How Latin America Fell Behind: Essays on the Economic Histories of Brazil and Mexico, 1800–1914* (Palo Alto, CA: Stanford University Press, 1997).
6. L. Prados de la Escosura, 'The Economic Consequences of Independence in Latin America', in V. Bulmer-Thomas, J. Coatsworth and R. Cortés Conde (eds), *The Cambridge Economic History of Latin America* (Cambridge: Cambridge University Press, 2006), vol. 1, pp. 463–504.
7. Coatsworth, 'Economic and Institutional Trajectories', p. 33.
8. S. Engerman, and K. J. Sokoloff, 'Factor Endowments, Institutions, and Differential Paths of Growth among New World Economies: A View from Economic Historians of the United States', in Haber (ed.), *How Latin America Fell Behind*, pp. 260–304.
9. Recently was published D. C. North, B. Weingast and J. J. Wallis, *Violence and Social Orders: A Conceptual Framework for Interpreting Recorded Human History* (Cambridge: Cambridge University Press, 2009), the most ambitious effort to interpret the causes of economic progress (or lack thereof) from a historical long-term perspective. The idea of a natural state, presented in the paper of 2005, proposes that forms of state, in the sense of political regime, which have not been able to move from the representation of a coalition of dominant private interests, act as an obstacle to economic development in that they impede the functioning of competitive markets with open competition. We will not be able to comment on this hypothesis here, but what has come to the fore is an idea which could have enormous relevance in the cases of Cuba and Chile.
10. J. Lynch, *The Origin of Latin American Revolution* (New York: Alfred A. Knopf, 1965); L. Prados de la Escosura and S. Amaral (eds), *La independencia americana: Consecuencias económicas* (Madrid: Alianza Editorial, 1993).

11. L. Bergad, F. Iglesias and C. Barcia (eds), *The Cuban Slave Market, 1790–1880* (New York: Cambridge University Press, 1995).

12. M. Góngora, *Origen de los 'inquilinos' del Valle Central* (Santiago: Editorial Universitaria, 1960); A. J. Bauer, *Chilean Rural Society: From the Spanish Conquest to 1930* (Cambridge: Cambridge University Press, 1975); G. Salazar, *Labradores, peones y proletarios. Formación y crisis de la sociedad popular chilena del siglo XIX* (Santiago: Ediciones Sur, 1985).

13. The personality of the leader of the sugar aristocracy or 'sacarócrata', to use the term coined by Moreno Fraginals, has been commented on by leading experts on Cuban economic history over the last two generations, from Julio Le Riverend, Historia económica de Cuba, La Habana: Edición Revolucionaria, 1974); to L. Marrero, *Cuba. Economía y Sociedad* (Madrid: Playor, 1972), vol. 11; M. Moreno Fraginals, 'El Ingenio', *Complejo económico social cubano del azúcar*, 3 vols (La Habana: Ciencias Sociales, 1978), and the more recent studies of A. Santamaría García and A. García Álvarez, *Economía y colonia. La economía cubana y la relación con España, 1765–1902* (Madrid: Consejo Superior de Investigaciones Científicas, 2004).

14. P. Fraile and R. and L. Salvucci, 'El caso cubano: exportación e independencia', in L. Prados and S. Amaral (ed.), *La independencia americana*, pp. 31–52.

15. Moreno Fraginals, 'El Ingenio'; and *Cuba/España, España/Cuba. Historia común* (Barcelona: Crítica, 1995).

16. Public Treasury problems were definitive in Spain's acceptance of the drafting of a new colonial treaty (J. Fontana, *La quiebra de la Monarquía Absoluta* (Barcelona: Ariel, 1977); H. Klein and J. Barbier, 'Recents Trends in the Study of Spanish American Colonial Public Finance', *Latin American Research Review*, 23:1 (1988), pp. 35–62; J. M. Fradera, *Gobernar colonias* (Barcelona: Península, 1999)), but the pressure of lobby groups in Spain were effective enough to hold onto dominance over Cuba and Puerto Rico (A. Bahamonde and J. Cayuela, *Hacer las Américas. Las elites coloniales españolas en el siglo XIX* (Madrid: Alianza Editorial, 1992) and J. Cayuela, *Bahía de Ulttramar. España y Cuba en eel siglo XIX* (Madrid: Siglo XXI, 1993)).

17. On this point we follow B. Lavallé, C. Naranjo and A. Santamaría, *La América española (1763–1898). Economía* (Madrid: Editorial Síntesis, 2002), who revise conventional theses on the reforms of the late nineteenth century, and highlight the Spanish Crown's capacity to economically order and exploit the colonies in a context of institutional and structural changes. In brief, they assert that the Bourbon reforms and many of the subsequent modifications in Cuba and Puerto Rica were applied as a last resort to preserve traditional privileges in a context where their continued existence was threatened, at least unless they were modified, adapting to these contexts and making certain concessions. In fact, in continental America these were not sufficient to conserve the Empire, at least in the state it was in when the Napoleonic invasion created a power vacuum.

18. The main threat to Spain came from England. The English occupation of Havana led the Spanish monarchy to support the independence movement of the 'thirteen colonies' of North America and go to war with England between 1796 and 1801 and later between 1804 and 1808. This was followed by the Napoleonic occupation of Spain until 1814.

19. Data from Santamaria García and García Álvarez, 'Economía y colonia', Table I.16.

20. M. Carmagnani, *Los mecanismos de la vida económica en una sociedad colonial. Chile 1680–1830* (Santiago: Dibam, 2001 – the first edition in French is from 1969), Annex p. 327.

21. D. Acemouglu, and J. A. Robinson, *Economic Origins of Dictatorship and Democracy* (Cambridge: Cambridge University Press, 2006).

22. The work of Acemouglu and his collaborators is incredibly rich, and here I have chosen to quote his work which synthesises his contributions prior to 2006.

23. J. Eyzaguirre, *Ideario y ruta de la emancipación chilena* (Santiago: Editorial Universitaria, 1957); S. Collier, *Ideas and Politics of Chilean Independence 1808–1833* (London: Cambridge University Press, 1967); and A. Jocelyn-Holt, *La Independencia de Chile: Tradición, modernidad y mito* (Madrid: Mapfre, 1992).

24. A. De Ramón, *Historia de Chile. Desde la invasión incaica hasta nuestros días (1500–2000)* (Santiago: Catalonia, 2003).

25. J. Barbier, *Reforms and Politics in Bourbon Chile, 1755–1796* (Otawa: University of Otawa Press, 1997 [1980]).

26. Á. Jara, in his book Á. Jara, *Guerra y sociedad en Chile* (Santiago: Editorial Universitaria, 1971), explained with the utmost rigour the function of the border wars in colonial Chilean society. Hereby social conflict was kept outside of the territories controlled by the landowners who were heirs to the colonial conquest.

27. Social exclusion was the path for those who did not submit to the social order. M. Gongora, 'Vagabundaje y sociedad fronteriza en Chile siglos XVII a XIX', *Cuadrenos del Centro de Estudios Socioeconómicos*, 2 (1966), pp. 1–41; Bauer, 'Chilean Rural Society'; B. Loveman, *Chile: The Legacy of Hispanic Capitalism* (New York: Oxford University Press, 1979).

28. Jocelyn-Holt, 'La Independencia de Chile'.

29. In Chilean historiography the 'Portaliano state' has been at the heart of debates throughout the twentieth century until today. Conservative histories such as A. Edwards, *La Fronda Aristocràtica en Chile* (Santiago: Ediciones Ercilla, 1936) and F. Encina, *Nuestra inferioridad económica* (Santiago: Editorial Universitaria, 1955) argued about the impersonal character of the regime established by Portales, whereas Sergio Villalobos in his book S. Villalobos, *Portales. Una falsificación histórica* (Editorial Universitaria, 1989) disputed the personal virtues of the minister and the merits of his management. More recent literature does not dispute the existence of a 'Portaliano order', but does attempt to reinterpret it (A. Jocelyn-Holt, *El peso de la noche. Nuestra frágil fortaleza histórica* (Santiago: Planeta/Ariel, 1997)) as a social order accepted by both the dominant and the dominated during the 'peso de la noche' ('weight of the night'); and Salazar as a simple police and military order – G. Salazar, *Construcción de Estado en Chile (1800–1837). Democracia de los 'pueblos'. Militarismo ciudadano. Golpismo oligárquico* (Santiago: Ediciones Sudamericana, 2005), p. 519.

30. J. Heise González, *Años de formación y aprendizaje político 1810–1833* (Santiago: Editorial Universitaria, 1978); and *150 años de evolución institucional*, 4th edn (Santiago: Editorial. Andrés Bello, 1979).

31. In the nineteenth century the Cuban and Chilean economies faced significant cyclical recessions as a result of the changes in the prices of their export products or the exhaustion of some of their exportable natural resources. For Cuba the most serious problem came when sugar cane had to face competition from the sugar beet. The growing world supply of sugar pressured international prices downwards, forcing Cuba to redouble its productive efforts so as to retain the competitiveness of its production. Added to this was Spanish colonial pressure to finance its public treasury with revenues from Cuban customs houses, which generated the dispute which would lead the Cuban elite to seek the support of the United States in their liberation strategy. In Chile, the silver cycle in

Chañarcillo ended when the mineral ran out, but the opportunities presented with the opening up of Australian and Californian markets replaced silver with wheat and flour exports. All of this came to an end when the United States and Australia began to produce agricultural products which they had previously bought in the South Pacific region. Chile still had the last resort of its copper exportations, but the poor technical evolution of extraction activities prevented it from maintaining international competitiveness. Finally, the nitrate cycle came to sustain the economic boom of the end of the nineteenth century and beginning of the twentieth.

32. Acemouglu and Robinson, 'Economic Origins of Dictatorship'.
33. M. Carmagnani, *Estado y sociedad en América Latina 1850–1930* (Barcelona: Crítica, 1984).
34. The modernizing reforms applied did not simply involve the implementation of technical change. The transformation of the regime of hereditary property was also important for the economic success of both countries. If the objective was to expand natural resources exports to above the levels of the end of the eighteenth century, political power had to be used to remove institutional obstacles of the Old Regime. Arango y Parreño in Cuba and Manuel de Salas in Chile noticed the close link between economic prosperity, the need to reform economic institutions and the protagonism of the elites (Le Riverend, 'Historia económica de Cuba', pp. 154 in the case of Cuba and Barbier, 'Reforms and Politics' in the case of Chile). Fiscal reforms were also consistent with the demands of change. Cuba and Chile managed to escape foreign debt crises and chronic public deficit. It could be said that the fiscal order reinforced the new political order. Cuba kept its public accounts balanced until the 1860s, and was even able to contribute positively to the Spanish accounts (I. Roldán de Montaud, 'España y Cuba. Cien años de relaciones financieras', in A. Bahamonde (ed.), *Cuba y el 98.* monográfico de *Studia Historica. Historia Contemporánea*, 15 (1997), pp. 35–69; and C. Saiz Pastor (1998), 'El imperio de Ultramar y la fiscalidad colonial', in S. Palazón and C. Saiz Pastor (eds), *La ilusión de un imperio. Las relaciones económicas hispano-cubanas en el siglo XIX* (Alicante: Universidad de Alicante, 1998), pp. 31–44)). Cuba, which until 1806 had received the 'Real Situado' from the Mexican treasury, then paid Spain the so-called 'sobrantes de Ultramar', to the sum of 37 million pesos fuertes between 1826 and 1866, according to Roldán de Montaud's calculations. As far as Chile was concerned, having had to resort to British loans in order to deal with the War of Independence, managed to balance its books in the 1830s thanks to Manuel Rengifo's management in the Treasury Ministry, without having to renege on its international commitments as happened in much of Latin America (J. Jofré, R. Lüders and G. Wagner, 'Economía Chilena 1810–1995. Cuentas fiscales', *Documento de Trabajo*, 188, Instituto de Economía, Pontificia Universidad Católica de Chile (2000); and Jofré, Lüders and Wagner. 2000; L. Ortega, *Chile en ruta al capitalismo. Cambio, euforia y depresión 1850–1880* (Santiago: Dibam-Lom, 2005). For both countries, fiscal difficulties appeared at the start of the 1860s.
35. E. A. Wrigley, *Continuity, Chance and Change: The Character of the Industrial Revolution in England* (Cambridge: Cambridge University Press, 1988).
36. C. Yáñez, and J. Jofré, 'Modernización económica y consumo energético en Chile, 1844–1930', *Historia* 396 1:1 (2011), pp. 127–65.
37. A. Maddison, <www.ggdc.net/maddison/Historical_Statistics/horizontal-file_03-2007.xls>.
38. A. Santamaría, 'Las cuentas nacionales de Cuba, 1690–2005', paper presented at the International Congress 'Análisis de series temporales de largo plazo y los problemas del

desarrollo latinoamericano', organised by C. Yáñez in Barcelona, Univertitat Pompeu Fabra, CIDOB and Universitat de Barcelona (1–2 July 2009).

39. Maddison , <www.ggdc.net/maddison/Historical_Statistics> [accessed July 15, 2009].

40. Yáñez and Jofré, 'Modernización económica y consumo energético'.

41. The apparent consumption of modern energies (ACME) consists of the local production of coal and hydroelectricity (in this case only Chile, as Cuba did not have its own production), as well as importations of coal and petroleum, excluding exportations of fossil fuels. For a global view of the ACME of Latin America and the Caribbean between 1890 and 1925, consult M. Rubio, C. Yáñez, M. Folchi and A. Carreras, 'Energy as an indicator of modernization in Latin America, 1890–1925', *Economic History Review*, 63:3 (2010), pp. 769–804.

42. Lavallé, Naranjo and Santamaría, 'La América española'; and Santamaría García and García Álvarez, 'Economía y colonia'.

43. L. Ortega, 'The First Four Decades of the Chilean Coal Mining Industry, 1842–1852', *Journal of Latin American Studies*, 14:2 (1982), pp. 1–32; Yáñez and Jofré , 'Modernización económica y consumo energético'.

44. O. Zanetti and A. García Álvarez, *Sugar and Railroad* (Chapel Hill, NC: North Carolina University Press, 1998).

45. I. Thomson and D. Angerstein, *Historia del ferrocarril en Chile* (Santiago: Dibam, 2000); G. Guajardo, *Tecnología, Estado y ferrocarriles en Chile, 1850–1950* (México: Fundación de los Ferrocarriles Españoles/UNAM, 2008).

46. Moreno Fraginals, 'El Ingenio'.

47. In Cuba, as in Chile, both the railways as well as productive activities adapted modern machinery which used vegetal fuels as an alternative to coal. Sugar cane bagasse and timber from natural forests were used to the limit of their technological viability.

48. Although there are no specific studies on social saving for the Cuban and Chilean railways, we could assume that these cases were no different from those of Brazil, Mexico and subsequently Argentina (W. Summerhill, 'Transport Improvements and Economic Growth in Brazil and Mexico', in Haber (ed.), 'How Latin America Fell Behind', pp. 93–114; A. Herranz, 'The Contribution of Railways to Economic Growth in Latin America before 1914: the Cases of Mexico, Brazil and Argentina', *Documentos de trabajo de la Asociación Española de Historia Económica*, 3 (2009)).

49. The case of Uruguay is probably similar, M. Rubio and Reto Bertoni, *Energía y desarrollo en el largo siglo XX. Uruguay en el marco latinoamericano* (Montevideo: Universitat Pompeu Fabra and Universidad de la República, 2008).

50. Two classic contributions to economic history are particularly relevant in this context: A. Pinto, *Chile un caso de desarrollo frustrado* (Santiago: Editorial Universitaria, 1973); and J. Nadal, *El fracaso de la revolución industrial en España 1814–1913* (Barcelona: Ariel, 1974), suggest that there would be a valid point of comparison between the Latin American leaders and the European peripherals.

51. This is being done in a project led by Albert Carreras of the Universitat Pompeu Fabra and until now has managed to offer new viewpoints from the perspective of energy, Rubio, Yáñez, Carrera and Folchi, 'Energy as an Indicator of Modernization'; and for capital formation X, Tafunell 'Capital Formation in Machinery in Latin America, 1890–1930', *Journal of Economic History*, 69 (2009), pp. 928–50.

52. Rubio and Bertoni, 'Energía y desarrollo en el largo siglo XX'.

53. It would be most interesting in the future to contrast the hypothesis of the existence of a 'natural state' in Latin America, to use the term recently employed by North, Wallis and Weingast, 'Violence and Social Order'.

8 Capital Goods Imports, Machinery Investment and Economic Development in the Long Run

1. Y. Alwyn, 'The Tyranny of Numbers: Confronting the Statistical Realities of the East Asian Growth Experience', *Quarterly Journal of Economics* (August, 1995), pp. 641–80.
2. J. B. De Long, and L. H. Summers, 'Equipment Investment and Economic Growth: How Strong Is the Nexus?', *Brookings Papers on Economic Activity*, 2 (1992), pp. 157–211.
3. Reference is made to the majority of economic aid programmes in the 1950s and 1960s, in Africa and Latin America, which accelerate capital accumulation, but the results in the medium run were unsatisfactorily if compared with the results in South Asian countries. However, several countries with very low or negative growth did not have high rates of investment in relationship with the GDP in the 1960–90 period. M. J. Oliver and D. H. Aldcroft, *Economic Disasters of the Twentieth Century* (Cheltenham: Edward Elgar, 2007).
4. See criticisms regarding the model in W. Easterly, *En busca del crecimiento. Andanzas y tribulaciones de los economistas del desarrollo* (Barcelona: Antoni Bosch Editor, 2003), who argues that the Harrod-Domar model was difficult to apply to the United States and other developed countries. An easy approach to the model as follows.

    The growth rate of the fixed capital stock (K) it will be determined by:

    $$\frac{\Delta K}{K} = \frac{\frac{\Delta K}{Y}}{\frac{K}{Y}} = \frac{S}{k}$$

    When Y is the output, k is the capital-output ratio and is constant. The growth rate of Y is equal to the growth rate of K, that is determined by s and k (savings, $s = k$).
5. One of the major problems in African countries was the evident lack of human capital and the lack of integrated markets, P. Collier and J. W. Gunning, 'Explaining African Economic Performance', *Journal of Economic Literature*, 14 (1999), pp. 64–111.
6. N. G. Mankiw, D. Romer and D. N. Weil, 'A Contribution to the Empirics of Economic Growth', *Quarterly Journal of Economics*, 107:2 (May, 1992), pp. 531–42.
7. The Allen proposal discards that the function used for the Soviet model can be a Cobb Douglas; it is more accurate to use a CES (constant elasticity of substitution) function in the form of $Y_t = A(Kh_t^{-p} + (1-h)L_t^{-p})^{-1/p}$, where Yt is GDP in year t, Kt is capital stock in year t, and Lt is labour in year t. Under this framework, Allen concludes that the substitution elasticity is too low (0.403). Implying that the lack of one factor (in the Soviet case the labour) causes increases in the other factor. R. C. Allen, 'The Rise and Decline of the Soviet Economy', *Canadian Journal of Economics*, 34:4 (2001), pp. 859–81.
8. J. Field, 'The Equipment Hypothesis and US Economic Growth', *Explorations in Economic History*, 44:1 (2006), pp. 43–58.
9. Implicitly equates machinery and equipment growth with IT (information technologies) growth. 'The end of the century surge in equipment investment, much of it IT related, did coincide with an accelerated growth in output per hour'. Ibid.

10. M. Blomstrom, R. E. Lipsey and M. Zejan, 'Is Fixed Investment the Key to Economic Growth?', *The Quarterly Journal of Economics*, 111:1 (1996), pp. 26–76.
11. In the Solow model the production for unity of effective work is in function of capital for unity of effective work. If capital per worker increases, output increases, but with diminishing returns in time.
12. J. Temple, 'Equipment investment and the Solow model', *Oxford Economic Papers*, 50:1 (1998), pp. 39–62.
13. J. B. De Long, 'Productivity Growth and Machinery Investment: A Long-Run Look, 1870–1980', *The Journal of Economic History*, 52:2 (1992), pp. 307–24.
14. Ibid.
15. In accordance with the classic Solow model.
16. Temple, 'Equipment Investment and the Solow model'.
17. J. Temple and H-J. Voth, 'Human Capital, Equipment Investment and Industrialization', *European Economic Review*, 42:7 (1998), pp.1343–62.
18. J. Greenwood, Z. Hercowitz and P. Krusell, 'Long-Run Implications of Investment-Specific Technological Change', *The American Economic Review*, 87:3 (1997), pp. 342–62.
19. The investment in machinery increases more than structures investment because indirect investment in human capital. J. B. De Long and L. H. Summers, 'How Strongly Do Developing Economies Benefit from Equipment Investment?' *Journal of Monetary Economics*, 32 (1993), pp. 395–415, and Temple and Voth, 'Human Capital, Equipment'.
20. J. Temple, 'The New Growth Evidence', *Journal of Economic Literature*, 37 (1999), pp. 112–56.
21. There are precedents of important industrial growth in the 'nitrate phase'.
22. Hofman, *The Economic Development of Latin America in the Twentieth Century* (Cheltenham: Edgard Elgar, 2000).
23. X. Tafunell, 'Capital Formation in Machinery in Latin America, 1890–1930', *Journal of Economic History*, 69:4 (2009), pp. 928–50.
24. A. Ducoing, 'Inversión en maquinaria y crecimiento económico en el largo plazo. Chile 1890–2005' (Thesis Master, Universidad de Barcelona, 2009).
25. The three series are available on request to the authors.
26. Gerschenkron, *Economic Backwardness in Historical Perspective, a Book of Essays* (Cambridge, MA: Harvard University Press,1962).
27. J-W. Lee, 'Capital Goods Imports and Long-Run Growth', *Journal of Developments Economics*, 48 (1995), pp. 91–110.
28. The methodology applied for subdividing the whole period was the following: first calculate the variance.

$$\frac{\sum_{i=1}^{117}(\Delta mch_i - \overline{mch})}{117}$$

where Δmch represents the growth rate of machinery, and 117 is the number of years for the whole period. Then, use the standard deviation to select the two main deviations to establish the three periods indicated above.

$$s = \frac{1}{117}\sqrt{117\sum_{i=1}^{117} mch_i^2 - (\sum_{i=1}^{117} mch_i)^2}$$

The sub-periods found with this methodology coincides with structural breaks in the years 1930 and 1975.

29. De Long and Summers, 'How Strongly Do Developing'.
30. A.C. Kwan, Y. Wu and J. Zhang, 'Fixed Investment and Economic Growth in China', *Economics of Planning*, 32 (1999), pp. 67–79.
31. To test a lag in the case of machinery, as for structures the effect of the infrastructures was estimated using a lag of one year. A. Herranz Loncán, *Infraestructuras y crecimiento económico en España (1850–1935)* (Madrid: Fundación de los Ferrocarriles Españoles, 2008).
32. The results of the Johansen cointegration test were as follows:

None *	34.29285
At most 1	3.823260
At most 2	0.43547
Test stat. **	4.5

    *(**) At 5% of null hypothesis and 1% of null hypothesis respectively.

33. The same model as J. B. De Long and L.H. Summers, 'Equipment Investment and Economic Growth', *Quarterly Journal of Economics*, 106:2 (1991), pp. 445–502, modified for one country in the long run.

$$\sum_{t=1}^{T} \left(y_t - s_t\right)^2 + \lambda \sum_{t=2}^{T-1} \left(s_{t+1} - s_t \right) - \left(s_t - s_{t-1}\right)^2$$

34. The filter is a smoothing method that is widely used among macroeconomist to obtain a smooth estimate of the long-term component of a series. In the equation y, (machinery) series is smoothed minimizing the variance. Granger Causality test for machinery and GDP.
35. Granger Causality test for machinery and GDP.

Null hypothesis:	Obs.	F-Statistic	Probability
machinery does not Granger Cause GDP	21	2.2019324752	0.142975076782
GDP does not Granger Cause machinery		1.10058589469	0.356586643131

36. P. Meller, *Un siglo de economía política chilena (1890–1990)* (Santiago: Editorial Andrés Bello, 1996), pp. 22–47.
37. C. W. J. Granger, 'Investigating Causal Relation by Econometric and Cross-Sectional Method', *Econometrica*, 37 (1969), pp. 424–38.

9 The Sugar Industry, the Forests and the Cuban Energy Transition, From the Eighteenth Century to the Mid-Twentieth Century

1. The author gratefully acknowledges the financial support received for this research which forms part of the Ministerio de Educación y Ciencias de España project: Importaciones y modernización económica en América Latina, 1890–1960 (SEJ2007–60445) co-funded by the European Union through FEDER. The main researchers on the team are: Albert Carreras, André Hofman, César Yáñez, Mar Rubio, Mauricio Folchi and Xavier Tafunell, and the researchers are: Anna Carreras, Carolina Román, Frank Notten, José Jofré and Marc Badia. A previous version of this document was presented at the XIV International Economic History Congress, Helsinki, Finland, 21–25 August 2006 in Session 99: 'Foreign Trade and Economic Growth in Latin America and the Caribbean until the Mid-Twentieth Century: Towards a System of National Accounts'.

2.   J. Coatsworth, 'Economic and Institutional Trajectories in Nineteenth-Century Latin America', in J. Coatsworth and A. M. Taylor (eds), *Latin America and the World Economy since 1800* (Cambridge: Harvard University Press, 1998), pp. 23–54.

3.   K. Sokoloff and S. Engerman, 'History Lessons: Institutions, Factors Endowments, and Paths of Development in the New World', *Journal of Economics Perspectives*, 14:3 (2000), pp. 217–32.

4.   D. S. Landes, *La Riqueza y la Pobreza de las Naciones* (Barcelona: Crítica, 1999).

5.   Q. Do and A. Levchenko, 'Trade, Inequality, and the Political Economy of Institutions', *World Bank Policy Research Working Papers*, 3836 (2006).

6.   Cuban historiography has paid scant attention to the environmental impact of the intensive and extensive sugar industry, particularly on the forests, with the exception of the work of R. Funes, 'Azúcar y deforestación. Una aproximación a la historia ambiental en Cuba', in M. González de Molina and J. M. Alier (eds), *Naturaleza Transformada* (Barcelona: Icaria, 2001), pp. 183–209; 'El espejo de las 'Sugar Islands'. El problema del combustible en los ingenios cubanos hasta mediados del siglo XIX y sus repercusiones paisajísticas', in A. Sabio and I. Iriarte (eds), *La construcción histórica del paisaje agrario en España y Cuba* (Madrid: Historia y Paisaje, Serie Estudios, 2003), pp. 257–83; R. Funes Monzote, *De bosque a sabana. Azúcar, deforestación y medio ambiente en Cuba: 1492–1926* (Mexico City: Siglo veintiuno editores S.A., 2004).

7.   Funes, *De bosque a sabana*, p. 61.

8.   Ibid., p. 40.

9.   Ibid., p. 45, footnote 27.

10. L. Marrero, *Cuba: Economía y Sociedad. Azúcar, Ilustración y Conciencia (1763–1868)* (Madrid: Editorial Playor S.A., 1984), vol. 10, p. 72. It was known as the Real Cédula de montes y plantíos.

11. Marrero, 'Cuba: Economía y Sociedad', vol. 10, p. 156.

12. Coffee production and exportation declined in relative importance in the early 1850s.

13. G. Cabrera, 'Población, Ambiente y Desarrollo en áreas tendientes a la desertificación en Cuba', paper prepared for debate in the meeting of the Asociación de Estudios Latinoamericanos, in the panel discussion: Población, medio ambiente y cambios en el uso de la tierra, Guadalajara (1997), p. 5 indicated that 19.5 per cent of the territory in 1991 was covered by forest, and in 1812 it was 89.2 per cent.

14. 1492 is used as a reference, since the information about the forests taken from Funes, 'Azúcar y deforestación', uses this focal point and because it permits us to have a very long term perspective on the impact of the economic activities being engaged in once the Spanish had occupied the island.

15. M. Moreno Fraginals, *El Ingenio. Complejo Económico Social Cubano del Azúcar* (Barcelona: Crítica, 2001), p. 42.

16. Ibid., p. 43.

17. Funes, 'De bosque a sabana', p. 78.

18. Moreno Fraginals, *El Ingenio*, p. 74. 1796 saw the arrival in Cuba of a steam engine to power the sugar mill.

19. The Spanish system consisted in each boiler for the cooking of the sugar-cane juice having its own direct furnace. By contrast, in the Jamaican system four or five boilers were lined up and the fire was directed along them, thus making the most of all the heat generated, with the minimum consumption of wood.

20. It is estimated that 6,710 hectares of forest were chopped down annually to be burned in the mills, and still more to be used in new factories, Moreno Fraginals, *El Ingenio*, p. 135.

21. The French 'train' became known as the Jamaican 'train' when the Havana-Matanzas region ran out of wood, Moreno Fraginals, *El Ingenio*, pp. 78. Marrero, 'Cuba: Economía y Sociedad', vol. 10. p. 144 points out that these systems became came into general use as from 1830 and this is when they became known as the Jamaican 'train'.

22. Residual sugar-cane after the juice or syrup has been extracted. In Cuba, until the end of the eighteenth century this was considered an industrial right. With the introduction of reverberos or the French 'train', bagasse became widely used as a fuel. (Taken from Moreno Fraginals, *El Ingenio*, p. 603.)

23. This variety was introduced to the island between 1796 and 1798. It has a woodier stem and is taller than the previously existing cane on the island.

24. Marrero, 'Cuba: Economía y Sociedad', vol. 10, p. 158.

25. Funes, 'De bosque a sabana', p. 262.

26. A. Santamaría García and A. García, *Economía y Colonia. La Economía Cubana y la Relación con España, 1765–1902* (Madrid: Consejo Superior de Investigaciones Científicas, 2004), p. 135.

27. Ibid., pp. 137. L. Marrero, *Cuba: Economía y Sociedad. Azúcar, Ilustración y Conciencia (1763–1868)* (Madrid: Editorial Playor S.A., 1985), vol. 12. In the case of coal they indicate that the Spanish customs tariff policy doubled its natural price.

28. Funes, 'De bosque a sabana', p. 26.

29. Marrero, 'Cuba: Economía y Sociedad', vol. 10, p. 61.

30. Ibid., p. 87.

31. *Caballería* is an agrarian unit of measurement. In Cuba, 1 *caballería* = 13.420 hectares. Funes, 'De bosque a sabana', p. 219.

32. Ibid., p. 221.

33. Ibid.

34. Santamaría García and García, 'Economía y Colonia', p. 177.

35. Ibid., p. 183.

36. The distinction used is that made by Funes, 'El espejo de las 'Sugar Islands'', in his article.

37. Marrero, 'Cuba: Economía y Sociedad', vol. 10, p. 179, 80% of the mills were powered by oxen and 0.3% of mills were hydraulic.

38. Marrero, 'Cuba: Economía y Sociedad', vol. 10, p. 159.

39. Funes, 'De bosque a sabana', pp. 217, points out that the introduction of this technological innovation meant that more fuel could be saved compared with the Jamaican boiler system although vaster extensions of sugar-cane fields were needed per farm.

40. Marrero, 'Cuba: Economía y Sociedad', vol. 10, p. 200.

41. Funes, 'De bosque a sabana', pp. 226–7 'the close connection with the promotion of the sugar industry was not the only reason why the railways had an effect on the forests. During the early years the only fuel they used was firewood which came from the trees on the island or was imported from the United States ... In time, most of the railway companies stopped depending on firewood although some used it exclusively or along with other energies sources in the 1880s and 1890s [in addition to being directly used as sleepers in the construction of new lines]... ' (Translation).

42. Funes, 'De bosque a sabana', p. 277.

43. Moreno Fraginals, *El Ingenio*, p. 140.

44. Marrero, 'Cuba: Economía y Sociedad', v. XII, p. 236, footnote 475 twice.

45. Monzote, 'El espejo de las 'Sugar Islands'', p. 278.

46. Santamaría García and García, 'Economía y Colonia', p. 199.

47. Juice obtained from the cane once the bagasse has been got rid of. This is described as raw juice. If the filter cake has also been removed it is known as clear sugar cane juice. A. Santamaría García, *Sin azúcar no hay país. La industria azucarera y la economía cubana (1919–1939)* (Sevilla: Consejo Superior de Investigaciones Científicas, 2001), p. 474.
48. Santamaría García and García, 'Economía y Colonia', pp. 190–1.
49. Ibid., p. 193.
50. Ibid., p. 201. *Arrobas* were a unit of weight between 11 and 16 kilograms.
51. Funes, 'De bosque a sabana', p. 291.
52. Ibid.
53. Information on the consumption of fossil fuels by the sugar industry is not available. Hence I have used as a reference the apparent consumption of fossil energies in the country in order to get an idea of what was happening in the industry. The same applies in the case of prices of these fuels, in order to get a long term idea of trends and so as to have some kind of quantitative indicator which allows one to get an idea of what lies behind the decisions to use substitute fuels in place of firewood.
54. Estimation carried out with information from the database of the project Importaciones y modernización económica en América Latina, 1890–1960, led by A. Carreras at the Universitat Pompeu Fabra.
55. In the mid-nineteenth century a sugar refinery measured up to 1,340 hectares on average, of which nearly half was sugar plantations. In contrast, in 1920 the average size of the 190 refineries was 134,00 hectares and some had 67,000 hectares of sugar-cane plantations, Funes, 'De bosque a sabana', p. 198.
56. Funes, 'De bosque a sabana', p. 340.
57. Ibid., p. 359.
58. Santamaría García and García, 'Economía y Colonia', p. 381.
59. Funes, 'De bosque a sabana', pp. 352–3, footnote 30.
60. This question could probably be clarified by analysing specific cases of refineries during this period, but for the moment this remains beyond the reach of this study.
61. On 13 April President Gerardo Machado signed Decree 495 absolutely prohibiting tree-felling in State or private highlands. This decree was extended until the 1930s, Funes, 'De bosque a sabana', p. 355.
62. Santamaría García, 'Sin azúcar no hay país', p. 381.
63. Funes, 'De bosque a sabana', p. 415.
64. The estimated growth rate for the period 1927–59 is 0.8% annually.
65. In the 1920s an average of 4,491,403 tons of sugar were produced annually, but the following decade this fell by 34.2 per cent. On comparing production levels of the 1930s with those of the 1910s, the former are 8.6 per cent higher.
66. Funes, 'De bosque a sabana', p. 34.
67. Ibid., p. 248.

10 Empirical Debate on Terms of Trade and the Double Factorial Terms of Trade of Colombia, 1975–2006

1. This paper is the result of a research project supported by the Programme Alban, the European Union Programme of High Level Scholarships for Latin America, scholarship No. E06D100950CO.

2. A. Smith, *An Inquiry into the Nature and Causes of the Wealth of Nations* (1776), ed. R. H. Campbell and A. S. Skinner (Oxford: Clarendon, 1976).

3. J. L. Love, 'Economic Ideas and Ideologies in Latin America since 1930', in L. Bethell (ed.), *Ideas and Ideologies in Twentieth Century Latin America* (Cambridge: Cambridge University Press, 1996), p. 208.

4. Where P_p is the price of the exports of the periphery and P_c the price of the exports of the centre. Following the expert literature on the subject, from now on we'll refer to this relation as the net barter terms of trade (NBTT).

5. Where q_p is the labour productivity in the periphery and q_c the labour productivity in the centre.

6. CEPAL, *América Latina: Relación de precios de intercambio* (Santiago: Naciones Unidas, CEPAL, 1976); O. Rodríguez, *La teoría del subdesarrollo de la Cepal* (Mexico City: Siglo veintiuno editores, 1980); J. Spraos, *Inequalising Trade?* (London: Clarendon Press, 1983).

7. From now on we'll refer to this relation as DFTT. By the other hand the simple factorial terms of trade (SFTT) are defined as the product of the NBTT and the labour productivity in the export country. In algebraic terms this is SFTT $= (Pp/Pc) \times qp$.

8. R. Prebisch, 'El Desarrollo Económico de la América Latina y algunos de sus principales problemas', *El Trimestre Económico*, 63:249 (1996), pp. 175–246. Translation made by the author. The original is as follows: 'los ingresos de los empresarios y factores productivos han crecido, en los centros, más que el aumento de la productividad, y en la periferia, menos que el respectivo aumento de la misma' and 'mientras los centros han retenido íntegramente el fruto del progreso técnico de su industria, los países de la periferia les han traspasado una parte del fruto de su propio progreso técnico'.

9. Nevertheless, Spraos argues that although Prebisch recognized the dimension of labour productivity on the subject, he focused its attention on the evolution of the NBTT. Spraos, *Inequalising Trade?*, p. 57.

10. This is common to almost all empirical studies since the 1990s. An important exception is J. A. Ocampo, and M. A. Parra, 'Los términos de intercambio de los productos básicos en el siglo XX', *Revista de la Cepal*, 79 (2003), pp. 7–35.

11. Rodríguez, 'La teoría del subdesarrollo de la Cepal'.

12. The author of this model is Prebisch in El Desarroleo Económico de la América Latina y algunos de sus principales problemas. However, the ongoing literature that explains the poor economic performance of Latin American countries focusing on the volatility of its export prices does not recall this cycling component of the old ECLA model, keeping in mind only what makes reference to the tendency of relative prices. See for example C. Blattman, J. Hwang and J. Williamson, 'Winners and Losers in the Commodity Lottery: the Impact of Terms of Trade Growth and Volatility in the Periphery 1870–1939', *Journal of Development Economics*, 82:1 (2007), pp. 156–79.

13. J. A. Ocampo and M. A. Parra, 'The Commodity Terms of Trade and Their Strategic Implications for Development', in K. S. Jomo (ed.), *Globalization under Hegemony: The Changing World Economy* (New Delhi: Oxford University Press, 2006), pp. 164–94.

14. Of course, this hypothesis is much related with that of Lewis about economies with infinite elasticity of supply of workforce. See A. Lewis, 'World Production, Prices and Trade, 1870–1950', *Manchester School of Economic and Social Studies*, 20 (1952), pp. 105–38.

15. Like, for example, A. Emmanuel, *El intercambio desigual: ensayo sobre los antagonismos en las relaciones económicas internacionales* (Madrid: Siglo XXI, 1973). S. Amin, *La acumulación a escala mundial* (Madrid: Siglo XXI Editores, 1977).

16. 'In the case of food, demand is not very sensitive to rises in real income, and in the case of raw materials, technical progress in manufacturing actually largely consists of a reduction in the amount of raw materials used per unit of output, which may compensate or even overcompensate the increase in the volume of manufacturing output. This lack of an automatic multiplication in demand ... results in large falls, not only cyclical but also structural.' H. Singer, 'The Distribution of Gains between Investing and Borrowing Countries', *American Economic Review*, 40:2 (May, 1950), p. 479. See also R. Prebisch, 'Commercial Policy in the Underdeveloped Countries', *American Economic Review*, 49:2 (May, 1959), pp. 251–73.

17. Ocampo and Parra, 'The commodity terms of trade'.

18. J. A. Ocampo, 'New Developments in Trade Theory and LDCs', *Journal of Development Economics*, 22:1 (1986), pp. 129–70.

19. Rodríguez, *La teoría del subdesarrollo de la CEPAL*, p. 68.

20. J. A. Ocampo, 'Los términos de intercambio y las relaciones centro periferia', in O. Sunkel (ed.), *El desarrollo desde dentro: un enfoque neoestructuralista para la América Latina* (Mexico City: Fondo de Cultura Económica, 1991), pp. 417–51, on p. 419. Another issue has been the lack of data on labour productivity in the primary products sectors of underdeveloped countries.

21. Actually, after thirty years since publishing his article, he declared: 'with the benefit of knowing further events, I should have avoided to use the "exchange relation", with its narrower professional meaning of net barter terms of trade related only to prices, and should have used instead the "trade framework" or some other similar concept. This was the real intention to avoid in the document title "exchange relation" and, instead, make reference to "investor and borrowing countries"', H. Singer, 'La controversia de la relación de intercambio y la evolución del financiamiento en condiciones concesionarias: los primeros años en la ONU', in G. M. Meier and D. Seers (eds), *Pioneros del desarrollo* (Madrid: Editorial Tecnos, 1986), pp. 273–303, on p. 286.

22. H. Singer, 'The Distribution of Gains from Trade and Investment Revisited', *Journal of Development Studies*, 11 (1974–1975), pp. 376–82.

23. P. Sarkar, 'The North-South Terms of Trade Debate: a Re-Examination', *Progress in Development Studies*, 1;4 (2001), pp. 309–27.

24. R. Lipsey, *Price and Quantity Trends in the Foreign Trade of United States* (Princeton, NJ: Princeton University Press for NBER, 1963).

25. C. P. Kindleberger, 'Planning for Foreign Investment', *American Economic Review*, 33:1 (1943), pp. 347–54, on pp. 349. Quoted in Sarkar, 'The North-South Terms of Trade Debate: a Re-Examination', p. 311.

26. J. Spraos, 'The Statistical Debate on the Net Barter Terms of Trade between Primary Commodities and Manufactures', *Economic Journal*, 90:357 (1980), pp. 107–28.

27. The articles in question were R. Prebish, 'Observaciones sobre los planes monetarios internacionales', *Trimestre Económico*, 11:2 (July-September 1940) and 'Panorama general de los problemas de regulación monetaria y crediticia en el continente americano: A. América Latina', in Banco de México, *Memoria: Primera reunión de técnicos sobre problemas de banca central del continente Americano* (Mexico City, 1946). Quoted in Love, 'Economic Ideas and Ideologies in Latin America since 1930', pp. 225–6.

28. Although Prebisch was already conscious by that time that the relevant measure was the DFTT instead of the NBTT, the evidence was elusive due to the lack of data on labour productivity. He conformed by quoting the 1949 UN report where it says that 'there is no doubt that productivity rose more quickly in industrialized countries than in those

producing primary products. This can be verified by the more pronounced raising pattern of life [in industrialized countries] during the long period elapsed since 1870.'

29. For example Lewis, 'World Production, Prices and Trade, 1870–1950', pp. 105–38.

30. C. P. Kindleberger, *The Terms of Trade: A European Case Study* (New York: Wiley, 1956); G. M. Meier, and R. E. Baldwin, *Economic Development: Theory, History, Policy* (New York: John Wiley, 1957); G. Haberler, *International Trade and Economic Development* (Cairo: National Bank of Egypt, 1959); Lipsey, 'Price and Quantity Trends'. Still, it is possible to find papers not that old in which one of the main arguments to re-examine Prebisch and Singer thesis is the inadequacy of the NBTT of UK used in 1949 to support the argument. See J. León and R. Soto, 'Términos de intercambio en la América Latina: Una cuantificación de la hipótesis de Prebisch y Singer', *El trimestre económico*, 62:246 (1995), pp. 171–99.

31. Meier and Baldwin, 'Economic Development: Theory, History, Policy'.

32. J. Viner, *International Trade and Economic Development* (Oxford: Clarendon Press, 1953). A research work that finds evidence supporting Viner's criticism is J. Williamson and Y. Hadass. 'Terms of Trade Shocks and Economic Performance 1870–1940: Prebisch and Singer Revisited', *Economic Development and Cultural Change*, 51:3 (2003), pp. 629–56, and a study that rejects Viner's idea is P. Sarkar, 'The Singer-Prebisch Hypothesis: A Statistical Evaluation', *Cambridge Journal of Economics*, 10 (1986), pp. 355–71.

33. CEPAL, 'América Latina: Relación de precios de intercambio'.

34. UNCTAD, *Handbook of International Trade and Development Statistics, 1972* (New York: United Nations, 1972).

35. Spraos, 'The Statistical Debate on the Net Barter Terms of Trade between Primary Commodities and Manufactures', pp. 107–28, and Spraos, *Inequalising Trade?*.

36. D. Sapsford, 'The Statistical Debate on the Net Barter Terms of Trade between Primary Commodities and Manufactures: A Comment and Some Additional Evidence', *Economic Journal*, 95 (1985), pp. 781–8; Sarkar, 'The Singer-Prebisch Hypothesis: A Statistical Evaluation', pp. 355–71.

37. D. Diakosawas, and P. Scandizzo, 'Trends in the Terms of Trade of Primary Commodities, 1900–1982: The Controversy and Its Origins', *Economic Development and Cultural Change*, 39:2 (1991), pp. 231–64; E. R. Grilli and M. C. Yang, 'Primary Commodity Prices, Manufactured Goods Prices, and the Terms of Trade of Developing Countries: What the Long Run Shows', *World Bank Economic Review*, 2:1 (1988), pp. 1–47.

38. J. T. Cuddington, and C. M. Urzúa, 'Trends and Cycles in the Net Barter Terms of Trade: A New Approach', *Economic Journal*, 99, 396 (1989), pp. 426–42.

39. A. Powell, 'Commodity and Developing Countries Terms of Trade: What Does the Long-Run Show?', *Economic Journal*, 101:409 (1991), pp. 1485–96.

40. The NBTT indexes used by these authors were published by the ECLA. León and Soto, 'Términos de intercambio en la América Latina', pp. 171–99.

41. For instance, D. Sapsford, , P. Sarkar and H. Singer, 'The Prebisch-Singer Terms of Trade Controversy Revisited', *Journal of International Development*, 4 (1992), pp. 315–32; J. T. Cuddington, 'Long-Run Trends in 26 Primary Commodity Prices: A Disaggregated Look at the Prebisch-Singer Hypothesis', *Journal of Developing Economics*, 39:2 (1992), pp. 207–27; P. G. Ardeni and B. Wright, 'The Prebisch-Singer Hypothesis: A Reappraisal Independent of Stationarity Hypothesis', *Economic Journal*, 102 (1992), pp. 803–12; P Sarkar, 'Long-Term Behaviour of Terms of Trade of Primary Products vis-a-vis Manufactures: A Critical Review of Recent Debate', *Economic and Political Weekly*,

29 (1994), pp. 1612–4; M.G. Lutz, 'A General Test of the Prebisch-Singer Hypothesis', *Review of Development Economics*, 3:1 (1999), pp. 44–57.

42. M. Bleaney, and D. Greenaway, 'Long-run Trends in the Relative Price of Primary Commodities and in the Terms of Trade of Developing Countries', *Oxford Economic Papers*, 45:3 (1993), pp. 349–63.
43. Ocampo and Parra, 'Los términos de intercambio de los productos básicos', pp. 7–35.
44. G. P. Zanias, 'Testing for Trends in the Terms of Trade between Primary Commodities and Manufactured Goods', *Journal of Development Economics*, 78 (2005), pp. 49–59.
45. P. Cashin, and C. J. McDermott, 'The Long-Run Behaviour of Commodity Prices: Small Trends and Big Variability', *IMF Staff Papers*, 49:2 (2002), pp. 175–99.
46. C. Blattman, J. Hwang and J. G. Williamson, 'The Impact of the Terms of Trade on Economic Development in the Periphery, 1870–1939: Volatility and Secular Change', *NBER Working Papers*, series 10600 (July, 2004), at <http://ssrn.com/abstract=563044> [accessed 3 February 2011].
47. Williamson and Hadass, 'Terms of Trade Shocks and Economic Performance', pp. 629–56.
48. Blattman, Hwang and Williamson, 'Winners and Losers in the Commodity Lottery', pp. 156–79.
49. Ibid., p. 177.
50. Ocampo, 'Los términos de intercambio y las relaciones centro periferia', pp. 417–51.
51. León and Soto, 'Términos de intercambio en la América Latina', pp. 171–99.
52. R. Ram, 'Trends in Developing Countries' Commodity Terms-of-Trade since 1970', *Review of Radical Political Economics*, 36 (2004), pp. 241–53.
53. P. Sarkar, and H. Singer, 'Manufactured Exports of Developing Countries and Their Terms of Trade since 1965', *World Development*, 19:4 (1991), pp. 333–40.
54. A. Maizels, 'The Manufactures Terms of Trade of Developing Countries with the United States, 1981–97', *QEH Working Paper Series*, 36 (2000), at <http://www3.qeh.ox.ac.uk/pdf/qehwp/qehwps36.pdf> [accessed 3 February 2011].
55. The SFTT are the NBTT multiplied by the labour productivity of a given country in its export sectors.
56. Ocampo, 'Los términos de intercambio y las relaciones centro periferia', pp. 417–51. León and Soto, 'Términos de intercambio en la América Latina', pp. 171–99. Ram, 'Trends in Developing Countries', pp. 241–53.
57. Grupo de Estudios del Crecimiento Económico del Banco de la República. GRECO, *El crecimiento económico colombiano en el siglo XX* (Bogotá: Fondo de Cultura Económica, 2002).
58. The NBTT series elaborated by Garay in 1980 is somewhat different, since he used a bigger basket of products for the period 1916–74. However there is no clear trend in this series either. L. J. Garay, 'Comportamiento de los términos de intercambio de Colombia durante el período 1916–1974', in *Ensayos sobre historia económica colombiana* (Bogotá: Fedesarrollo, 1980), pp. 231–42.
59. In Spraos's words, it is 'the rate at which one national man-hour of work is exchanged for foreign man-hours of work through trade intermediation'. Spraos, *Inequalising trade?*, pp. 93–4.
60. These numbers are obtained by calculating the share of all the CIIU groups beginning with number 3 in the total exports of Colombia, excluding groups 3111, 3114, 3116, 3530, 3539 and 3540, which is the regular procedure made by the central bank in Colombia (Banco de la República).

$$NBTT = \frac{P_{EXP}}{P_{IMP}}.$$

Of course,

61. J. Atack, and F. Bateman, 'Chapter Dd. Manufacturing', in S. Carter, S. S. Gartner, M. R. Haines, A. L. Olmstead, R. Sutch and G. Wright (eds), *Historical Statistics of the United States: Millennial Edition* (Cambridge: Cambridge University Press, 2006), pp. 583–617.

62. G. Bonilla, J. M. Silva and J. Villamil, 'Análisis metodológico y empírico de la medición de productividad en Colombia', in R. Chica (ed.), *El crecimiento de la productividad en Colombia: resultados del estudio nacional sobre determinantes del crecimiento de la productividad* (Bogotá: Departamento Nacional de Planeación, Colciencias, Fonade, 1996), pp. 319–38.

63. Because the mentioned sources present aggregate value in nominal terms, the manufacturer's Producer Price Index published by the Banco de la República was used as deflator (in the case of Colombia) and, in the case of the United States, the wholesale price index published by Mitchell for the 1975–1993 period and the manufacturer's Producer Price Index available in the Bureau of Labor Statistics (<http://www.bls.gov>) for the remaining years. The two indexes were connected in 1993. See B. R. Mitchell, *International Historical Statistics: The Americas, 1750–2000* (New York: Palgrave Macmillan, 2003), p. 704.

64. Available at <ftp://ftp.bls.gov/pub/special.requests/opt/lpr/histmfgsic.zip>.

65. The difference between the two DFTT series is that in the calculations of the number (1) we used the mentioned 'output per person' in the United States published by the Bureau of Labor Statistics while in the number (2) we employed United States labour productivity index published in Atack and Bateman, 'Chapter Dd. Manufacturing', pp. 583–617.

66. Banco de la República, *Subgerencia de Estudios Económicos, Principales Indicadores Económicos* (Bogotá: Centro de Información, version 1.0, 1998).

67. See Maizels, 'The Manufactures Terms of Trade of Developing Countries with the United States, 1981–97' and Sarkar and Singer, 'Manufactured Exports of Developing Countries and Their Terms of Trade since 1965', pp. 333–40. However this does not invalidate their results, because they make reference to a broader sample of countries. It just sets Colombia into the group of countries whose manufacturing NBTT don't show a clear downward tendency during the last three decades as a whole.

68. This figure is not reported here, but is available upon request to the author.

69. The Colombian labour productivity in Appendix A was elaborated by the author using data from DANE, Encuesta Anual Manufacturera, various years. US Output per person was taken from data available at <ftp://ftp.bls.gov/pub/special.requests/opt/lpr/histmfgsic.zip>. US labour productivity was author's elaboration using data from Atack and Bateman, 'Chapter Dd: Manufacturing', pp. 573–610.

70. Spraos, *Inequalising trade?*.

71. Rodríguez, *La teoría del subdesarrollo de la CEPAL*, p. 233. Translated by the author.

11 Public Revenues in Bolivia, 1900–31

1. Economic History Departament, Universitat de Barcelona. Financial support was provided by Universitat de Barcelona (Ajut per Personal Investigador en Formaciò, 2008–2012) and the Innovation and Science Ministry of Spain (Project ECO2009–13331–C02–02). The author thanks Alfonso Herranz Loncán for his continuous

support. The author also thanks César Yañez and Albert Carreras for their stimulus to present this work at the XVth World Economic History Congress, held in Utrecht in August 2009. The standard disclaimer applies.

2. M. Rubio, C. Yáñez, M. Folchi, and A. Carreras, 'Energy as Indicator of Modernization in Latin America (1890–1925)', *Economic History Review*, 63 (2010), pp. 769–804.

3. B. Hildreth and J. Richardson, 'Economic Principles of Taxation', in B. Hildreth and J. Richardson (eds). *Handbook on taxation* (Nueva York: Marcel Dekker, 1999), pp. 21–30.

4. D. De Ferranti, G. Perry, F. Ferreira, and M. Walton, *Inequality in Latin America and the Caribbean: Breaking with history?* (Washington, DC: World Bank, 2003), pp. 132–40.

5. International Monetary Fund, *Government Finance Statistics Manual* (Washington, DC: IMF, 2001).

6. M. Moore, '¿Cómo afecta la tributación a la calidad de gobernación?', *Trimestre Económico*, 294 (2008), pp. 281–328. In relation to this, a tax is defined as a transaction which entails a compulsory payment (IMF, 'Government Finance Statistics Manual', pp: 27–8). It does not imply an immediate or equivalent retribution by the government. The particularity of a tax is its compulsory nature, the uncertainty on the 'return' of the payment and the non-existent balance between payment and profit.

7. Given the copiousness and richness of the primary data, each of these categories was divided in different subcategories as proposed by the IMF. The sources here used and the classification criteria of the several taxes are stated in the Annex.

8. In any case, the evolution of fiscal revenues was analysed under different schemes and greater differences did not arise when establishing the main stylized facts.

9. L. Peñaloza, *Nueva Historia Económica de Bolivia. El Estaño* (La Paz-Cochabamba: Los Amigos del Libro, 1985), pp. 188–90.

10. Although it is also possible to identify a significant leap in the collections made from internal indirect taxes, the relative importance of these taxes on the total amount was stabilized around 13 per cent.

11. The reform entailed a series of controversial concessions to international lenders, particularly the transfer of the control on the main revenue sources of the country. 'To obtain loans for such an extremely underdeveloped and risky economy, Bolivia had to surrender exceptional sovereignty to foreign financial houses and inspectors', P. Drake, 'Exporting Tin, Gold, and Laws from Bolivia, 1927–1932', in *The Money Doctor in the Andes: The Kemmerer Missions, 1923–1933* (Durham, NC: Duke University Press, 1989), p. 175. However, it cannot be denied that in the end, the government knew how to make the most of the pressure to legitimate itself and increase the fiscal pressure. See, M. Contreras, 'Debt, Taxes, and War: The Political Economy of Bolivia, c. 1920–1935', *Journal of Latin American Studies*, 22:2 (1990), pp. 265–87.

12. OECD, *Perspectivas Económicas de América Latina 2009* (Paris: OECD, 2008), p. 37.

13. J. Jimenez And V. Tromben, 'Fiscal Policy and the Commodities Boom: The Impact of Higher Prices for Non-Renewables in Latin America and the Caribbean', *Revista de la CEPAL*, 90 (2006), pp. 61–86.

14. Peñaloza, 'Nueva Historia Económica de Bolivia', pp. 192–193.

15. R. Cortés Conde, 'Fiscal and Monetary Regimes', in V. Bulmer-Thomas, J. Coatsworth and R. Cortés Conde (eds), *The Cambridge Economic History of Latin America* (New York: Cambridge University Press, 2006), Vol. 2, pp. 209–47.

16. L. Whitehead and M. Dos Santos, 'El impacto de la Gran Depresión en Bolivia', *Desarrollo Económico*, 12:45 (1972), pp. 58–60.

17. J. Coatsworth and J. Williamson, 'Always Protectionist? Latin America Tariffs from Independence to Great Depression', *Journal of Latin American Studies*, 36 (2004), pp. 205–32.
18. R. Barragán, and J.A. Peres, 'El armazón estatal y sus imaginarios. Historia del Estado', in PNUD, *Informe Nacional de Desarrollo Humano 2007. El Estado del Estado* (La Paz: PNUD, 2007), pp. 127–218.
19. The Presupuestos and Cuentas Generales, show that some of the aforementioned specific contributions showed uneven collection levels throughout time and even short duration.
20. The same conclusions arise using more sophisticated indexes of volatility.
21. W. Gómez, *La minería en el desarrollo económico de Bolivia* (La Paz-Cochabamba: Los Amigos del Libro, 1978).
22. This series is subdivided in three categories: export duties, direct taxes and public services. The first category adds the total exports duties derived from the mining exports. The second category adds several taxes that the government tried to levy on the utilities or dividends of the mining companies. The last category adds several payments for services or duties charged by the government to the mining sector: mining patents, mining plans, publication of mining assignments, etc.
23. In order to make a comprehensible reading of the fiscal information and analyse the process, we added export taxes in five large categories: tin, rubber, silver, other ore and other farming products.
24. Contreras, 'Debt, Taxes, and War.'.
25. Banco Minero, *Tasas e impuestos sobre la industria minera en Bolivia* (La Paz: Imp. artística, scs. de A.H. Ofero, 1941).
26. Cortés Conde, 'Fiscal and Monetary Regimes'.
27. The subsequent consolidation of the International Tin Council (ITC) stresses the oligopoly nature of the tin market and the need for an international agreement to have an effect on the global prices.
28. Before the Great Depression, two of the so-called 'Tin Barons' controlled a considerable portion of the export offer of Bolivian tin. Simon Patiño controlled more than a 25 per cent of the Bolivian mining production In 1924, thanks to the acquisition of the producing centres of Uncía and Llallagua it took over almost half of the Bolivian export Carlos Víctor. Aramayo controlled between 8 and 10 per cent of the national mining production (J. Dunkerley, *Orígenes del poder militar. Bolivia 1879–1935* (La Paz: Plural, 2003), p. 106).
29. As we mentioned before, the fiscal needs made the government get into massive debts in the foreign markets throughout the 1920s. The debt entailed a higher pressure by international loaners which the government used to impose higher taxes to the mining sector. The Impuesto a las Utilidades Mineras, for instance, was basically laid to attend the 1922 credit (C. McQueen, *Bolivian Public Finance* (Washington, DC: Government printing office, 1925), p. 24.
30. The initial intention was to group the general interest of the whole sector. However, as time went by, it came to basically represent the demands of only the great mining producers.
31. H. Klein, *Historia General de Bolivia* (La Paz: Juventud, 1982), p. 218.
32. Drake, 'Exporting Tin, Gold', pp. 205–6.
33. Barragán and Peres, 'El armazón estatal y sus imaginarios'.
34. H. Delgadillo, 'Apéndice Estadístico', in H. Huber, N. Pacheco, C. Villegas, A. Aguirre and H. Delgadillo (eds), *La Deuda Externa de Bolivia: 125 años de renogociaciones*

y ¿cuántos más?. Desde la Operación secreta del gobierno y los Meiggs hasta la iniciativa HIPC (La Paz: CEDLA/OXFAM, 2001).

35. McQueen, 'Bolivian Public Finance'.
36. J. Palenque, 'Análisis numérico del presupuesto nacional', *Estadística Boliviana. Primera Parte. Años 1911–1931* (La Paz, 1931).
37. McQueen, 'Bolivian Public Finance', pp. 19–27.

12 The Consumption of Durable Goods in Latin America, 1890–1913

1. This chapter is part of the Master Thesis 'Imports of Durable Consumption Goods and Economic Growth in Latin America (1890–1913)', from the Programme on Economic History and Institutions at the University of Barcelona. In addition, this research and its database are part of the Project 'Imports and Economic Modernization in Latin America, 1890–1960' (BEC 2003–0190) coordinated by A. Carreras. I am very grateful for comments and suggestions made by its members and by A. Herranz.
2. B. Haig, and J. Anderssen, 'Australian Consumption Expenditure and Real Income: 1900 to 2003–2004', *Economic Record*, 83:263 (2007), pp. 416–31; A. Deaton and S. Zaidi, 'Guidelines for Constructing Consumption Aggregates for Welfare Analyses', *LSMS Working Paper*, 135 (Washington, DC: The World Bank, 2002); N. Rossi, G. Toniolo and G. Vecchi, 'Is the Kuznets Curve Still Alive? Evidence from Italian Household Budgets, 1881–1961', *Journal of Economic History*, 61:4 (2001); C. Shammas, 'Changes in English and Anglo-American Consumption from 1550 to 1880', in J. Brewer. and R. Porter (eds), *Consumption and the World of Goods* (London: Routledge, 1993); J. Mokyr, 'Is There Still Life in the Pessimist Case? Consumption during the Industrial Revolution 1790–1850', *Journal of Economic History*, 48:1 (1998), pp. 69–92; A. S. Deaton, 'Estructura de la demanda en Europa, 1920–1970', in C. M. Cipolla (ed.), *Historia Económica de Europa*, 5, El Siglo XX (Barcelona: Ariel 1981), pp. 105–50.
3. Engel's Law was named after Ernest Engel (1821–1896) who formulated his law in 1857 after a study of 200 household budgets of workers in Belgium. H. S. Houthaker, 'An International Comparison of Household Expenditure Patterns, Commemorating the Centenary of Engel's Law', *Econométrica*, 26 (1957), pp. 531–51.
4. Deaton, 'Estructura de la demanda en Europa', p. 138.
5. Brown and Deaton, 'Surveys in Applied Economics'; Mokyr, 'Is There Still Life in the Pessimist Case'.
6. Deaton, 'Estructura de la demanda en Europa', p. 139.
7. J. S. Duesenberry, *Income, Saving and the Theory of Consumer Behavior* (Cambridge, MA: Harvard University Press, 1949).
8. D. Raff and M. Trajtenberg, 'Quality-Adjusted Prices for the American Automobile Industry: 1906–1940', in T. F. Bresnahan and R. J. Gordon (eds), *The Economics of New Goods* (Chicago, IL: University of Chicago Press, 1997), p. 73.
9. Bresnahan and Gordon (eds), *Economics of New Goods*.
10. T. Halperín Donghi, W. Glade, R. Thorp, A. Bauer, M. Moreno Fraginals, C. M. Lewis, V. Bulmer-Thomas, R. French-Davis, O. Muñoz, and J. G. Palma, *Historia económica de América Latina: desde la Independencia a nuestros días* (Barcelona: Crítica, 2002).
11. Mokyr, 'Is There Still Life in the Pessimist Case?'.
12. Shammas, 'Changes in English and Anglo-American consumption'.

13. V. Bulmer-Thomas, *Historia Económica de América Latina desde la Independencia* (Mexico City: Fondo de Cultura Económica, 1998), p. 98.
14. The share of France, Germany, Great Britain and the United States in total imports was calculated for three benchmarks: 1890, 1900 and 1910. The information for determining these percentages is based on the United Kingdom, *Statistical Abstract for the Principal and Other Foreign Countries* (London: HMSO 1895, 1905 and 1924).
15. Several authors have used this methodology based on the trade statistics of the exporting countries, for example, A. Carreras, A. Hofman, M. Folchi, M. Rubio, X. Tafunell and C. Yañez, 'Importaciones y modernización económica en América Latina durante la primera mitad del siglo XX. Las claves de un programa de investigación', *Serie Estudios Estadísticos y Prospectivos*, 44 (Santiago: CEPAL, 2006); C. Yáñez and M. Badia-Miró, 'Las importaciones de relojes y automóviles en América Latina durante 1925. Una aproximación desde el punto de vista de la renta y su distribución', *Revista de Historia Industrial*, 35:3 (2007), pp: 143–64; and 'El consumo de automóviles en la América Latina y el Caribe (1902–1930)', *El Trimestre Económico*, 310 (2011), pp. 317–42.
16. M. Badía-Miró and A. Carreras-Marín, 'Geographical Deviations in Foreign Trade Statistics: A Study into European Trade with Latin American Countries, 1925', Working Paper, 884 (Barcelona: Departament d'Economia i Empresa, Universitat Pompeu Fabra, 2005); and AEHE, 'Fiabilidad de las estadísticas de comercio exterior referentes a América Latina y el Caribe (1908–1930): Una aproximación al patrón geográfico de las discrepancias distributivas a través del carbón', *Documentos de trabajo*, 0801 (2008).
17. Shammas, 'Changes in English and Anglo-American Consumption' includes vehicle transport (including horse carriages and carts if these were used for transporting people) in the analysis of the evolution of durable goods between 1550–1880 in Great Britain and its colonies.
18. B. R. Mitchell, *International Historical Statistics: The Americas 1750–2000*, 5th edn (New York: Palgrave Macmillan, 2003).
19. We were unable to calculate the unit values from the French and German statistics because they report quantities expressed in kilograms and not in units.
20. This result is based on C. Román, 'Importación de bienes de consumo duradero y crecimiento económico en América Latina (1890–1913)' (Master dissertation, University of Barcelona, 2006), where the evolution rates of consumption of durable goods in nineteen Latin American countries between 1890 and 1913 were compared.
21. A. S. Deaton, 'The Measurement of Income and Price Elasticity', *European Economic Review*, 6 (1975), pp. 261–73.
22. T. D. Logan, 'Food, Nutrition, and Substitution in the Late Nineteenth Century', *Explorations in Economic History*, 43 (2006), pp. 527–45; Shammas, 'Changes in English and Anglo-American Consumption'; Deaton, 'The Measurement of Income and Price Elasticity'; Brown and Deaton, 'Surveys in Applied Economics'; A. S. Goldberger and T. Gamalestos, 'A Cross Country Comparison of Consumer Expenditure Patterns', *European Economic Review*, 1 (1970), pp. 357–400, among others.
23. Brown and Deaton, 'Surveys in Applied Economics'.
24. We have estimations of GDP between 1890 and 1913 for four countries: Argentina, Brazil, Chile and Uruguay. In addition, we include Mexico with information since 1895 and Cuba since 1900 (see the sources in the annex).
25. As explained below we draw up this weighted index based on export prices for industrial products in four industrialized countries.

26. Previously we made several analyses. We tested the correlation between the individual effects and the other regressors with the Hausman test, and the result allowed us to reject the null hypothesis of no correlation and used the fixed effects model. In addition, we tested the significance of the individual effects computing the F test statistic. To control for heteroscedasticity we used robust standard errors.

27. Following the methodology used by Rubio, in M. del M. Rubio, 'Protectionist but Globalized? Latin American Custom Duties and Trade during the Pre-1914 Belle Époque', *Economics and Business Working Papers*, 967 (Barcelona: Universitat Pompeu Fabra, 2006), we calculate the ratio of customs income to total imports and use this as a proxy for the tariff ratio. We used information from the United Kingdom: 'Statistical Abstract for the Principal Foreign Countries and Others' (London: HMSO, 1900, 1905, 1911 and 1924).

28. A. S. Goldberger and T. Gamalestos, 'A Cross Country Comparison'. R. H. Clarida, 'Consumption, Import Prices and the Demand for Imported Consumer Durables: a Structural Econometric Investigation', *The Review of Economics and Statistics*, 78:3 (1996), pp. 369–74.

29. L. Bértola and J. A. Ocampo, *Desarrollo, vaivenes y desigualdad. Una historia económica de América Latina desde la independencia* (Madrid: Secretaría General Iberoamericana, 2010), p. 132, Table 3.15.

30. The transport group includes 'carriages, vehicles and parts, motorcycles, bicycles and parts'.

31. We did not obtain information to be able to construct specific relative prices for each group. For transport we adjusted the relative prices by the unit value of the cars. For the other categories we used the general prices calculated for the aggregate demand.

32. According to the results of the Hausman test we do not reject the null hypothesis that individual effects are correlated with the explicative variables, so we estimated the model of random effects. In addition, we tested the significance of the individual effects computing the Breush-Pagan test. Finally, we used heteroscedasticity-consistent standard errors.

33. Deaton, 'Estructura de la demanda en Europa'.

34. Yáñez and Badía-Miró, 'Las importaciones de relojes y automóviles'.

35. Ibid.

36. Halperín Donghi and others, 'Historia económica de América Latina'.

37. R. Cortés Conde, *La economía argentina en el largo plazo* (Buenos Aires: Universidad de San Andrés, 1994); A. Maddison, *Monitoring the World Economy, 1820–1992* (Paris: OECD, 1995); Dirección General de Estadística, *Anuario del comercio exterior de la República Argentina* (Buenos Aires, 1903 and 1913); L. Bértola, L. Calicchio, M. Camou, and G. Porcile, 'Southern Cone Real Wages Compared: A Purchasing Power Parity Approach to Convergence and Divergence Trends, 1870–1996', *Documento de Trabajo*, 44 (Montevideo: Universidad de la República, 1999); and M. Flandreau and F. Zumer, *The Making of Global Finance 1880–1913* (Paris: OECD, 2004).

38. Maddison, 'Monitoring the World Economy'; Directoria de Estatistica Commercial, *Commercio exterior do Brazil* (Rio de Janeiro: Ministerio de Fazenda, 1910 and 1913); and Bértola, Calicchio, Camou and Porcile, 'Southern Cone Real Wages Compared'; Flandreau and Zumer, *The Making of Global Finance*.

39. R. Lüders, 'The Comparative Economic Performance of Chile: 1810–1995', *Estudios de Economía*, 25:2 (1998), pp. 217–49; Maddison, 'Monitoring the World Economy'; Oficina Central de Estadística, *Anuario Estadístico de la Reública de Chile, Comercio*

Exterior (Valparaíso: Imprenta y Litografía Universo, 1902 and 1913); J. Díaz, R. Lüders, and G. Wagner, 'La República en Cifras', *Mimeo* (Santiago: Universidad Católica, 2004).

40. A. Santamaría García, 'El crecimiento económico de Cuba republicana (1902–1959). Una revisión y nuevas estimaciones en perspectiva comparada (población, inmigración golondrina, ingreso no azucarero y Producto Nacional Bruto)', *Revista de Indias*, 219 (2000), pp. 505–45; Secretaría de Hacienda, *Comercio Exterior* (Havana: Imprenta Carasa y Cia., 1903 and 1913); OXLAD, <http://oxlad.qeh.ox.ac.uk/search.php>; Santamaría and García Álvarez, *Economía y colonia. La economía cubana y la relación con España, 1765–1902* (Madrid: Consejo Superior de Investigaciones Científicas, 2004), p. 344.

41. Instituto Nacional de Estadística y Geografía, *Estadísticas Históricas de México* (Mexico CITY: INEGI, 1985) (p. 884 for ER); A. Maddison, *The World Economy: A Millennial Perspective* (Paris: OECD, 2001) for 1900–1910 and Maddison, 'Monitoring the World Economy' for 1910–1913; Departamento de Estadística Nacional, *Anuario Estadístico: Comercio exterior y navegación* (México: 1894 and 1913); A. Gómez-Galvarriato and A. Musacchio, 'Un Nuevo Índice de Precios para México, 1886–1929', *El Trimestre Económico*, 67:265 (2000), pp. 45–91.

42. A. Maddison, *The World Economy: Historical Statistics* (Paris: OECD, 2003), based on L. Bértola, L. Calicchio, M. Camou, and L. Rivero, 'El PBI uruguayo y otras estimaciones: 1870–1936' (Montevideo: Universidad de la República, 1998); Dirección General de Estadística, *Anuario estadístico de la República Oriental del Uruguay* (Montevideo: Dirección General de Estadística, 1903 and 1911); Bértola, Calicchio, Camou, and Porcile, 'Southern Cone Real Wages Compared'.

43. Direction Générale des Douanes, *Tableau générale du commerce et de la navigation* (Paris : Direction Générale des Douanes, Several years); Y. Breton, 'Indices de prix de produits industriels (1847–1938) et des produits agricoles (1815–1938) en France', in 'La croissance Francaise 1789–1990, Nouvelles estimations', *Economies et Societes, Histoire economique quantitative*, Serie HEQ, 1:11 (1997), pp. 189–259.

44. *Der Auswärtige Andel Deutschlands* (Berlin, several years); W. Hoffmann, *Das Wachstum der deutschen wirtschaft seit der mitte des 19 jahrhunderts* (Berlin: Springer-Verlag, 1965).

45. Department of Commerce, *The Foreign Commerce and Navigation of the US* (Washington, DC: Government Printing Office, several years); *Historical Statistics of the United States: Earliest Times to the Present: Millennial Edition* (Cambridge: Cambridge University Press, 2006), vol. 5.

46. Statistical Office of the Customs and Excise Department, *Annual Statement of the United Kingdom with Foreign Countries and British Possessions* (London: several years); B. R. Mitchell, *British Historical Statistics* (London: Cambridge University Press, 1990).

INDEX